# TEACHING CHINESE SECOND LANGUAGE

Grounded in analysis of Chinese and international educational concepts and classroom techniques currently used to teach Chinese as a Second Language, and a thorough review of recent research in the field, this volume identifies the learning challenges of the language for native English speakers. Orton and Scrimgeour assess the gap in knowledge and skills between learners' initial and future proficiency levels as L2 Chinese speakers, map their needs as learners towards achieving a high language proficiency, and set out an informed, integrated teaching orientation and practice for the Chinese classroom that responds to those needs. Chapters in the volume address curriculum design, teaching diverse learners and levels, the learning challenges of Chinese oral and literacy skills, grammar and vocabulary, discourse development, cultural understanding, and the affordances of a visit to China. Filled with original and engaging teaching and learning tools and techniques, this book is an essential and rich content resource for primary and secondary teachers, and teacher candidates and educators in Chinese as a Second Language education.

**Jane Orton** is an Honorary Fellow and former Director of the Chinese Teacher Training Centre at the University of Melbourne, Australia.

**Andrew Scrimgeour** is a Lecturer in Languages Education and Chinese at the University of South Australia, Australia.

**ESL & Applied Linguistics Professional Series**
*Eli Hinkel, Series Editor*

For more information about this series, please visit: www.routledge.com/ESL-Applied-Linguistics-Professional-Series/book-series/LEAESLALP

# TEACHING CHINESE AS A SECOND LANGUAGE

## The Way of the Learner

*Jane Orton and Andrew Scrimgeour*

Routledge
Taylor & Francis Group

NEW YORK AND LONDON

First published 2019
by Routledge
52 Vanderbilt Avenue, New York, NY 10017

and by Routledge
2 Park Square, Milton Park, Abingdon, Oxon, OX14 4RN

*Routledge is an imprint of the Taylor & Francis Group, an informa business*

© 2019 Taylor & Francis

*Library of Congress Cataloging-in-Publication Data*
A catalog record for this book has been requested

ISBN: 978-0-8153-8304-8 (hbk)
ISBN: 978-0-8153-8305-5 (pbk)
ISBN: 978-1-351-20687-7 (ebk)

Typeset in Bembo
by Apex CoVantage, LLC

# CONTENTS

# 1

# EMPOWERING LEARNING

## Introduction

In this opening chapter, the overarching framework of education, teaching, and language learning that shapes the work in this book is set out and the demands of learning Chinese considered within these parameters. It is proposed that special preparation is needed for speakers of European languages if they are to learn Chinese successfully. Apprenticeship exercises which might be undertaken ahead of and then concurrently with the start of language learning are introduced.

The educational framework presented reflects the historically and socio-culturally shaped beliefs, values and practices of current teaching and learning that have evolved in the West and are generally held in Western schools and colleges where Chinese is taught. Yet the vast majority of the teachers of Chinese in these institutions were raised and educated in China, according to beliefs, values and practices that evolved there and which, as has been widely acknowledged by both Chinese and non-Chinese writers, are in important ways different from and also partly in conflict with the Western framework presented here (e.g. Grant, Stronge, Xu, Popp, Sun, and Little, 2014; Hall Haley and Ferro, 2011; Chen and Yeung, 2015a; Zhou and Li, 2015; Orton, 2016; Yue, 2017). Resolving these differences is of paramount concern if the field of Chinese as a Second Language is to advance. However, the authors are aware that resolution cannot be achieved by seeking just to laminate one culture's ideas over the top of another's, or to have new practices blindly adopted. It can only be achieved through interculturally sensitive dialogue informed by serious study of propositions. To advance this dialogue, in the second part of the chapter sources of difference in the two broad traditions of teaching are identified, as well as areas of commonality, and the suggestions made by various writers to deal with areas of mismatch are discussed.

It is hoped that this opening chapter will assist teachers, firstly, to appreciate the principles supporting the discussions and suggestions they find in the other chapters of the book; secondly, to become more aware of the framework of knowledge and perspectives that form their own professional knowledge base; and, thirdly, to perceive where and how they may need to reconsider and extend their current understanding if they are to be successful in following the lines of action proposed.

## Part 1: The Overarching Framework

### Language Learning in Education

Language learning belongs in the school curriculum not simply as 'training' for a job or even for life in an interconnected world. As acknowledged in *The Common European Framework of Reference for Languages* (Council of Europe, 2003–2009), the American *National Standards for Foreign Language Learning* (ACTFL Inc., 2012) and the *Australian Curriculum for Languages* (ACARA, 2014), the value and affordances of modern language study are understood first and foremost to be potentially educational: it leads to desirable cognitive and affective growth in the learner.

Specifically, a central purpose for language study in schools is the raising of students' awareness of the nature of language—how it names and frames those matters the language user groups believe, value, and enact in practice and the things they make use of; how it constructs, develops, negotiates, and stores knowledge; how knowledge is presented via different modes of communication and different types of texts; how it carries the power divisions that exist between groups; and how it is also open to being re-formed and made to serve new purposes. It is with these possibilities in mind that educators such as Michael Young (2012) in the UK include *acquiring the ability to speak and read a foreign language*, as 'powerful knowledge', which, like the study of History and Literature, has the potential for *giving students the tools to 'think the un-thinkable'*.

### Teaching Principles

Education is a social practice. As educators, teachers draw on a range of complex bodies of knowledge, which they synthesise in their design of curricula and lessons. These designs are based on probabilities drawn from research and theory and from actual past experience. But while there are routines that can be carried over from prior lessons, all lessons are also new creations and hence, actual teaching is a combination of applied science and artistry. While proceeding on an 'as if it will be predictable' basis, teachers in practice must also be ready to perceive and analyse situations which arise at the time that are novel, unexpected or uncertain, and on the spot design, test and assess quite a new action in response to them (Schön, 1984).

This way of thinking about teaching presupposes a meaning for the word 'to teach' which encompasses not only 'presenting content to students', but also 'taking responsibility to help students to learn content'. Thus, 'to teach' means presenting knowledge in activities which are most likely to make it learnable by the students, and at the least cost to them in terms of time and effort. In practice it assumes that work in the classroom will be interactional and active, creating a two-way dialogue between students and teacher and students and students. It is often in the dialogue and in the experimental activities in which students try things out for themselves that novel situations arise in a lesson.

The knowledge bodies that teachers draw on are from the broader dimension of education and from the more concentrated dimension of their own discipline area. In language teaching, the former involves theories of education and studies in pedagogy, curriculum design and assessment, as well as work in psychology on topics such as child development, learning norms and interpersonal communication. In the field of foreign and second language learning, teachers draw heavily on bodies of knowledge created by a range of linguists such as phoneticians, grammarians, and semanticists, as well as research by applied linguists in areas such as discourse analysis, lexicography and language acquisition. They also seek practical knowledge in the teaching methods of experienced practitioners. Knowledge from both the broader and the more concentrated bases are used in planning teaching and are engaged in acts of artistry to provide direction and clues as to what might need to be changed in the teaching practice if student work is to improve. Developing artistry requires practice, but it will only be effective if it is being informed by sound knowledge and a good repertoire of strategies for action.

## The Practice of Teaching

As a number of educators over many decades have proposed, the key tenet of successful teaching in this way is that it must be subordinated to learning:

> If teaching is to be effective, the activity to which it is addressed should be perceived as meaningful, satisfying an intrinsic need in the learner and 'incorporated into a task that is necessary and relevant for life' as perceived by the learner.
>
> (Vygotsky, 1930/1978: 118)

> Unfamiliar concepts and ideas need to be grounded within the scope of ordinary life-experience if students are to be able to grasp them.
>
> (Dewey, 1938: 26)

> If real success is to attend the effort to bring a person to a definite position, one must first of all take pains to find him where he is and begin

there . . . so that you may understand what he understands and in the way he understands it.

(Kierkegaard, 1959)

You must be with them where they are.

(Gattegno, 1972)

The central point of this advice is that it requires the teacher to find the student, not the other way around. The route forward along the learner's way from where the student is to somewhere beyond their current experience is initiated by effective teacher scaffolding of activity that

mostly takes the form of supporting or challenging, in 'joint involvement episodes'. . . . The former serves to maintain the student's current behaviour and to facilitate it [and] in the latter, the adult gears demands to those aspects of the task that lie just beyond the level that the child has currently attained, in order to carry the child forward in a series of carefully graduated steps at a pace appropriate to that individual

(Schaeffer, 1996: 266)

This kind of teaching presupposes that, during the lesson, there are times when the teacher is available to observe and create effective suggestions for students who are at work independently. It also proposes a clear separation of roles for teacher and student: the teacher (T) works on the student (S) while the student works on the knowledge (K), as shown in Figure 1.1 below.

Of course, the teacher will have already worked on the knowledge (the content) to ensure that it can be made independently available and accessible to the students in class.

**FIGURE 1.1** Teacher, student, knowledge relationship

*Source:* Adapted from Gattegno, 1970

# Chinese Language Learning

## *The Reality*

Faced with the noble aspirations set out earlier, engagement with the reality of Chinese learning is often a cold shower. In international publications and conference papers, evidence constantly shows that what most school age and undergraduate learners from Europe, North America and Australia find to be 'hitherto unthinkable' in their encounter with Chinese language are the overwhelming challenges they meet when trying to learn it. Far from being led along an empowering path, many end up despondent about success. This can lead them to discontinue their Chinese studies. Even those who do persevere often remain dissatisfied, feeling that they only 'half know' what they have studied and despairing of making real progress to new levels. High school graduates of Chinese learned in a classroom do not normally come near the level of proficiency that their peers taking a European language attain. In undergraduate courses, teachers have long noted that 'students ultimately hit a bottleneck as they find it more and more difficult to increase their Chinese language level' (Yin, 2003). Typically, 'some students who make it to advanced level Chinese classes . . . have problems finding effective strategies [for] reading and writing . . . and continue using lower level vocabulary learned in beginner Chinese' (Xing, 2003). And at the pre-tertiary level: 'The lack of success in the majority of K-12 programs in terms of helping students attain a functional level of proficiency has become a challenge for CSL programs in US elementary and secondary schools' (Ke, 2016).

This sobering assessment of current CSL outcomes holds true in other English-speaking countries as well (e.g. CILT, 2007; Orton, 2016) and in Western Europe more broadly (e.g. 徐(Xu) and Kooi, 2017; Gabbianelli, Formica, and Chang, 2017; She, 2017; Rukodelnikova, 2017). While not all students are willing to put in the effort required, especially among those dragooned into learning the language at school, it remains clear that even students who do apply themselves still only achieve a level of Chinese proficiency well below that of students of other languages. Considering this state of affairs from a professional perspective, we can say that this is primarily because it is still early days in the field of CSL, and there is a great deal yet to be discovered about the teaching and learning of Chinese internationally, especially at the pre-tertiary level. International English, at the same stage, was not the success it has since become, either; and when English did begin to spread internationally it was able to draw on the very extensive English teaching to adult and child immigrants that had already been going on inside English-speaking countries for decades. Although also reaching back many years, teaching Chinese to foreign learners was a particularly narrow field in China until quite recently and the experience and resources within it are virtually limited to the teaching of self-motivated, educated young adults already in tertiary institutions.

The authors of this book believe that there are three main areas in which CSL needs to develop if learning outcomes are to improve. One is *continuing analysis and description of the language in use*, especially very modern Chinese, of itself and in relation to the first language of the major groups studying Chinese; a second area is a *much greater focus on the nature of the learning* that Chinese demands of foreign students; and the third area is the *informed preparation of knowledgeable and able teachers*. The line of development devoted to language analysis is beyond the scope of this book. Instead it is focussed on the second area needing to be opened up: the nature of the learning tasks that Chinese demands of foreign learners from the perspective of the learner not the native speaker; this also provides an important but little recognised part of the knowledge and skills of an able teacher, the third area needing development.

## Chinese Language and Resources

Chinese is a language long used by a very large, very diverse set of people in China and in many countries beyond China's borders. Historically, there have been periods of intense work on analysing and organising the language and in the past three decades as the digital age emerged, a great deal of documentation of the modern language has been achieved. While there is still more to be done to bring knowledge of Chinese usage up to par with our knowledge of some other languages, the work undertaken to date to codify what is said and what will be accepted as a public standard has been very useful for the field of Chinese as a Second Language (L2 Chinese). This knowledge forms our understanding of the goal of language teaching, the finishing line for learners, which is located in the contemporary language of today's first and international users of Chinese.

When we look at resources for teachers—coursework for teacher candidates and textbooks and other materials for actual teaching—we find most exercises and activities offered at all levels are no more than the presentation of pieces of the final goal—the perfect Chinese text—combined with opportunities for the student to hear, say, read or write them in gradually larger chunks. Thus, the resources do not start where the students are, on the starting line, nor do they even consider what it is that the learners on the starting line need to master in order to reach the perfect texts on the finishing line. As a result, exercises and activities often do not form a scaffolded path between starting line and finishing line. In fact, the learning path has been far less regarded or studied, so much of the necessary information about it is simply not available. Instead the finishing line is presented with an underlying assumption that the learners will already have available what is needed to attain the goal and all that needs to be added is determination and diligence.

From a range of countries across the globe the evidence is that, at least those learners of Chinese with a European first language, do not have what is needed to easily adopt what is required to master Chinese. Indeed, there is ample evidence that the skills and strategies that first language speakers of a European language developed in learning their first language to a high degree of expertise and automaticity are an insufficient base for perceiving and producing even simple Chinese. As Orton (2016: 109–112) has shown, to develop the most basic capacities in Chinese—to hear and utter, to read and write—requires these foreign learners as a starting point to *extend fundamental motor skills* and to *change long ingrained habits in perception and production* of spoken and written language. Understanding Chinese *as an object of learning,* in this way, involves perceiving the demands that learning the various elements of the language will make on learners as speakers of their own particular language. This is the crucial link between knowledge of the language as content to be taught (the finishing line) and the design of methods and techniques, which will allow students eventually to progress along the way of the learner from their starting line to development of proficient Chinese on that finishing line and a concurrent development of their identity as a bi- or multi- lingual, bi- or multi- cultural, person.

The lack of a recognised learners' path in Chinese is the result on the one hand of ignorance on the part of Western language educators of the very real differences in the nature of Chinese language and the nature of European languages, and on the other of low appreciation of the challenges of Chinese by those who teach it, the vast majority of whom are themselves native speakers. Thus, the former proceeds to ask the Chinese language field to produce courses and resources that follow the familiar shape and structure of their own second European language courses, not realising that these will prove to be inadequate to the task. And the latter, like all first language users, blithely unaware of the demands on a learner posed by the language they have used since birth, do as bidden, producing courses and learning activities that resemble the English and other European language courses they themselves have followed as second language learners. When L2 students of Chinese falter, their teachers can only encourage them to be more diligent and sigh over the evidence that Chinese is a difficult language to learn. They often fall back on proposing students adopt the study habits they themselves acquired as children in China. In many cases, these did prove at least partly effective for mature and dedicated L2 learners who went to China some decades ago, who were able to adapt themselves to high repetition and committing texts to memory while aided by the immersive language rich and highly academic environment they were in. Still found in contemporary textbooks, these methods, however, place characters at the heart of learning and ultimately expect L2 learners to process characters in order, not only to read aloud, but also to *speak*. This approach is not suitable for younger, less dedicated and less experienced learners in overseas contexts, partly because the learning task of an L2 student who already has the habits of their own first language does not match that of a native-speaking child developing literacy, and partly because few Western students these days are strong in memorising skills.

Schoenfeld (2014) argues that instead of looking to students or the content to improve a situation where teaching is failing to develop powerful learning, we should look to the teachers and the resources. The failure, he says, is likely to be the result of inappropriate teaching materials and a teacher's, or a group of teachers', lack of domain-specific knowledge and content knowledge. In this view, the failures in the field of Chinese as a Second Language indicate that teachers and resource creators need to improve their understanding of the concepts of education and language teaching and of the formal linguistic concepts of language and culture that are involved, as well as to develop their grasp of what in the whole endeavour merits being called powerful. Teachers' mastery of content specific knowledge—here, the nature of Chinese language and of the students' own first language—would also need to be augmented. The starting point for this will be to recognise and understand the demands of Chinese and the natural deficits in learners' skills that result from their first language mastery. Only when this has been achieved can a pedagogy be prepared which will create a learner's path along which challenges to progress will be successfully mitigated. As always, creating such a path will require synthesising various aspects of formal knowledge into practice with actual students, and the use of congruent resources. The nature of the challenges Chinese presents to learners that teachers and resources need to target are set out in the next section.

## Chinese: Creating a New Skill Base

For speakers of a European language to take even the first steps along the way to learning Chinese means encountering two challenging new phenomena: *tones* and *characters*. The argument here is that these are not only new linguistic forms for learners from European language backgrounds, but that they are formidable learning challenges which require scaffolded re-education of basic cognitive and production skills if they are to be mastered. A third such challenge comes from Chinese grammar and vocabulary. Each of these aspects is dealt with in detail in later chapters in this book. Here just the basic pieces of the argument are presented showing that they need to be seen as requiring development of new basic skills involving detailed, targeted work.

### Tones

In Chinese language courses in the primary years, tones are rarely explicitly taught. Instead, students are expected to pick up correct pronunciation from being exposed to natural flows of Chinese. In many cases, they can largely do this, but it is noticeable that even after some years in a bilingual program, where they use several hours of Chinese every week to learn ordinary school subjects, most children often still make tonal errors of perception and production. If these young learners are to be able to discern and reproduce tone, especially the reduced tones of rapid speech, like older students, they also need to have regular, scaffolded exercises which specifically target tones. The work on tone set by most teachers and textbooks comprises explanations about pitch entry and contour—often accompanied by Y. R. Zhao's famous graph of tone lines (1968)—and recordings of syllables which students are to listen to and repeat, or Pinyin transcriptions of syllables with tones marked on them, which they are to read aloud. Nowhere does one find information on what it is that a speaker needs to do to produce tone or to hear tones in multi-syllable words and connected speech spoken at varied speeds. Nowhere does one find an understanding that what the learner will need to do is to put aside the well-developed competence they have in their mother tongue, in which in order to understand the words being uttered, tonal variation in a word is *ignored* so that the segmental sounds of the utterance are perceived. For example, to hear as one does in English the high pitched voice calling out 'Jāne', the query 'Jáne?', the cry of disbelief 'Ja-ǎne?' and the peremptory command 'Jàne!' as all referring to the same person (or at least, to the same name) is to stress recognition of what in those utterances is common—the sounds (*dʒ ei n*)—and to ignore the glaring differences in intonation. L1 English speakers become so adept at doing this at such an early age that they forget that there is nothing natural about it. It is a learned skill. When L1 speakers of a European language transfer this skill to listening to another European language, it is a strength, but when they use it, as European language speakers naturally do, for listening to spoken Chinese, it turns into a liability. It is just what is not needed if they are to understand Chinese. For Chinese, they need to undo this skill and reverse it: to listen intently for the intonational differences and only then attend to the segmental sounds. To do this requires the metalinguistic knowledge about what needs to be done, plus the cognitive flexibility to shift aural attention from the sounds to the pitch and contour.

The first lesson is thus to *know* what to do and the second lesson is learning *how* to do it. Contrary to what is often believed, European learners of Chinese can quite quickly perceive shifts in tone accurately. What they find difficult, especially in real life interaction, is to *remember to attend to tone* instead of falling back onto mother tongue habits and letting tone filter through as they zero in on just the segmental sounds. The noticing skill to be developed involves basic habits of perception, and it is developed through exercises, which concentrate on teaching students to shift primary attention from sounds to tone. These are similar to exercises in visual perception of black and white field-background illustrations, where viewers can see two quite different objects depicted depending on whether they look hard at the black as field and see the white as background, or vice versa. Tone production, especially in flows of speech, requires similarly targeted exercises as are done for visual perception, combined with metalinguistic knowledge of what is required of the body in the form of pitch entry point, breath intensity, length and contour. Utterances in which there is an emotional intensity that in a European language might require additional stress are particularly likely to evoke mother tongue habits which interfere with learners' tonal production, unless students are also taught to use the modal particles in Chinese available for just this purpose. Such a deep re-routing of cognitive processes which have become automatic and virtually invisible will only be developed gradually. But constant, regular short exercises over time aimed at the problem do enable learners to successfully develop high level tonal capability.

## *Characters*

Reading and writing characters also demand from the European language learner the use of motor skills that lie outside those developed to master literacy in their own language. The fact that beginning Chinese literacy pushes even adult learners back to pre-school level is most evident in their slow and higgledy-piggledy attempts to write characters. While the fact that they are also slow to recognise characters in reading is well known, there is rarely any appreciation that this is due to their being as equally lost about to how even to begin to tackle reading characters as they are in knowing how to write them. The tightly packed information provided in a uniform sized square space that characters present requires very different eye movements to absorb than do the linear strings of Roman alphabet letters mostly based on the circular shape (o). What those who succeed in setting out on the path to Chinese literacy learn to do is to perceive the character as structured, and the components as arranged in one particular structure, some of which contain information about the meaning and possibly how the syllable is sounded. Knowing this, however, is of no use to the young learner with limited vocabulary—at best it may assist in differentiating between related characters but is hardly likely to assist the novice in sound or meaning identification. Just like learning tones, the task of basic literacy skill development—of knowing to look for the structural clues and knowing what they are, plus noticing them at the time of meeting a character—all need to be taught and practised. Just as with learning tones, this is also most effective if preliminary exercises are undertaken which only require noticing and remembering structure and structural patterns, without the burden of stroke shapes or components, let alone any need to know the sound of the syllable or what it means.

Activities which comprise looking, noticing, discriminating and remembering create the students' way into literacy from their starting line. General exercises targeting these skills can make a good start on this development. For example, looking at two copies of an illustration in which certain features have been altered or deleted in one and finding these differences demands looking at detail. This can be followed by specifically Chinese-targeted exercises where, for example, flashcards are presented that show character-like squares filled with abstract signs that are arranged in the ways that characters are, although at this point *the only task is to train the eye to look and remember a pattern* (see Figure 1.2). In the most basic task, students are asked just to look and to point with their fingers on a designated space (e.g. their book or table) the arrangement they see. Thus, for the card in Figure 1.3 they would point twice, with the second point directly to the right of the first; and for the card in Figure 1.4 they would also point twice, this time with the second point directly below the first. They would practise marking a variety of structures in this way (Figures 1.5–1.7).

Such activities would both prime students for the task of character learning, and also assist the teacher in identifying students for whom basic visual information processing tasks create challenges, and who would thus require additional scaffolding before undertaking the challenge of character learning.

A second exercise would ask students to look at a flashcard and then say whether the following card shown (which replaces the first) depicts the same structure as the first one or not (e.g. Figures 1.3 and 1.4). Then a third card is shown and they need to say whether it shows the same structure as the one before (e.g. Figures 1.4 and 1.5), and so on. As students become very quick at succeeding in this task, the demands of the exercise are gradually extended by adding more structures to the pack being shown, and further extended by decreasing the time available to look at any card. Another increase in demand can be created by gradually moving from cards sequenced to show very dissimilar structures to ones which are more and more alike.

A third type of exercise would have students marking on a worksheet showing only blank squares the dots and divisions of the cards they look at. This is

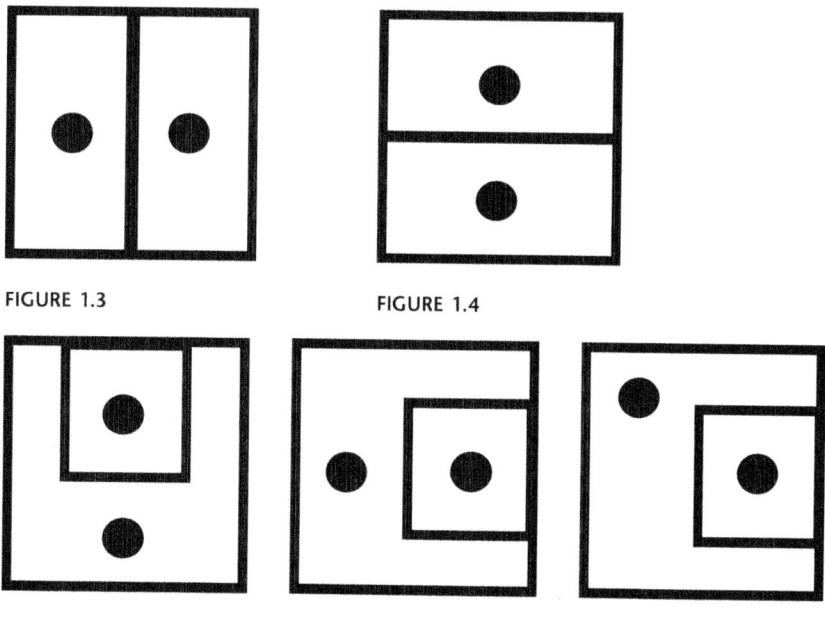

FIGURE 1.3                    FIGURE 1.4

FIGURE 1.5              FIGURE 1.6              FIGURE 1.7

FIGURE 1.2 Pattern perception training (includes Figures 1.3–1.7)

simply a 'looking and noticing' exercise. Once it is successful, the card being shown is removed from view and students have to reproduce its structure from memory. Increasing the speed, and then the complexity of the structures are ways to stretch the demands, as is making cards which follow each other in the sequence more and more alike.

## Grammar and Vocabulary

A final area which needs the same kind of kindergarten level field extension in order to create a sound foundation, is working with the challenges of Chinese grammar and vocabulary. While in some respects the grammar of Chinese is less of a challenge to speakers of English because it often follows a similar word order in the two languages, there are features of Chinese which are very different to those found in European languages. Yet very little attention is given to developing in learners any feel for the expressive power of the structures which are different from those of their mother tongue. Instead, all the energy is concentrated on form. In textbook after textbook, a great deal of attention is paid to teaching measure words, and it is true that, initially, speakers of languages that do not use these as they occur in Chinese can forget to insert them, and often find themselves not knowing the measure word they need. But measure words are not structurally difficult to comprehend and their mastery is far less elusive in the longer term than, for example, the lack of a word in Chinese for *Yes* (requiring an attention to the verb used in the interrogative sentence), or the lack of articles; verb complements and particles expressing aspect; modal particles; and *de*-segments. While students can develop competence in processing and even producing these structures as sentence *forms*, they often fall back onto L1 norms in independent expressive use, because they still lack a sense of the expressive power of Chinese structures.

With respect to vocabulary, what seems rarely to have been acknowledged in the teaching of Chinese is that Chinese Pinyin words look very unfamiliar to European language speakers. Just like characters, they present a very small number of features that look and sound remarkably similar and very different from the words the learners are used to: they are short, use only a small number of sounds, many starting with x, y or z (new to English speakers, at least) and do odd things with familiar letters like e, i, j, q and x. This all makes them hard to remember and as there are so many of them to be remembered (far more than is required when learning a second European language where cognates abound), plus each has its own character, a massive burden on memory is the key problem of acquiring Chinese vocabulary. To be efficient, students need help developing their memory skills, and if help is to be successful, it needs to be provided in ways which connect with the learners' existing cognitive style. That is, it needs to provide high frequency engagement and the involvement of higher order categories of thought: not just memorising lists of words, but quizzes which keep the mind active in looking carefully and making judgments. Recognising these challenges also makes evident the importance of accurate Pinyin processing as a tool for engaging with new (spoken) words, for recording the sounds of words encountered, and for accurate and efficient production of digital (character) texts. Activities that can assist in this development include dictation—writing down sounds with tones—and working on rhythm and sounds through narratives and dialogues presented in Pinyin alone, removing the character 'burden'.

*

More detailed work on all these challenges, as well as on the demands of Chinese and culture learning, are set out in the chapters which follow. The aim of each is to allow teacher educators, teachers, and teacher candidates to gain deeper knowledge and expanded perspectives on their field through an examination of the relevant research that needs to inform and underpin their planned practices and classroom artistry. With this strengthened base, teachers will be able to present Chinese using powerful instruction which will enable learners to create their own way from starting line to finishing line, and to do so effectively in terms of results, and economically, in terms of effort required.

## Part 2: The Culture of Education

### *Origins*

The way of teaching proposed in this book is grounded in a traditional Western perspective on human nature and the goal of education, which has survived its origins in religious beliefs. The origins can be found in the key text of the Jewish, Christian and Islamic religions, the Bible. Its first chapter, *Genesis*, sets out the story of God's creation of human beings, the first of whom were the man and woman, Adam and Eve, who lived in Paradise. Adam and Eve were free to choose their own course of action and, in fact, they chose away from God and fell into sin. They thus lost the right to Paradise for all human beings. Thereafter the only way for people to get to Heaven after death has been to earn it by avoiding evil and leading a good life. The central cultural orientations that emerge from the story of Adam and Eve are that (i) human beings are individuals, who (ii) can and must exercise will and agency to choose their own path in life, (iii) for which they alone will be held responsible. Neither parents nor position nor wealth can influence the outcome of a life. Each person must learn independently to resist the temptation to do bad things. There are some direct conflicts with the traditions of Chinese philosophy here that need to be recognised. Modern Confucians such as Xie (1967: 321) reject the values in the story of Adam and Eve, claiming that, 'No ethics of any kind would allow freedom to do evil'; and the eminent modern Confucian philosopher, the late

Tang Junyi, summed up the situation by saying: 'Our two forms of self-assertion each imply that the other is pathological' (in Metzger, 1977: 43).

The previously mentioned traditional Western orientations are evident still in the practice of modern education, a process described by the American educational psychologist Howard Gardner as one providing ' . . . a series of situations in which one has to learn to think for oneself, to solve problems on one's own, and even to discover new problems for which creative solutions are wanted' (1989: 5). Imbued with the ideas of individual will and agency, since the 18th century Western educators such as Rousseau, Pestalozzi and Froebels have promoted the assumption that children are individuals, natural learners with an active, curious mind which needs to be engaged in any learning to develop. Learning is understood to be a gradual, iterative process of gaining ever greater control through knowledge, understanding and skill, and this proceeds in irregular stages which include backtracking at times. Mistakes and failure are accepted as natural by-products of this learning process. Chinese educators often note that not making more overt use of the superior knowledge of the teachers involved to instruct directly, the Western process takes time and seems inefficient, and when students encounter false starts and dead ends, even undesirable. The Western argument is that these are a necessary part of learning because the goal is student internalisation of what is being taught so that they can *own* it and so make use of it in the new situations in which they find themselves at times with no teacher to fall back on, circumstances which are the reality of modern life. While intuition and ways of knowing embedded in action—usually practical activities, often in forms of play—are accepted as how our understanding of matter is acquired, there is also a belief in conscious reflection—metacognitive awareness—as a necessary auxiliary means to grasping and controlling knowledge so that results are not accidental but can be replicated at will and can be accurately passed on to others. At least part of this knowledge is often produced inductively by the students after they have first engaged with the topic themselves.

It is essential that first language speaking teachers of Chinese understand these basics of the Western learning tradition because it can help them see the line of logic in the behaviour they find in the practices of Western schools and universities. *To encourage this understanding does not imply an expectation that these views will simply be adopted.* However, for the discussion of the learner's path set out in this book to be effective in increasing a Chinese teacher's mastery of professional knowledge and their ability to use it in their teaching, it *is* necessary to address the conflict between the educational beliefs, values and experience of teachers of Chinese from China and those held by the field of language teaching in the countries outside China in which many of them teach. As noted in the introduction to this chapter, the differences have been publicly acknowledged over some time. More recently a growing volume of writing by China-educated teachers of Chinese (e.g. Lü and Lavadenz, 2014; Ma, 2014; Chen and Yeung, 2015a, 2015b; Yue, 2017) has revealed the practical difficulties and ethical dilemmas they face when they find themselves in overseas schools, as well as their openness to engage with creating resolutions to them. The authors of this book recognise all these discussions as active steps in creating dialogue over the issues and intend their book to be a reciprocal step in furthering the dialogue.

## *Principles and Practice*

What all the writers mentioned show very clearly is that 'teachers approach and understand teaching and learning from their own culturally specific points of view' (Yue, 2017) and that the points of conflict encompass beliefs, knowledge, theories, assumptions and attitudes. This is hardly surprising, given that education is a crucial social practice in which a society's older generation prepares a younger generation for life, handing on received knowledge and wisdom and at the same time trying to ready their young to deal with an unknown future. As this work is carried out within a specific sociocultural and historical perspective, it can be expected that a quite different set of educational beliefs, values and practices will have emerged from an ancient civilisation like China which has been through considerable turmoil in the 20th century, to that developed in the relatively young, European heritage pioneer nations of the United States, Canada, Australia and New Zealand, where the 20th century was largely a time of peace and prosperity (Gao, 2010; Zhang and Yin, 2014). Thus teachers raised in a traditional Chinese spirit of '苦苦苦，不苦如何通今古' [*bitter, bitter, bitter, without suffering no way to reach knowledge past and present*], and '学 海无涯苦作舟' [*to sail the boundless sea of knowledge, bitterness must be your vessel*] will not easily fit into a system imbued with the creative ideas of Dewey and Malaguzzi derived from a tradition grounded in calls by Plato and Rousseau for children to be taught through play and to be let out of stuffy rooms to run about outside (Gao, 2010; Zhang, 2018).

At the level of classroom practice, the differences between the two broad approaches are manifest in the style of instruction, the view of learning, the roles of teacher and student, and the relationship between them. In short, they lie in the very concept of what to teach means, as these examples show:

L1 Chinese Teacher discussing pedagogy with the author:
I see what you mean: It's not just to *teach*, right, but it's also to help students learn?

By contrast, the Western view is that:

The unique *work of teaching* involves the 'core tasks that teachers must execute to help pupils learn'.

(Ball and Forzani, 2009: 497)

Despite ongoing moves in China towards developing more independent thinking, traditional views such as that good teaching centres on presenting knowledge is still both practised and advocated:

培养和提高
　　只有掌握丰富的专业学科知识,才能更好地驾驭教材,处理教,才能完整准确, 生动有校地传授知识:才能时刻面对和清晰解决学生随时可能提出的疑惑, 满足学生得求知欲, 启发学生思维。(甲 2007: 40) *[Training and Improvement—Only if you master rich professional scientific knowledge can you manage the teaching content, handle the resources, and transmit knowledge completely accurately, vividly and efficiently; and be ready to face students' questions, at all times solving their problems and queries; satisfying students' learning needs, catering to their craving for knowledge, and stimulating and inspiring students in their thinking.]*

I don't use the science equipment very much. I deliver the knowledge and I write on the board in a very traditional fashion. It's all done in books and paper and note taking, 'cos I can go fast, deliver quickly, in a very structured manner.

[Mainland Teacher Yang, BBC 2, 2015]

There are also differences in terms of expectations about the student's role and motivation. For example:

My neighbour walks her 8-year old son to school every morning at the same time as I am leaving. In China, the mother would say to her child, 'Now study hard and obey the teacher'. But at the school gate, my neighbour kisses her son goodbye and says, 'Have a good day'.

　　I learned each of those words in my first month of English 15 years ago, but actually I don't know what she means: what will happen if he has a good day—or if he doesn't't? I have no idea! [*Fudan University graduate in the author's Australian teacher education program*]

Some of the students [in China] have better English learning abilities. . . . I would call one of these high performing students to answer my questions; they will give the correct answer. Then I will ask the whole class to give a round of applause, so that students can see some classmates are ahead of them in learning and thereby will have more enthusiasm for learning.

(Grant, Stronge, Xu, Popp, Sun, and Little, 2013: 109)

The proposed action in this last example is expected to be motivating, but in many Western classrooms, such a technique would be counterproductive, the teacher resented as patronising by the students and possibly leading to the teasing of the singled-out student. Many Western teachers would also be uneasy about the competitiveness underlying such an action, just as they are often unhappy with the heavy focus on competitions run in Chinese language teaching.

Studies of teachers handling interactions with students, especially problematic behaviour (e.g. Zhou and Li, 2015; CTTC, 2015; Chen and Yeung, 2015a; Yue, 2017), reveal high anxiety on the part of Chinese teachers that they will not know what to say at these moments, will not understand what is being said to them, and that they might lose face by making mistakes in their English. As a result of this, and in keeping with the power distance held by teachers in China, many do not talk directly to individual students about their work, nor do they do so on a social level before class, in the playground or on the bus. Even during language exercises, many do not appear to listen to what students actually say to them in English or Chinese. In light of their own tradition, their behaviour is understandable, but maintaining it means they miss out on knowing their students well and letting students assist them with behaviour issues, both of which are sources of the effective soft power exercised by their local colleagues—as some Chinese who have yielded have discovered (e.g. Chen and Yeung, 2015a).

A number of writers in the field have been concerned with how to 'help [Chinese] teachers not only understand the concepts but also reframe their teaching practice in terms of teaching and learning goals that are substantially different from those that native speaker teachers aimed toward as learners of Chinese' (Yue, 2017). But the teachers often find that, deep down, although they agree that the Chinese way does not fit their students, 'in their hearts, they could not discard their belief in rote learning, which is deeply rooted in Chinese educational culture' (Yue, 2017: 615). Furthermore, some feel that they are teaching Chinese and so it is right that they should teach it in a Chinese way, and it is the students who should adjust. However, with little external pressure or reward for learning Chinese, when students find the work involved tedious and their results unsatisfying, most do not adjust: they simply give up.

The view taken here is that there is a strong case to be made for asking teachers of Chinese to adapt to Western ways, firstly on the grounds that they have entered a non-Chinese educational system and need to meet its demands, which cannot be changed to suit thinking from outside. Secondly, and more importantly, as set out in the earlier section of this chapter, on both principled and practical grounds: if they are to have any hope of success, teachers of Chinese need to initiate engagement with students, meeting them where they are and creating with them a viable learning path, not expecting students to find *them*. What this means is starting in accordance with the students' usual learning habits, which are that:

- They have been taught to exercise their curiosity.
- They expect to solve problems and to have their own view on matters.
- They remember things through being interested in them and using them frequently, in slightly different ways.

- They have rarely been asked to memorise matter and hence are poor at it.
- They expect learning material, which has been prepared to allow them direct access.

Hence teachers should:

- Provide only what students cannot provide for themselves.
- Allow opportunities for students to play with the new learning.
- Monitor and challenge student efforts appropriately.
- Correct errors by targeting the learner, not the language.
- Talk directly and personally to students.

The chapters in this book are designed to fill out the meaning of these statements with respect to various aspects of Chinese linguistic knowledge and knowledge of Chinese as a learning object.

Suggesting this line of action, it might be noticed, is no more than suggesting that the field of CSL follow very much along the path of ESL in China since its early years, where the same differences caused similar problems in reverse that were hotly debated in many Chinese public forums and in the privacy of university staffrooms, as well as discussed internationally (e.g. Simpson, 2008; Hu, 2002). The outcome in many Chinese institutions has been to have local staff teach the basics of English in the first two years and then have teachers from overseas work with the more advanced students in their final two years.

In taking this stand, the authors also acknowledge that there is more to be said than making a simple binary decision. What is required is to create dialogue that over time develops a viable synthesis of the two perspectives. The basis for this is to understand the source of differences and also to recognise the commonalities.

## Commonalities

If it is to be successful, the teaching of any subject has to start from where students are and this means that the teaching of Chinese in Western schools needs to begin by attracting the attention of students in a Western style, which will include intellectual development; not just language acquisition. But saying this does not mean that Chinese habits of diligence should be disregarded, nor deny that there is a need for memorisation in some parts of language learning. Both have a clear place in any student's learning scheme. Furthermore, it is agreed that longer term students will need to go beyond their current experience and encounter contemporary Chinese learning culture as part of their studies, which may well mean working in ways new to them. However, the introduction and exploration of new cultural practices in learning must be recognised as being just that—very new, and so this, too, must occur in a style and at a pace that leads to productive development over time.

An important area of commonality has emerged in just the last decade or so, as Chinese educational thinking undergoes quite a few fundamental changes due to modernisation. Modernisation has meant that better educated, younger people with much greater access to the world through their skills in English and technology, are challenging their subordination to their parents and even older colleagues. Well-paid and able to enjoy a lifestyle that has emerged to cater to their age and discretionary income, and frequently living in a different city from their family or moving around the country, they have quickly become more individualistically oriented. This social reality and the skill set needed to staff modern enterprises have led to considerable convergence in contemporary Chinese government thinking and aspiration with Western educational principles and practices (中华人民共和国政府 (*Chinese Government*), 2001; Guan and Meng, 2007). New practices derived from the new perspectives can already be observed

**TABLE 1.1** Modern Chinese educational thinking

---

**Retired Teacher:**

看到了吧，老关！孩子们都玩疯了。

You must have seen it, Old Guan: The kids went crazy playing!

**Teacher Guan:**

*玩物丧志啊！* 小时候玩的多，长大就要受苦。

*People lost in play will lose their aims.* If they play too much in childhood, they will suffer when they grow up.

**Retired Teacher:**

老关！看到你，我就看到了从前的我自己呀！该醒一醒了。

Old Guan, when I see you, I see my previous self! It is time to wake up.

**Teacher Guan:**

简直是在浪费*生命*啊！

Playing is such a waste of life!

**Retired Teacher:**

生命！说的没有错！对于我而言，每一个孩子，都是含苞待放独特的生命体！可是*扪心自问*，我们真正尊重过他们吗？我们真正像生命一样对待他们了吗？

Life! You are right! To me, every child is a special life that's about to blossom. But let's ask ourselves from the heart: Do we really respect their individuality? Do we treat them as if they each are a life?

---

*Source: Tiger Mom, Pussy Cat Dad* episode 45 (Dragon TV, Shanghai). Reproduced with permission of the author, Shen Jie.

in key schools in China's major cities, while such a big reorientation inevitably has constantly been debated by those involved (e.g. Hu, 2002; Tan, 2016). A dialogue in a contemporary Chinese TV drama series between two teachers watching as their young students come in from playing in an orchard explains and advocates the new perspective very clearly:

In light of this development especially, the authors suggest that teachers of Chinese who find themselves facing a dilemma because the teaching style advocated in the West conflicts with their own educational tradition will need to consider whether, in this 21st century, all their views are still validly 'Chinese educational thinking and practices', inside or outside China.

## Professional Development

The proposal that Chinese teachers should adjust their teaching style is made here with some confidence of it being adopted because many of the teachers who participated in the various studies cited earlier in this section make it clear that they are willing to adapt their practice to local conditions, but just do not know how to. Most teacher education courses offer only generic language teacher training and there is a dearth of developed material to help with the linguistic issues in teaching Chinese specifically, and virtually no understanding of the intercultural factors at play. Many teachers trained in China have built no repertoire of strategies for motivating students and have no experience of seeing teachers engage students, and so they lack an understanding of the underlying triggers which could help generate active student learning. As a result, when they embrace the goals of a modern style of teaching, they are able only to imitate the apparently 'fun' activities they see on the surface, and then fall back on carrot-and-stick gimmicks such as competitions and rewards or tests and punishments to jolly students into compliance. A further difficulty they face are classes comprising mixed level groups including competent home speakers, novice learners, students whose English is not strong, and special needs students, which they also feel unprepared to manage—a situation shared by local teachers as well. There is much that could be done in teacher education to better assist these teachers in pre-service and in-service professional development programs. To be effective, however, both sides must be informed by an understanding of the linguistic and intercultural dilemmas involved and find ways to make them regularly discussable.

## Conclusion

The outcomes reported around the world show that the need for the field of CSL to develop is critical and, as Shoenfeld proposes, the way to develop will be through better teaching practices grounded in knowledge and assisted by well-designed resources. However, a teacher's practice does not all derive from knowledge and logical reasoning but also, and often more deeply, from emotional attachment to ways of being in the classroom derived from their own experience as a student. In many cases, teachers are not even aware of this and, in all countries, even those teachers who espouse contemporary practices may actually, unawares, behave in quite the opposite way in their teaching. This means that, even when accepted, real change will be gradual. A further complication to progress is that with the advent of the electronic age and globalisation, more radical social changes in both China and the West are underway, and these are putting new pressures on education to develop further.

The authors believe that if there is to be any advance in Chinese language teaching internationally, both L1 and L2 teachers of Chinese and language teacher educators in the CSL field, have to be willing to work together to consider the propositions being put forward in this book about Chinese from the learners' perspective, and about issues in the wider educational framework which support the teaching outlined. Recognising their common intent is to motivate and facilitate students' learning of Chinese, and their common need to develop their professional knowledge and artistry, all involved need to be willing to acknowledge the limitations of their own practice and its outcomes, as well as to recognise their mutual strengths. Only then can they together create ways to try something really new, monitor it, and continue dialogue about what it produces.

## References

American Council on the Teaching of Foreign Languages. (2002) *Program Standards for the Preparation of Foreign Language Teachers*. Alexandria, Va: American Council on the Teaching of Foreign Languages.

Australian Curriculum Assessment and Reporting Authority. (2014) *Australian Curriculum for Languages*. Preamble. Retrieved 31 December 2014 from www.australiancurriculum.edu.au/languages/preamble

Ball, D.L., and Forzani, F.M. (2009) 'The Work of Teaching and the Challenge for Teacher Education', *Journal of Teacher Education*, 2009(60): 497.

BBC 2. (2015) *Are Our Kids Tough Enough? Episode 1*. DVD. Retrieved 17 December 2016 from www.youtube.com/watch?v=pHTVnB4SvuA

Chen, Z. and Yeung, A. (2015a) 'Learning to Teach in a Research-Oriented School-Based Language Teaching Programme', *Electronic Journal of Foreign Language Teaching*, 12(2): 183–199.

Chen, Z. and Yeung, A. (2015b) 'Self-efficacy in Teaching Chinese as a Foreign Language in Australian Schools', *Australian Journal of Teacher Education*, 40(8): 24–44.

CILT. (2007) *Mandarin Language Learning Research Study*. London: UK Report.

Council of Europe. (2003–2009) *The Common European Framework of Reference for Languages*. Cambridge: Cambridge University Press. Retrieved 31 December 2014 from www. coe.int/t/dg4/linguistic/source/framework_en.pdf

CTTC. (2015) 'Intercultural Challenges for L1 Teachers of Chinese in Australian Schools', *A Digest of Chinese Teacher Training Centre Research, Resources and Publications 2009–2015*, 23. Melbourne: University of Melbourne.

Dewey, J. (1938) *Education and Experience*. New York: Touchstone.

Gabbianelli, G., Formica, A., and Chang, Y. (2017) 'Difficulties and Expectations of First Level Chinese Second Language Learners', Paper presented at the *Being and Becoming a Teacher of Chinese as a Foreign and Second Language Today—From the Weakest to the Strongest Link Conference*, University of Helsinki, 22–23 May 2017.

Gao, B. (2010) *China's Teacher-Student Relations in the Period of Modernisation (1982–1992) A Comparative Study*. Lewiston, Queenston, and Lampeter: The Edwin Mellen Press.

Gardner, H. (1989) *To Open Minds*. New York: Basic Books.

Gattegno, C. (1970) *What We Owe Children*. New York: Outerbridge and Dienstfrey.

Gattegno, C. (1972) *Teaching Foreign Languages in Schools the Silent Way*. New York: Educational Solutions, Inc.

Grant, L., Stronge, J., Xu, X., Popp, P., Sun, Y., and Little, C. (2014) *West Meets East: Best Practices From Expert Teachers in the U.S. and China*. Alexandria, Va: ASCD.

Guan, Q. and Meng, W. (2007) 'China's New National Curriculum Reform: Innovation, Challenges and Strategies', *Frontiers of Education in China*, 2(4): 579–604.

Hall Haley, M.H. and Ferro, M.S. (2011) 'Understanding the Perceptions of Arabic and Chinese Teachers Toward Transitioning Into U.S. Schools', *Foreign Language Annals*, 44(2): 289–307.

Hu, G. (2002) 'Potential Cultural Resistance to Pedagogical Imports: The Case of Communicative Language Teaching in China', *Language Culture and Curriculum*, 15(2): 93–105.

Ke, P. (2016) 'Chinese as a Foreign Language in K-12 Education', in J. Ruan, C. Leung, J. Zhang (eds.), *Chinese Language Education in the United States*, 123–140. Cham, Heidelberg, New York, Dordrecht, and London: Springer.

Kierkegaard, S. (1959) *The Journal of Kierkegaard* (trans. A. Dru). New York: Harper.

Lü, C. and Lavadenz, M. (2014) 'Native Chinese Speaking K-12 Language Teachers' Beliefs and Practices', *Foreign Language Annals*, 47(4): 630–652.

Ma, W. (ed) (2014) *East Meets West in Teacher Preparation Crossing Chinese and American Borders*. New York and London: Teachers College Press.

Metzger, T.A. (1977) *Escape From Predicament: China's Evolving Political Culture*. New York: Columbia University Press.

Orton, J. (2016) 'Chinese Language Education: Teacher Training', in Chan Sin-Wai (ed.), *The Routledge Encyclopedia of Chinese Language and Culture*, 177–197. Abingdon, Oxon: Routledge.

Rukodelnikova, M. (2017) 'How to Strengthen the Interest in the Study of the Chinese Language?', Paper presented at the *Being and Becoming a Teacher of Chinese as a Foreign and Second Language Today—From the Weakest to the Strongest Link Conference*, University of Helsinki, 22–23 May 2017.

Schaeffer, H.R. (1996) 'Joint Involvement Episodes as Context for Development', in H. Daniels (ed.), *An Introduction to Vygotsky*, 251–280. London and New York: Routledge.

Schoenfeld, A.H. (2014) 'What Makes for Powerful Classrooms, and How Can We Support Teachers in Creating Them? A Story of Research and Practice, Productively Intertwined', *Educational Researcher*, 43(8): 404–412.

Schön, D.A. (1984) *Educating the Reflective Practitioner*. San Francisco: Jossey Bass.

She, J. (2017) 'Chinese as a Foreign Language in Europe—Challenges Faced by Native Chinese Teachers', Paper presented at the *Being and Becoming a Teacher of Chinese as a Foreign and Second Language Today—From the Weakest to the Strongest Link Conference*, University of Helsinki, 22–23 May 2017.

Simpson, S.T. (2008) 'Western EFL Teachers and East-West Classroom-Culture Conflicts', *RELC Journal*, 39(3): 381–394.

Tan, C. (2016) 'Tensions and Challenges in China's Education Policy Borrowing', *Educational Research*, 58(2): 195–206. doi:10.1080/00131881.2016.1165551

Vygotsky, L.S. ([1930] 1978) *Mind in Society: The Development of Higher Psychological Processes* (trans. M. Cole, English). Cambridge, MA: Harvard University Press.

Xie, Y. (1967) 'The Status of the Individual in Chinese Ethics', in C. Moore (ed.), *The Chinese Mind: Essentials of Chinese Philosophy and Culture*, 307–322. Honolulu: East-West Centre Press, University of Hawaii Press.

Xing, Z.Q. (2003) 'Toward a Pedagogical Grammar of Chinese: Approach, Content and Process', *Journal of Chinese Language Teachers Association*, 38(3): 41–67.

Yin, J. (2003) 'Methods Used by American College Students in Memorizing Chinese Characters', *Journal of the Chinese Language Teachers Association*, 38(3): 69–90.

Young, M. (2012) *The Curriculum—'An Entitlement to Powerful Knowledge': A Response to John White. New Visions for Education*. Retrieved 31 December 2014 from www.newvisionsforeducation.org.uk/2012/05/03/the-curriculum-%E2%80%98an-entitlement-to-powerful-knowledge%E2%80%99-a-response-to-john-white/

Yue, Y. (2017) 'Teaching Chinese in K—12 Schools in the United States: What Are the Challenges?', *Foreign Language Annals*, 50(3): 601–620.

Zhang, H. and Yin, J. (2014) 'K-5 Literacy Education: A Comparison Between American Common Core State Standards and Chinese National Curriculum Standards', *Universal Journal of Educational Research*, 2(7): 521–525.

Zhang, L. (2018) *The Affordances of TV Drama in Building L2 Chinese Learners' Intercultural Competence*. Unpublished PhD thesis, Melbourne: The University of Melbourne.

Zhao, Y.R. (1968) *A Grammar of Spoken Chinese*. Berkeley: University of California Press.

Zhou, W. and Li, G. (2015) 'Chinese Language Teachers' Expectations and Perceptions of American Students' Behavior: Exploring the Nexus of Cultural Differences and Classroom Management', *System*, 49: 17–27.

中华人民共和国中央人民政府 (Chinese Government). (2001) 教育部关于印发《基础教育课程改革纲要(试行)》的通知 (Announcement of the Publication of the Basic Education Curriculum Reform Program (Trial)). Retrieved from www.gov.cn/gongbao/content/2002/content_61386.htm

申继亮 (主编) (Shen Jiliang) (ed.). (2007) 新世界教师角色重塑 (Remodeling the Role of the Teacher in the New Century). 北京：北京师范大学出版社.

徐天就 (Xu Tianjiu) and Kooi, R. (2017) '学习动机与学生辍学的关系初探：以荷兰汉语专业学生为例', A Preliminary Probe Into the Relationship Between Motivation and Drop Out: the Example of Dutch Majors in Chinese). Paper presented at the *Being and Becoming a Teacher of Chinese as a Foreign and Second Language Today—From the Weakest to the Strongest Link Conference*, University of Helsinki, 22–23 May 2017.

# 2

# ESTABLISHING ORAL SKILLS

## Introduction

Teaching students to 'speak a second language' is a term which conflates mastery of two aspects of oral language—firstly, there is mastery of the fundamental components of speech, the phonological system, and secondly, there is mastery of interactional use of the language in spoken communication with others. The two aspects are intimately linked: control of the phonological system is required in order to ensure basic comprehension of what is being said, and control of the vocalic options within the system—how the voice is used—is needed to ensure that the speaker's emotional state about what is being said is also conveyed. In addition to controlled articulation, competence in interactional use of the language requires knowledge of vocabulary and grammar and takes the learner into the social domain, which requires knowledge of cultural norms and appropriate behavior. Both aspects are complex and competence can only be developed gradually through a great deal of practice. Although intimately connected, for the purposes of this book it is possible and useful to separate these two aspects of oral language and to consider each in turn before discussing them in combination.

## The Phonological System

There are three principal domains of speech common to teaching the phonological system of any language: *prosody, intonation*, and the *pronunciation of segmental sounds*. In this section, the nature of each of these domains will first be considered and then the important facts of the domain within Chinese and what they demand of the learner will be discussed. Finally, the specifically Chinese feature of *tone* will be examined. The section concludes with a summary of the learning tasks and challenges in the Chinese phonological system for the English-speaking student and the principal teaching approach and techniques needing to be adopted if they are to be met and conquered.

## Prosody

### The Basics

Prosody, or the rhythm of the language, is found in the pattern of stressed and unstressed syllables in an utterance. The key features of prosody are:

1. Chunking—words are uttered in sense groups. E.g. 我明天 /八点钟/给他打电话. I will phone him/at eight/tomorrow morning /
2. Key words in a chunked sense group are stressed. Like a telegram, these words carry the main message. The words stressed can vary depending on the thrust of the message, e.g. I can be arguing that it is *I* who will phone him, or that *he* is the person I will phone, or that I will *phone* him, not go to see him; but without any of these particular emphases added, in the example sentence 明八打话 *phone eight tomorrow morning* carries the main message and they will be the stressed words.
3. Within a word, stress falls on one or more key syllables in the key word. E.g. *míng bā dǎ huà*, phone **eigh**t tomorrow **mor**ning.
4. Being 'stressed' means a syllable is made salient due to breath intensity, length and contour (the rise and fall of the voice).
5. There are degrees of stress (primary, secondary, tertiary). E.g. the three 'o' sounds in the word 'tomorrow' are all pronounced with different levels of stress, usually tertiary, primary and secondary, respectively. The first 'o' might even be unstressed.
6. There are unstressed words and unstressed syllables in an utterance.
7. Lesser stressed and unstressed syllables have a reduced quality of articulation. E.g. 干什么? *gàn shénme* is often actually said '*gàshme*'. *It's for you* is very often said *It's f'you*. In these cases, words such as '*shén*' and 'for' are unstressed so their syllable '*en*' and '*or*' are barely pronounced.
8. When a syllable is unstressed, what is pronounced is tied to the next word in the sense group and said without a break between them.
9. When uttered, a stressed syllable is naturally synchronised with any movement of the body, that is, it occurs at the same time as the movement, whether it is a large movement like walking, or small like a slight hand gesture, turn of the head or eyes, or blinking. Furthermore, in conversation, when the hearer moves, that movement is also in synchrony with the speaker's speech rhythm (Condon and Ogston, 1966).
10. Words that are stressed in an utterance are normally the lexical items (adjectives, nouns, verbs, adverbs). These words appear in the utterance according

to the grammatical rules, so the pattern of stressed and unstressed syllables is directly linked to the grammatical patterns of the language.

## The Role of Prosody

Prosody is the very fundamental component of a language. Newly born babies can be seen to tune in to the rhythm of their mother's speech as early as 14 days after birth: when their mother speaks, not only does the infant listen, but it moves its body (e.g. shoulder turn, blink) in time with the stresses in the mother's speech (Condon and Sander, 1974). Furthermore, before they use words, babies babble, producing strings of sounds, and their babbling uses the common rhythmic patterns of their mother tongue, its intonation patterns and, in Chinese, its tonal system (Cruttenden, 1997). Prosody is thus the net that holds everything together: the voice, the body and the grammatical arrangement of the words. It is prosody that governs the production of a coherent message, uttered in chunks, which helps the listener process the basic message, and with only certain items stressed, which draws the listener's attention to the main points the speaker is wanting to make. It is prosody that connects speaker and listener.

## Stress in Chinese

Within a multisyllabic Chinese word, the strongest stress falls on the last syllable, the second strongest on the first syllable, and the weakest comes out as a neutral tone on the syllables in between. Thus in a system where the numeral 1 represents the most prominent syllable and 3 the least prominent (usually a syllable with reduced or no tone), disyllabic Chinese words are commonly pronounced 2–1, with the second syllable more prominent than the first; trisyllabic words are pronounced 2–3–1; and quadra-syllabic words follow a pattern of 2–3–3–1 (Švarny, 1991). It must be noted that certain words, such as particles, never take stress. As well there are about 50 high-frequency monosyllabic function words that are normally not stressed. Called *cliticoids* (Triskova, 2017), these are:

- Personal pronouns
- Classifiers
- Conjunctions
- Prepositions
- Some post prepositions (上, 下, 里)
- General verbs (是, 有, 在)
- Modal verbs
- Grammaticalised adverbs (就, 都, 很)

(Triskova, 2017: 35).

## Learning Chinese Prosody

Students' greatest learning challenge in the mastery of Chinese prosody is managing to give full tonal value only to stressed syllables, reducing the tonal value of unstressed syllables, and tying these unstressed syllables to the stressed syllable ahead of them in the chunk. For example, in normal speech when the listener knows who is being spoken about, *tā shì Zhōngguó rén* becomes *tashZhōng guorén*, with only two stressed syllables getting full tonal value to carry the message— **Zhōng rén**—and no spaces between *ta* and *shi* and *Zhōng*, or between *guo* and *rén*. Leaving a space around a syllable automatically lengthens it, which makes it salient, i.e. gives it stress. If it is isolated, a syllable also requires full tonal value, another feature of stress in Chinese.

A first principle for language teachers is to respect the role of prosody as the base of all spoken language. They also need to note that in perception and production of language, prosody is the first phonological feature that babies acquire in their mother tongue, that they perceive it and produce it *in the whole body*, and that they tackle acquiring grammar and vocabulary already armed with the rhythmic patterns into which these must fit if speech is to be intelligible. Thus, to understand and be understood it is essential that students master the common prosodic patterns of Chinese. While they cannot go back to being infants in a new language, development of oral skills in their new language can be productively guided by a teacher who understands the nature and role of prosody and is trained in techniques which help them override the natural inclination to continue to use the prosodic forms of their first language.

One of the two most common Chinese learner errors in speech is having too many fully tonal syllables in one utterance: *tā shì Zhōng guó rén*. The other is not chunking sense groups, instead saying something like 我明 /天 八点 /钟 给 /他 打 /电/话. While this is acceptable as the first stage of a newly created utterance, too often students are permitted to stop there and not helped to polish their production by chunking the sense groups 我明 天/八点 钟/给 他/打电 话 and finally saying them smoothly 我明 天 八点 钟 给 他 打电 话. When what they are to say has been provided for them, it should be introduced in its chunks made by the teacher using his/her hands like brackets: [我明 天] [八点 钟] [给 他] [打电 话]. Once the chunks can be said with the appropriate syllables stressed and de-stressed, it can be practised as a whole fluent utterance: just as students are finishing the first chunk, the teacher's left hand is moved along, letting the first chunk flow into the second, then stopped to keep the first half of the utterance together: [我明 天 八点 钟; and then the second half: [给 他 打电 话; and finally with the left hand gradually moving left: [我明 天 八点 钟 给 他 打电 话].

Using the natural phenomenon of synchrony of voice and body, stress patterns can be perceived and practiced using hand beats, arm movements and stepping. It is also useful to concentrate on the rhythm (the patterns of stressed and unstressed syllables) without worrying about segmental sounds, simply using a single syllable for all. So 他是中国人 *tash**Zhōng** guorén*, for example, can be practised as dada**DĀ** da**DÁ**.

As the voice will follow the contour of the movement, it is critical in Chinese that any gesture used with speech mirrors the tonal contour of the stressed syllable it is being used with, i.e. *not* just be a set of downward beats of the hand ꜚꜚꜚ, which would only match a fourth tone contour. A second essential is that the body makes only one movement per syllable. So, for example, a downward hand beat ꜚ used when saying 对! *duì!* must go downwards and then remain down and still, not immediately rise again. This is because the voice will follow the body and a second movement (moving the hand back up) will produce a further sound, so 对 will come out as a jerky down-up *duì-í* or at least *duì-á*.

Some further teaching techniques for prosody will be discussed in the section on tone.

## Intonation

A second basic feature of spoken language is *intonation*. Intonation occurs in all languages and refers to the rise and fall of the voice—the pitch—over a whole utterance. Intonation must not be confused with Chinese *tone*, a phenomenon which occurs within a single syllable. Like prosody, there are common patterns of intonation in a language, rising, falling, or both, in either order, each with a relatively consistent meaning (Cruttenden, 1997: 7). Thus, in English, a rising pitch pattern is used to express a question even if the words remain in the declarative form: You're going home *now?* A determined statement such as an order—You're going home *now!*—is said using a falling intonation. A speaker's strong surprise is expressed by a rising-falling-rising intonation pattern: You're going home *no-ow?* The basic content remains the same in all three utterances and intonation is used by the speaker to indicate differences in his or her attitude to what is being said.

There are three basic intonation patterns in Standard Chinese: *Pattern 1* for statements, which starts with a mid-key and ends low: 他现在会家; *Pattern 2* for yes-no questions, whether marked by 吗 or not, which starts with a mid-high key and ends high or mid-high: 他现在会家吗?; and *Pattern 3* for alternative questions (他是中国人,不是?), Wh-questions (他是哪国人?), and A-not-A questions (他是不是中国人?), which starts with a mid-high key and ends low (Triskova, 2008: 527). Intonation in Chinese is constrained by the tonal contour of the specific words in the utterance and thus intonation pitch contour is not freely available for expressing a speaker's attitude. As a consequence, to become questions, declarative sentences need an additional particle such as *ma*, *ya* or *ne* at the end, and the intonational peak will include the particle—他是中国人吗?

你现在回**家啊**? 你现在回**家呢**? A persistent tendency to rely on whole utterance English intonation patterns to convey feeling is one of the strongest interferences to learners correctly speaking Chinese, as doing so often changes the pitch of specific syllables, leading to listener confusion. For example, an emphatic 我想买水果, which should be said *wǒ xiǎng mǎi* **'shuíguǒ'**, comes out *wǒ xiǎng mǎi* **shuìguò**; or a surprised 你要 问他? *nǐ yào wèn tā? (You want to ask* **him?)** becomes *nǐ yào wěn tā? (你要 吻他?) (You want to kiss* **him?)**. The problem here is not that the learners don't know the correct tone, it is that they have changed it to fit the English intonational contour with the intention of conveying the emphasis or surprise they are feeling and do not know how else to convey.

To master Chinese intonation, learners firstly need to be aware of their erroneous tendency to rely on English intonation and consciously practice modifying their speech to integrate the demands of different tones into a Chinese intonation contour that will not be as expansive as the one they are used to. As well, they need to become sensitive to the use of Chinese particles and make use of their power to convey feelings. This is a particularly neglected aspect in teaching oral skills at all levels.

Bent (2005: 33) found that in listening to Chinese, native English speakers mostly attend to the pitch pattern of the whole utterance—the intonation contour—whereas Chinese first language speakers attend to the tone of the stressed lexical words. Students therefore need practice in Chinese with both declarative statements and with questions that end in different tones so that they can become sensitive to the interplay of tone and intonation.

### Pronunciation of Segmental Sounds

Learners of a second language need to be introduced to the range of sounds that are used in the language and be taught how to pronounce those that are new to them. While a great many of the sounds of modern standard Chinese are the same or very close to sounds that are used in English, there are a small number that need special instruction. Most importantly it is essential to recognise that Chinese people hear tone embedded as an integral part of any syllable, so that a toneless syllable such as *a* or *ao* does not exist in Chinese: there is only *ā, á, ǎ,* or *à*; so it isn't '*a* with a first tone', it is simply *ā*; not 'second tone *ao*', but *aó*, and so on.

Many textbooks give tips for teaching pronunciation, so all that will be mentioned here are some more recent observations from phonological scholars and some remarks on teaching drawn from Kubler (2011), Triskova (2011), Sanders and Yao (2009) and the author's own experience.

1.  While students can initially be left using essentially English pronunciation of the Chinese sounds written in Pinyin as **b, m, f, d, n, l, g,** they should be

coached from the start to use the breathier **p, t, k, ch, c,** and **s** and the more throaty **h.**

2.  As they progress, they can refine their **b, m, d** and **g** to be unvoiced. A trick from Kubler (2011) to help them make these sounds unvoiced is to practice with English words like (for **b**) *spies*, (for **m**) *smile*, (for **d**) *still* and (for **g**) *skite*, where those sounds are unvoiced; then to exaggerate the hissing 's' sound at the start—for example, *ssspies, sssmile*—and then say the same word without the 's': *ssspies-pies; sssmile-mile; ssstill-till; ssskite-kite*.

3.  Learners can be helped to feel in their mouth how they make certain sounds so that they can practice making them correctly and gradually become accustomed to the new arrangements of tongue and teeth. For example, Triskova (2011: 101) suggests a more successful way of teaching *j, q, x* than the usual contrasting with the retroflex *zh, ch* and *sh*, is to teach learners to contrast both these sets with the dental *z, c, s*. The dentals are sounds generally familiar to English speakers and they are able to feel their tongue behind their teeth when they say them and, using that reference point, they can move their tongue to the flat palatal position for saying *j, q, x*, or back from the alveolar ridge to say *zh, ch* and *sh*.

4.  Among the vowels, usually the 'ü' in 女, *nü*, 绿, *lü*, etc., the apical vowel in *chi, shi*, and *ci*, and the vowel in *che, she*, and *ce*, need to be taught explicitly, while other vowels need coaching to keep them pure and said with more lip tension than in English. The common trick with 'ü' is to ask students to switch between saying for example, 'seat-suit-seat' or 'leek-luke-leek', then asking them to say the first word (seat) and to keep their tongue in the same position and to then say the second word (suit); and then, from the same position, to isolate the vowel 'ü' in the second word. Said with lips spread for saying 'seat' or 'leek', the words 'suit' and 'luke' will be said using the vowel 'ü'. The apical vowel is best introduced as a consonant syllable, so that no effort is made to produce a vowel but the correct sound will come naturally as the consonant finishes. The 'e' of *che* is not difficult, but attention needs to be drawn to its length in its full stressed form in contrast to both *chi* and the unstressed 'e' of *le, ne*, etc.

5.  The key to correct pronunciation of diphthongs (e.g. **ei, ai, ou**) and triphthongs (**iao, uai**) is that each sound gets an equal share of time, whereas in English the first vowel sound in a diphthong, for example (**ao**) in 'now' or (**ei**) in 'ray', is given more time—is said longer—than the second vowel.

6.  At the beginning of a word (the initial position) the **n** and **f** sounds of Chinese are very like their equivalents in English, but said with the tip of the tongue a little more forward. At the end of a word, **n** is lighter than in English when in the final position and it is closed off more quickly by putting the tongue behind the teeth. In final position **ng** is also lighter than in English and it is also closed off more quickly at the back of the throat so it resonates less.

## *Tone*

In addition to the previous three features of oral language, which Chinese shares with other language—albeit each with patterns unique to itself—learning Chinese also means coming to grips with learning to be tonal. Of the four basic Chinese phonological features of prosody, intonation, segmental sounds and tone, tone is the most addressed feature in the teaching of Chinese and yet it is not very successfully learned, even by the keenest students. This is partly because using tone to change meaning is an entirely new concept for an English speaker, but it is mostly the result of very limited teaching in terms of what using tone really involves, especially as tonal articulation needs to be combined successfully with the correct use of prosody, intonation and pronunciation of segmental sounds if an utterance is to sound native-like. On the matter of what tone involves, most Chinese textbooks provide some version of Figure 2.1 below and a brief description of the pitch and contour of each tone in words and numbers from the chart: e.g. first tone is flat, 5–5, second tone is mid-pitch rising, 3–5, and so on.

The most common types of change (sandhi) are also described:

- 一 *yī,* as a cardinal number, sounds as *yì* before a fourth tone, and as *yí* before the other tones;
- a third tone sounds as a second tone before another third tone, and has only a short fall + flat contour preceding a first, second or fourth tone;
- 不 *bù* sounds as *bú* before another fourth tone.

Textbooks then typically provide lists of Pinyin syllables to be listened to and repeated, after which some bisyllabic words may also be practised. Many publications come with audio recordings, which students can play for their own practice.

In terms of the articulated components of proficient Chinese speech, this information comprises just a tiny portion of what using tone actually involves. For example, tone changes when used in connected speech according to a number of co-occurring features, most notably according to the position of the syllable in the utterance (initial, medial, final), to the segmental sounds and tones of the

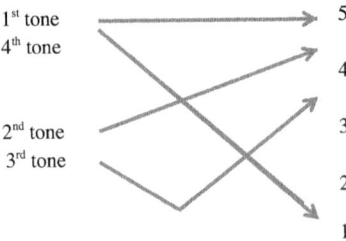

**FIGURE 2.1** Chart showing relative tone pitch entry and contour

adjacent syllables in relation to its own, and in relation to the intonation contours of declarative and interrogative utterances. Most importantly, a tone changes radically according to the degree of stress or de-stress it receives. Research has shown that variations because of these factors all have an effect on learners' capacity to hear and recognise tones, and they can even affect first language speakers' perceptions. When it comes to production, analysis shows more and finer distinctions between what different levels of learner can manage to control.

## Learning to Become Tonal

Many of the outcomes of these detailed studies are beyond the scope of knowledge needed by most classroom teachers, but there are three findings common to many of the studies (e.g. Bent, 2005; Yang and Chan, 2010; Liu, Wang, Perfetti, Brubaker, Wu, and McWhinney, 2011), which show students learning to become tonal experience certain significant problems and which all teachers need to be aware of:

1. Speakers of English have difficulty even noticing tone, and most have trouble recognising or reproducing a tone well into their study of Chinese. Many, though not all, do improve over time, but even by third year most are still making a lot of mistakes in their perception and production of tone.
2. After their initial phase learning to hear and produce tones, the biggest difficulty L2 learners have in both the perception and production of tones correctly is managing the switches that occur in connected utterances between fully tonal syllables and reduced or even atonal syllables.
3. The changes that need to be managed involve how a tonal syllable should be sounded:
   a. when the syllable is stressed or not stressed;
   b. when it occurs in different positions in the sentence;
   c. when surrounded by syllables using different tones and segmental sounds;
   d. in relation to intonational contouring.

## Teaching Tone

To make an overall improvement in this fundamental area, the critical issue is to teach students to perceive and produce tone accurately, and to do this means providing both metacognitive information that is sufficiently comprehensive to cover the features listed earlier, and to accompany explanations with long-term, regular, guided practice in scaffolded, targeted exercises. The key techniques for teaching tone are:

1. Working on perception first, then production.
2. Providing regular opportunities for flows of Chinese to be listened to without demands to perform.

3. Paying special attention to the starting pitch of a syllable—too often this is simply ignored, or if hand gestures are used to indicate tone, they all start at or close to the same point, whereas in fact only Tone 1 and Tone 4 start at the same point.

4. Tone 3 is only rarely said with the V-contour shown on the chart (falling and then rising 2–1–4). Most third tones fall and stay flat: 2–1–1. Only when Tone 3 falls on a stressed final (e.g. 一,二,三,四,五 (1,2,3,4,5) 别 给他,给我! (don't give it to him, give it to me)) will it rise: 2–1–4.

5. Moving from working on monosyllabic to bi- and multi- syllabic utterances.

6. Providing graded development using various tone combinations, e.g.

| **1+1** | **1+2** | **1+3** | **1+4** |
|---|---|---|---|
| *fēijī (plane)* | *qīshí (70)* | *yībǎi (100)* | *chīfàn (eat)* |

7. Using the prosody to determine stressed syllables and using hands to mark off the chunking of phrases, and gestures to mirror the tonal contour of stressed syllables.

8. Working on sounds and tone using Pinyin not characters, because characters do not present segmental sounds or tones.

9. Ensuring that students learn Pinyin thoroughly and accurately, because they are totally reliant on it for providing the accurate pronunciation of new vocabulary and characters.

10. In content, the use of monologue recitation can provide excellent opportunities to work on fluency and phonological features without the disturbance of having to deal with another person's responses. Useful material for such an exercise includes verses and rhymes and sequences of instructions in the process of making something—a simple paper cut, for example, or a short recipe.

11. Warning: Like instructions presented to a large group of people, verses and rhymes that are recited are usually expressed at a much slower pace than interpersonal conversation and this slower pace will affect the chunking of the utterance and the number syllables that are de-stressed, resulting in more, fully tonal syllables per line of speech. Indeed, a five-syllable line of classical poetry will have a regular chunking of 2 + 3 syllables, with every syllable stressed: 一 望 二 三 里; and a seven-syllable line will chunk 4–3 with every syllable stressed: 玉露凋伤枫树林.

## Meeting the Phonological Challenges

### *Techniques*

The phonological system of a language constitutes its core. Having learned to control the prosody, intonation and segmental sound systems of their mother tongue in their first few years, even early primary school second language students have difficulty adapting to the full range of phonological demands of the new Chinese system. If they hear enough natural language spoken around them and to them, if they are read stories, recite verses, and watch videos, they are likely to pick up the rhythm of the language and the intonation patterns, especially as modern spoken Chinese is not too dissimilar to English in these respects. Tones, however, prove a challenge even for learners who have been in immersion programs for some years. Very young children do not usually develop completely native-like proficiency in tones and it is common to find persistent errors among all students even after some years of immersion learning, especially with Tone 4. One of the major obstacles to their developing greater sensitivity to tone in listening and control of it in speaking is that *teachers rarely listen carefully enough to what their students say and even let errors pass when they do hear them, or at most just say it correctly themselves, but leave the student no better off and often not even aware of their error.* This is often because teachers do not know what to do beyond saying the correct thing themselves.

Effective techniques put forward by experienced practitioners for working on phonological features include the following:

1.  Do not ask students to 'Listen' or 'Listen to me', but rather say, 'Listen to my voice', 'Listen to the voice on the recording', 'Listen to your own voice'.
2.  Ask students to listen to the teacher's model and a classmate repeating the teacher's model. This can often allow them to perceive a learner's error in relation to the correct utterance and this helps them avoid making the same error themselves, or at least improve in that respect. Where it can be arranged, visualisation using speech analysis software of their own efforts against the model can also be effective in raising awareness of error leading to improvement (e.g. Chun, Jiang, and Ávila, 2013).
3.  Prosody is expressed in the whole body, so using the body (arm movements, hand beats, hand shapes, walking) is a very effective way to mark out the chunking of words, stressing of syllables, and tone contours, and to have them absorbed into the body.
4.  Have students change incorrect pronunciation (sound, tone and intonation) by using gestures which mirror the starting pitch, duration and contour of a stressed word synchronised with their uttering of the word. If the gesture is formed correctly, the voice will follow the body and the pronunciation will also be correct.
5.  Refusing to accept a syllable without its correct tone, or the separating of segmental sounds and tone ('*man* **with** a fourth tone' instead of just *màn*), is critical to students' learning to attend to tone as fundamental to meaning. Likewise, explaining to students that in English just as we don't say, 'My brother is going to marry Jan—that's J-n with an "A"', as if otherwise the listener might have thought he was marrying Jen or Jane, Chinese don't say *tā pǎo de màn*, that's *man* with a fourth tone'. This can be helpful in getting students to appreciate what tone really does—i.e. it changes the

meaning—and hence how important it is that they listen for tone, not just for the sounds.

6. Correcting tone by referring to meaning not tone number, e.g. 'No, that's *shì*, matter, this is *shí*, time'.

Research shows that if students are taught the phonological aspects well, they can acquire very good, natural spoken Chinese (Miracle, 1989; Wang, Spence, Jongman, and Sereno, 1999; Yang and Chan, 2010). Hence teachers of Chinese need to recognise that not teaching phonological features well means they are failing their students, not the other way around. However, because it is so new to them, improvement in both perception and production of the various phonological features only occurs if students' attention is constantly and explicitly drawn to these aspects and there is some pressure applied to having them learn to produce them accurately. It can seem tiresome to be pulling students up all the time, but if the teacher doesn't do that, they will never change. That said, of course there are times when the focus will be on getting out an utterance with a certain set of vocabulary or using a particularly structure, and how it gets said is not the important thing. But that is only at first. Once an utterance has been created and can be said, it needs to be polished to become a naturally expressed utterance, with phrases chunked, only certain words stressed and the tones and intonation working well together.

## *Teacher Education*

Teachers must know the fundamentals concerning Chinese phonological features, plan for them in their unit and lesson designs, and be able to recognise them in the efforts of their students. As few have been thoroughly introduced to the linguistic facts and learning challenges of Chinese phonology in their teacher preparation, both L2 and L1 teachers often need to study the features identified earlier—prosody, stress and de-stress, intonation, sounds and tones—as well as become familiar with the demands they present for students. While L1 teachers have a natural facility with producing all the phonological features accurately and can usually perceive errors in student utterances, virtually all have considerable difficulty in identifying the rhythm, tone and intonation of their own or others' utterances when spoken or even recorded and replayed. In addition to these same failings, L2 teachers of Chinese are often unable to produce sufficiently accurate utterances themselves to be of help to their students. This is a serious professional weakness that needs to be remedied by the means proposed here. A sense that they 'don't sound right' even after months of study leaves learners feeling inhibited from speaking in real situations and this, and the inability even to understand what is said to them due to weaknesses in phonological perception skills, leaves them despondent and often leads them to decide to quit.

Teachers also need to understand that to teach basic spoken Chinese well is a complex matter because it demands from learners a very new use of the body, and to master this, students need to discover the new domains that exist in Chinese, explore them and practice them over time. Listening plays a critical role in this learning and it useful to ask learners daily just to surrender to a whole flow of Chinese so they can become sensitive to how they are supposed to sound. Just 30 seconds at a time of this kind of listening is enough. Apart from the exercise of 'surrender listening', most phonological exercises also need the input of metacognitive information if they are to bring about development. That is because much that is involved in learning to speak Chinese lies outside the students' experience as English speakers and hence, it is either not attended to, or it is changed to meet the norms of English. In addition to 30 seconds of every lesson spent listening, plus the constant requirement for them to attend to and polish the phonological features of their own utterances, a dedicated segment of time (15–20 minutes) should be solidly devoted to phonological exercises every week, or at absolute minimum, every two weeks. The exercises should include explicit work on rhythm and chunking, articulation of specific sounds, articulation of tones and tone combinations, tone and intonation combinations, and practising moving between stressed and unstressed syllables. Resources are still lamentably scarce for this work, but Orton (2013) and Triskova (2008, 2017), for example, do provide some content to be used in such activities, as well as information on goals and how to attain them. It is important to realise that the content does not need to be long. Just reading numbers (17, 145, 1,298, 3,620 . . .) from the board offers opportunities for most of these challenges, provided they are said normally and not allowed just to be droned.

## The Goal

The starting premise of this book is that the most basic elements of Chinese language use require English speaking learners to extend the fundamental skills they have acquired to a high level of automaticity in their use of English, and in some cases to substitute new skills for these ones already acquired. A second premise is that because this very deep re-learning is often omitted, indeed the need for it often not even recognised, many learners do not achieve mastery of the basics and as a consequence their language learning proceeds on very shaky foundations that eventually cannot support them going further. The articulatory system of Chinese presents the English-speaking learner with a totally new way of using the body and thanks to their expertise in English there are obstacles to them even perceiving what it is they have to acquire. It is therefore, not surprising that they learn to speak so poorly unless they are well-taught by a teacher who not only knows the facts of the Chinese language, but is also aware of what mastering them requires of such a learner, *and* has the strategies and techniques for meeting them on the starting line and leading them in developing whole new aspects of their physical and mental capacities, and in reflecting on the wider growth in awareness that this work brings them. Unfortunately, this rarely happens. Instead, despite being the core of the language, the learning demands of the phonological system are commonly neglected. This is the result of five main faults in teaching:

- Firstly, as noted, there is a lack of awareness that learners need this deep re-learning, that is, teachers and resource creators don't appreciate just how different speaking Chinese is from speaking English;
- Secondly, not enough work on articulation is provided for students to develop mastery;
- Thirdly, what awareness teachers have often centres exclusively on *tone*, neglecting the other phonological aspects of language and how they work together with tone;
- Fourthly, the teaching of tone is incomplete, too often aimed exclusively at the pure form used in uttering single syllables; and,
- Finally, the means of teaching of any aspect of articulation is too often reliant on the single technique of *listen and repeat*.

With such a limited notion of what there is to be learned and how it might be achieved, it is not surprising that the learning of basic oral skill competence is generally ineffective.

What needs to occur is teaching the phonological system from an understanding of learning. This will mean assisting students to create an auditory and felt image from hearing flows of spontaneous speech, explicitly listening for and identifying stressed syllables and their tone and the overall intonational contour of the utterance leading to comprehension. Mastery in producing accurate spoken Chinese will require work on chunking and allocation of stress and de-stress by using movement and gesture to support control. Retraining the body to be sensitive to Chinese prosody, intonation and pronunciation, teachers will seek to correct the voice through the body by relying on the natural synchrony of body and voice.

*

## Communicating

Many teachers of Chinese would say they use 'a communicative approach' in their teaching and most textbooks for school learners are based on communicative encounters between people similar to the learners, often including some native speakers. The underlying assumption about this content is that this is the language the learners need and that they will be encouraged to learn by imitating the Chinese used by people like themselves. Yet many students fail to relate to such content. If we consider the issue from the learners' perspective, we may realise that this is hardly surprising. Few of them at this stage in their life share the adult perception that they need Chinese at all. They lead busy lives inside and outside school engaged largely, if not entirely, with people who speak their own language. Any meaningfulness of oral activities in the classroom is further eroded by there being only one competent speaker in the room and the limitations of students' language to say all they would like to.

It takes a broad leap of imagination for students to enter the make-believe world in the language classroom where they need to use Chinese to address their teacher and classmates. The task is often made all the harder by the artificiality of dialogues in which, for example, they must ask someone they know well what their name is, or role play someone beyond their experience, such as a travel agent. All too often, as well, they do not need to do more than get the words out once as best they can, with no requirement to chunk the utterance, handle the stressed and de-stressed words to fit what they are supposed to be communicating, and utter the whole fluently and with accurate pronunciation. Their utterances are very often accepted even if quite ragged and no work is done to polish them. At most the teacher might say the lines correctly him- or her- self, which makes evident the inadequacies of student's utterance but does nothing to improve it.

From a learning perspective, to be successful, classroom oral work needs to be meaningful at two levels: firstly, to be remembered, the words of the interaction need to have meaning for the learners, and that requires them to be uttered in context, with all the articulatory features assisting in conveying the speaker's message. Secondly, the whole activity needs to be perceived as meaningful in itself, something that won't have students muttering to one another, 'What are we supposed to do?' 'What are we doing this for?' The fundamental teaching problem in this area of communicating is thus, *how to create meaningful spoken interaction* in class.

There are books filled with techniques for arranging oral practice in a classroom and they will not be duplicated here. Instead, just four suggestions are set out, all of which address the fundamental problem of creating meaningful activities that will greatly increase students' success in learning to speak Chinese fluently, accurately and appropriately. The suggestions involve both choice of material and approach to teaching. They are:

- Teaching *the real thing*
- Creating an imagined community
- Using conversational formulas
- Sounding good.

## Teaching the Real Thing

### The Real in the Room

If speaking to one's Chinese teacher in Chinese carries some element of normal behaviour, there is no getting away from the initial artificiality of students using Chinese to speak to one another. The key to this is the teacher creating a

Chinese world in the classroom by using Chinese him/herself and insisting on students doing likewise in so far as they are able. To do this, the teacher needs to systematically present the language of the classroom as the course goes along, starting with the most frequent. The most natural communications to begin making in Chinese are those that need to occur among teacher and students: greetings, farewells, roll call; directions for movement around the room and for doing activities and using things; asking permissions, and so forth. Using Chinese in these genuine exchanges creates both a solid meaning base for the words used as well as a rationale for speaking at all. Everyday classroom management provides constant opportunities to listen and speak and there is naturally a high frequency recycling of language learned. Research has shown that as few as 150 words cover most of what will be needed to run activities in a Chinese classroom (Cui and Orton, 2013). Furthermore, the language has embedded in it a wealth of vocabulary and structures—for example, 把 本子拿出来／放回去; 把桌子上的书给我—that can be exploited to advance learning more generally. Much of this language can be understood by all but the very youngest of students just from the given situation and their knowledge of classrooms, but it will need to be introduced gradually, with plenty of practice given to students to speak as well as listen. Having students work in pairs with one speaking and the other doing, and then reversing the roles, and then switching pairs, are simple techniques to get the various commands and action sequences established and mastered efficiently.

Human beings are naturally playful and games are an authentic activity which demand the use of language. There are several card and board games that can be played in a classroom in their Chinese version (or with Chinese modified materials). Once how to play and the language needed for taking part have been learned, games such as Snakes and Ladders or Happy Families can be tailored to require provision of information that has been taught about Chinese geography, culture or history, or use of language learned for presenting personal information or the vocabulary of any topic. A profusion of games and adventure stories are available on line, some of which have been designed for learners. Other situations where language is used for real include targeted listening and viewing of activities such as a sports match of a game known to the learners, a pop concert, or children's cartoons. These have the potential for providing useful practice in receptive skills and offer the chance to learn odd phrases that can be used in students' own speech. To gain benefit from these programs, however, it is essential that they be carefully selected, of intrinsic interest to the learners involved, and not go on for too long.

## Organised Opportunities

A second kind of real use of the language is designed encounters where students need to speak in Chinese. One of the simplest ways of arranging for this is to invite a Chinese person to the classroom for a conversation that is within the students' capacity. For beginners, there may only be very brief input on their part, but the visitor could show a map of China and give a little talk about where their family comes from. The whole event may be no more than five minutes long but its power will be considerable just because it is real—everything they know about this person the students learned through Chinese. While they could rehearse their questions beforehand, it is essential, of course, that the teacher does not destroy the whole point of the activity by telling students in advance information about the visitor that they would otherwise have to use Chinese to find out! Knowing the answers in advance—what the person's name is, where they come from, etc.—would render asking those questions of the visitor quite meaningless and this would rob the students of the motivating triumph from finding out through Chinese alone.

Most schools have a sister school in China and a regular meeting via a program such as Skype with classmates there, or at another school anywhere in the world where the students will speak Chinese, provides an authentic need to use the language. Such encounters, however, do not usually go well without help, and to reap benefits meetings need to be organised and the conversations practised in advance. They also need to be fairly brief. If students have the chance to meet these other students personally, by visiting their school or hosting them at their own school, there is the chance that friendships might develop and individuals will be able to chat more often and without teacher supervision. But in the initial stage and at the group level, there needs to be structure, including time limits so that several students from both sides have the chance to speak. If the other students want to practise their English as well, it is psychologically easier if a session runs in only one language and then the next session is run in the other language. This allows each group to have a session tailored to their level of proficiency and avoids problems arising from the other students' English being stronger than the learners' Chinese, as is often the case. It must be a rule that reverting to English is not permitted and for this to happen, it is probable that the teacher of Chinese needs to liaise with the teacher in the other school and make sure that the questions asked and information given are within the repertoire of their learners' Chinese language abilities.

Organised opportunities for using Chinese can also be created around excursions to places such as a China Town or a specific commercial venue like a restaurant or grocery shop. It is particularly valuable if those working in some of these venues have been briefed and will participate in speaking to the students using language within their range. Apart from speaking to people at the venue, prepared tasks to be undertaken en route, such as sign reading, using digital information booths, noting the names of Chinese places or people in the street, or having to request directions, can provide opportunities for direct real use of the language.

## *Creating an Imagined Community*

One of the motivating forces that keeps a second language learner going through the hard times is an inner image or sense of themselves in future as a member of a group who uses the language for real to which the learner would like to belong. Not all students spontaneously create this 'imagined community' (Norton, 2000) on their own, and even those who do may not always explicitly recognise that they have. Talking to students, even very young students, about themselves in an imagined Chinese speaking community and helping them develop a sense of one that fits their personal dreams is an important way to increase motivation and give classroom work real-life meaning. Once students have been encouraged to create their own image, the teacher can evoke it in support of speaking practice to provide meaningfulness to both the activity and the actual words: 'We are doing this because we are getting ready for meeting our Chinese friends/our sister school classmates'. 'Keep in mind that you are learning/practising what you want to be able to say/what you imagine you will need to be able to say, to these people about yourself and your life'.

Typically, the first 'imagined community' students hope or expect to join will be a group of young Chinese people like themselves, and they envision talking to them, their parents and their teachers in real life contact and also on Skype, as either the beginning of the contact, or as a way of maintaining a relationship created on a visit. With this as the goal, in addition to any textbook dialogues that are used, students' oral skills should be gradually built up through learning to make fluent, naturally articulated, accurately spoken, true, short presentations about themselves. For example:

- Basic self-presentation: *My name is [XX], I am [X] years old. I live in [city X, state X] with my family: Mum, Dad, and my younger sister/with my mother and older brother/with my grandparents.*
- Basic information about school: *I go to [X] school in [district X, city X]. I am in Year [X]. We learn English, Chinese, Math, Science, History, Geography, Computer Studies, Music, Art and PE. I like Chinese and History (best).*

Over time, the repertoire can be extended to include:

- My daily life—Monday to Friday (morning routine, school times, meals, chores).
- My life at weekends (hobbies, sports, shopping, job).
- My life during the holidays (staying with friends, going away, relatives, Christmas and Easter).

It is important that students learn to say the things they genuinely want to say or are likely to need. For example, they should know how to describe things that they care about that their hearers may not already know, such as an outline of the local code of football, local food specialties, the kind of leisure activities they like, or particular features of their locality that are significant to them. Personal information relevant to them that are met in the textbook can be added to their repertoire as the words are learned.

## Using Conversational Formulas

A third kind of real, or at least realistic, language for developing interactional skill in communicating involves conversational formulas and routines. These are conventional expressions that are used in a fixed form to fill up spaces in conversations (e.g. My goodness! 那太好了!) or make or reply to routine enquiries.

## Learning Formulas

From a learner's perspective a conversational formula is a very economical acquisition as it doesn't require any kind of grammatical construction at the time, it is a chunk of language that can be produced whole, on the spot at the time it is needed; and if it has been well-taught and is used correctly, it is a comfortable piece of language to say because the learner knows it is appropriate and will keep the other person feeling relaxed, confident this second language learner they are speaking to is understanding what they are saying and able to connect with them. Formulaic expressions can occur as an opening line, a response, or the coda in a short A-B-A dialogue, where A speaks first, B responds and A wraps up the interchange. For example:

1.  A: **好久没见了。**
    B:
    A:

1.  A: 你好吗?
    B:  **我很好, 谢谢。你呢?**
    A:

2.  A:
    B:
    A:  **那太好了!**

(For actual use, these dialogues should be contextualised.)

Other standard expressions that make good coda include:

糟糕!
麻烦你!
太可笑!
真奇怪!

真好玩儿!
可不是吗?

Fillers like 反正 (anyway) and conjunctions such as 要不然 (otherwise) are also useful to learn, and gradually, age-appropriate idioms and four-character expressions can beneficially be learned in a similar way.

Apart from getting the right words in the right order, the central learning tasks of acquiring this kind of formulaic expression are (i) *being really clear what it means to use it*: literally, emotionally, and in terms of formality-informality, intimacy-distance, the speaker's age and status, and so on; and, (ii) *getting the phonological features right*, so that, when uttered, it does convey the intended message.

### Teaching Formulas

To achieve these tasks, the students must know who the people are, what their relationship is, and why they are speaking to one another. This is because, in the previously mentioned simple example (2), A will have had to decide whether to use 你 or 您, and that it is all right to turn the greeting into a question by adding 吗, which implies a right to expect B to say something about his/her state of being, while B's 你呢 implies a level of equality between speakers. The response of each, however, is perfunctory and provides no real information as to how they are, suggesting the relationship is not very close. Teachers need to be attentive to this kind of contextual planning and able to discuss the social implications of choice of expression and then ensure that the utterance is said in a way that matches that. As well, any dialogue is much easier to imagine and hence to learn if the people are given names and their location spelled out, not simply sentences said by an anonymous A and B.

### Sounding Good

The fourth essential to learning the complex set of aspects that go into speaking Chinese for real even in a classroom is learning to speak well, so that utterances sound good. This gives meaning to both the language used and to the activity itself. Direct work on articulation and the polishing of communicative utterances for real use are integral to all speaking development. A side benefit of this work is that classmates listening to a student being coached are also learning, and correct use of the language by all students is strengthened from hearing the language used well by others.

## Conclusion

To be effective, activities of any kind intended to develop spoken language must be real or at least realistic. That means that for monologue presentations or dialogues to be practised meaningfully, the speaking event must be *contextualised*:

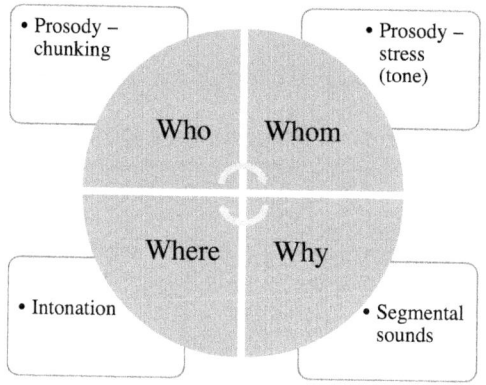

**FIGURE 2.2** Factors combining for effective communication in spoken language

students must know who they are in the conversation—where they are, whom they are speaking to—and what their speaking to that person is intended to achieve. This information frames the choice of words, the speed of utterance and how close to the listener the speaker will stand. The manner of articulation must be congruent with the speaker's intention and thus support communicating the message. As well, bounded interchanges involving use of the language in real ways in their own classroom and beyond offer graduated opportunities to practise communicating in Chinese. Creating and developing a strong sense of imagined community can be a great help in fulfilling these demands. Knowing some formulaic expressions can ease pressure at the time of performance, and an internalised sense of Chinese prosodic patterns will ensure that the language chosen to say will come out sounding right and meaning what is intended.

## References

Bent, T. (2005) *Perception and Production of Non-native Prosodic Categories.* Unpublished Ph. D dissertation, Department of Linguistics, Northwestern University. Retrieved 27 September 2018 from www.linguistics.northwestern.edu/about/events/past%20conferences/mcwop10/bent.txt

Chun, D.M., Jiang, Y., and Ávila, N. (2013) 'Visualization of Tone for Learning Mandarin Chinese', in J. Levis and K. LeVelle (eds.), *Proceedings of the 4th Pronunciation in Second Language Learning and Teaching Conference, August 2012*, 77–89. Ames: Iowa State University.

Condon, W.S. and Ogston, W. (1966) 'Sound Film Analysis of Normal and Pathological Behaviour Patterns', *Journal of Nervous and Mental Disease*, 143(4): 338–347.

Condon, W.S. and Sander, L. (1974) 'Neonate Movement Is Synchronized With Adult Speech: Interactional Participation and Language Acquisition', *Science*, 183: 99–101.

Cruttenden, A. (1997) *Intonation.* Cambridge: Cambridge University Press.

Cui, X. and Orton, J. (2013) *Classroom Chinese Language.* Melbourne: Chinese Teacher Training Centre, University of Melbourne, 3010, Australia.

Kubler, C. (2011) *Basic Spoken Chinese*. Tokyo, Rutland, and Singapore: Tuttle.

Liu, Y., Wang, M., Perfetti, C., Brubaker, B., Wu, S., and McWhinney, B. (2011) 'Learning a Tonal Language by Attending to the Tone: An in Vivo Experiment', *Language Learning*, 61(4): 119–1141.

Miracle, W.C. (1989) 'Tone Production of American Students of Chinese: A Preliminary Acoustic Study', *Journal of Chinese Language Teachers Association*, 24: 49–65.

Norton, B. (2000) *Identity and Language Learning: Gender, Ethnicity and Educational Change*. Harlow: Pearson Education.

Orton, J. (2013) 'Developing Chinese Oral Skills—A Research Base for Practice', in I. Kesckes (ed.), *Research in Chinese as a Second Language*, 3–26. Berlin: Mouton de Gruyter.

Sanders, R. and Yao, N. (2009) *Fundamental Spoken Chinese*. Honolulu: University of Hawaii Press.

Švarny, O. (1991) 'The Functioning of the Prosodic Features in Chinese (Pekinese)', *Archiv Orientalni*, 59(2): 208–216.

Triskova, H. (2008) 'The Sounds of Chinese and How to Teach Them', *Archiv Orientalni*, 76(4): 509–544.

Triskova, H. (2011) 'The Structure of the Mandarin Syllable: Why, When and How to Teach It', *Archiv Orientalni*, 79(1): 99–134.

Triskova, H. (2017) 'De-stress in Mandarin Clitics, Cliticoids, and Phonetic Chunks', in I. Kecskes and C. Sun (eds.), *Key Issues in Chinese as a Second Language Research*, 29–56. New York and London: Routledge.

Wang, Y., Spence, M., Jongman, A., and Sereno, J. (1999) 'Training American Listeners to Perceive Mandarin Tones', *Journal of the Acoustical Society of America*, 106(6): 3649–3658.

Yang, C. and Chan, M. (2010) 'The Perception of Mandarin Chinese Tones and Intonation by American Learners', *Journal of the Chinese Language Teachers Association*, 45(1): 7–36.

# 3

# DEVELOPING LITERACY SKILLS

## Introduction

One of the more challenging features of learning Chinese as a foreign language is learning to be literate: to be capable of understanding messages in Chinese characters and communicating ideas through Chinese characters. For the novice learner, characters loom large as both an object of great interest and a great challenge. The challenge is due to the learners' experience with literacy development in their own language having been so fundamentally different that it makes a very inadequate foundation for building the knowledge and skills to read and write in Chinese.

This chapter explores the path that English-speaking learners need to take to reach competency in Chinese literacy. It describes the nature of the system and current understandings of learning to read in an additional language, and in Chinese in particular. It explores representations of the character system in contemporary textbooks and the learning processes that are imposed in order to *memorise* the characters required to engage in communicative activity in Chinese. It questions whether these representations and processes of learning are adequate or appropriate, given the experiences of literacy learning in an alphabetic language that the novice learners bring to the task. The nature of the task is then explored from the learner's perspective, and ways in which the theoretical debates can inform classroom practice are examined, in order to find how the learning and use of characters can be made more effective and meaningful in that context.

The chapter concludes by reflecting on how teachers might proceed with the task of scaffolding learning of the character system to make the process a more positive and productive experience, leading learners along a new path of literacy yet drawing on relevant aspects of their existing knowledge and experience in reading and writing in English.

## Learning to Read

Developing reading skills in a language, be it one's first or an additional language, depends on some basic universals, described as *the general mapping principles*, which include the realisation that print relates to speech. In a particular language these principles are represented as language-specific mapping details, which identify how the language is mapped onto its particular writing system. Learning to read involves a number of sub-skills, including lower-level processing skills which involve a learner's abilities in word recognition. Word recognition skills are a necessary precursor to the higher-level processes used to build text comprehension and are thus essential for effective reading. Word recognition involves three distinct but interrelated processes: orthographic, phonological, and semantic processing. Orthographic processing involves the ability to extract sound and meaning information from print. This process relies on the other lower level processes of understanding speech sounds and how these are mapped onto the writing system, and understanding units of meaning in the language and how these relate to sounds (Koda, 2005). Learner efficiency in these lower-level word recognition processes is an important predictor of later reading ability and is crucial in both first and in second language contexts (Grabe, 2009). Hence, a fundamental skill in learning to read in a language is orthographic awareness: knowledge of the graphic units that make up the writing system, and understanding how these units are organised to represent the sounds and meanings of the language.

### Learning to Read in a Second Language

The orthographic knowledge needed to develop reading competence in a particular language depends on the nature of the writing system involved. Depending on their age and literacy experiences, English-speaking novice learners come to the study of Chinese with a significant level of orthographic awareness of English writing, and of the specific ways in which spoken language elements are graphically represented in the English alphabetic writing system. The orthographic knowledge and the processes involved in accessing sounds and meaning via the Chinese writing systems are very different. Language transfer theory (Koda, 2008) suggests that learners rely on their first language linguistic resources and cognitive patterns to learn to read in a second language. Their ability to transfer orthographic knowledge from a language such as English to another language such as Chinese is constrained by three factors: the orthographic distance between the structure and features of the English alphabet and those features in the new writing system; the learners' (relatively extensive) experience with their first language writing system; and their (relatively brief) experience with the new writing system. In fact, novice learners' experience with English writing can provide little basis or support for developing orthographic knowledge in Chinese.

So, without a systemic understanding of how the character system works and how that knowledge should be applied to their learning, to decoding characters, and to reading and writing in Chinese having been established, novice learners have only blind memorisation with which to master Chinese writing. Thus, they find themselves confronted with an, often, overwhelming demand on their time, mental energy and interest as they try to commit to memory a large number of character forms, and their sounds and meanings, supported only by their knowledge of the English alphabet and text processing skills.

## The Importance of Language-Specific Knowledge

In any language, orthographic awareness is typically developed through extensive input and exposure to the language in print. While writing in Chinese, like English, represents a code for conveying sound and meaning, the actual mapping of these elements in Chinese is substantially different, necessitating a new and different level of orthographic knowledge than learners have developed through extensive exposure to and use of English. Novice learners in school-based foreign language settings, however, are likely to be exposed to just a few hundred characters at most over their first few years of study. From this limited exposure they are unlikely to be able to elicit much reliable, generalisable information about the structures and features of the Chinese writing system to contribute to development of their orthographic knowledge. Unless their attention is drawn to the salient features of the Chinese system, learners' orthographic awareness will remain at a foundational level, and this in turn runs the risk of slowing progress in reading and writing performance and undermining motivation to continue. Given the absence of extensive input and exposure in this context, a particular goal of reading and writing instruction for classroom-based learners needs, therefore, to be awareness-raising of the particular mapping patterns that apply to Chinese, and how to use this knowledge effectively in order to develop greater efficiency in lower-level processing and consequent acceleration in their reading comprehension and writing.

Before we turn to this goal, we need first to establish a common picture of the orthographic knowledge involved in the Chinese writing system.

## The Nature of the Chinese Writing System

Chinese characters are composed of a sequence of strokes, which are written in a generally well-defined sequence within a square space. The majority of characters contain between five and 13 strokes. These strokes are used to create stroke sequences, which are referred to as *components* (部件, *bùjiàn*),[1] what Bai (2005) describes as the basic graphs in characters, with a status equivalent to the letter graphemes of western alphabets. Components, the individual 'graphs' or symbols, like letters (rather than the strokes which compose them), are the actual 'building blocks' of characters within the system. Unlike letters, however, components are written in a square space rather than in a string on a line. And unlike letters, components are not phonemes although they can potentially be cues to sound or meaning depending on their location within a compound character. By contrast with the 26 letters in lower and upper case (plus the 10 number symbols and numerous additional logographs such as $, &, %) of the English alphabet, the Chinese writing system is considerably more complex, being comprised of more than 400 individual components. The total number varies according to the level of deconstruction into ever simpler forms. *The Practical Dictionary of Chinese in Graphic Components* (Zhou, 2003) lists a total of 420 components. A large number of components are themselves used as characters; others are known as *bound forms* (非成字, *fēichéngzì*), such as 宀, 亻, 灬, that only occur in compound characters. Fei (1996) identifies 384 components, of which 162 are themselves basic characters. Each individual character is composed of between one and six components. Single component characters are typically referred to as *basic* or *integral* characters, and multi-component characters are referred to as *compound* characters. For example, the characters for the word *component* (部件, *bùjiàn*) are comprised of three components: 立+口+阝 ; and two components 亻 + 牛, respectively.

Compound characters are composed of two or more components organised into a particular structural sequence, arranged into two sides (偏旁, *piānpáng*). The character 新 (*xīn*), for example, displays a left-right arrangement, while 音 (*yīn*) displays a top-bottom arrangement. One side of a compound character is the semantic radical (部首, *bùshǒu*), which is likely to suggest broadly the semantic meaning of the character and is usually used to classify the character in a dictionary. Traditional dictionaries use 214 radicals to classify characters and modern simplified character dictionaries may use anywhere between 188 and 227 radicals. Semantic radical knowledge thus serves a practical as well as functional purpose. Over 80 per cent of compound characters are considered to be semantic-phonetic compounds. In these characters, the other (non-semantic radical) side is generally a phonetic radical (声旁, *shēngpáng*), which has the potential to suggest the sound of a character. Estimates vary, but it is generally accepted that around 800 phonetic sides (Shu, Chen, Anderson, Wu, and Xuan, 2003) are evident in the full range of semantic-phonetic compound characters.

Given the complexities and unreliability of relations between a character's form and its sound and meaning, the lack of transparency in orthography-phonology (form to sound) correspondence, and the limited access to morphological (meaning related) information within individual characters, the Chinese writing system is recognised as a *deep orthography*. Degrees of semantic transparency or phonetic reliability vary considerably, depending on the number of characters included in the analysis and the measure of transparency or reliability used to make judgements. An important study by Shu, Chen, Anderson, Wu, and Xuan (2003) of 2,570 characters taught in primary school found 58 per cent of compound characters to be usefully related to the meaning of the semantic radical, with 39 per cent of semantic-phonetic compound characters showing a regular relationship (same sound, if not same tone) with the phonetic side. Knowledge of the cueing function of semantic and phonetic radicals does, however, provide useful information for a native speaker during text processing.

## Representation of Chinese Orthographic Knowledge

The orthographic knowledge of the Chinese writing system needed by novice learners can be represented in two possible ways. One is a native speaker representation of the structures and features of the Chinese character system that represent the way that first language learners learn it and understand it. The other representation entails some consideration of how the system might be viewed, or best understood, by novice learners for whom English (or another alphabetic language) is their native tongue, and for whom reading alphabetic representations of sounds and meanings forms the foundation of their literacy skills.

### The Native Speaker Representation

The general mapping principles that the meaning of the majority of compound characters is related to the general semantic classification suggested by its radical, and the sound of the majority of compound characters is suggested by its phonetic, are the basic principles of the Chinese character system as understood by native speakers. These principles are taught to native speaker children as they learn to map their well-developed spoken lexicon onto the large number of characters they learn each year in primary school.

The native speaker representation tends to focus on awareness of *function*: how sound and meaning are mapped onto characters. This approach assumes there is less challenge to the young native speaker learner in the perceptual demands of recognising and remembering the physical, graphic properties of characters. It focuses on how sound and meaning cues are represented or accessed in characters, particularly in compound characters, which make up the vast majority of characters in common use.

### The Novice Learner Representation

With no internalised lexicon available, the novice learner representation, by contrast, places greater priority on *form*: how to deal with the perceptual demands of the unfamiliar and extensive graphic information that characters represent. The graphic information bears no relationship at all to the learners' experience of English writing, and consequently places a significant demand on their visual information processing capabilities, and a significant burden on their memory. For these novice learners, information related to the function of the semantic radical and the phonetic side is rendered next to meaningless, not only because transfer of sound or meaning information is unreliable, but, more importantly, because learners simply have not encountered sufficient related characters for such transfer or reliabilities to become evident. Also, unlike young native speaker children at the stage they begin to develop literacy skills in Chinese, the novice second language learner lacks a command of oral language, and therefore lacks any foundation for relating sound and meaning information to each character encountered. Learners are left with the burden of attempting to learn to identify an unfamiliar character form, and to map a sound, and a meaning onto each new form with very few reliable clues to assist them. It is fair to say reliable information for the novice about the actual sound (tone-syllable) of the character or its meaning is not readily available, and that the only reliable, constant information available to assist the novice learner to remember the character is *the form*.

Even at the orthographic level the challenge for the novice learner is, thus, significant. Building orthographic knowledge for character recognition and recall depends fundamentally on becoming aware of the physical structural properties of each character. That is, learners need to be alert to the number and arrangement of components in each character they encounter and the graphic properties of each component, including the sequence of strokes from which it is composed and their arrangement. This is the foundation of the character system as seen from the novice learner's perspective.

For the novice second language learner, thus, what matters most of all is: What can I see? How can I remember what I see? How can that orthographic information help me remember what it means? While learning the sound of the character must remain a task of rote memory, what novice learners primarily need to learn to do is to focus on the individual graphic units from which all characters are constructed: the *components*. Being able to identify the nature, number and arrangement of components is the basic, essential orthographic information that provides a foundation for efficient character recognition and recall from the earliest stages of learning, and in learning to read and to write using this complex and very distinctive orthography over time.

### School-Based Learners' Orthographic Awareness

The author was discussing learning Chinese with a student who had studied Chinese for six years in an intensive immersion program, where the key learning areas of Geography, Science and Mathematics were taught in Chinese. In order to understand the student's knowledge of Chinese characters, the author wrote down the characters (斜率 (*xiélǜ*, slope, or *gradient*), as shown in A, Figure 3.1. The student had encountered these characters in a mathematics class taught in

Chinese some years prior. The author asked the student if she could identify the characters. The student wasn't sure of the meaning or sound, until advised by the author. Once the sound and meaning had been established and the student agreed the word was familiar from mathematics class, the author covered the characters he had written and asked the learner to write the same characters herself. The student hesitated and then attempted to reproduce the characters, which had been the centre of attention for the last few minutes. Her first effort, character B1, Figure 3.1, is shown beside the author's characters. The author then uncovered the characters and asked the student to focus on the characters again for a moment, before repeating the cover, write, check procedure. The student's second attempt at writing the characters is shown in B2, Figure 3.1.

The work in Figure 3.2 was done when the author was assisting another senior secondary student who spoke Mandarin at home with his mother and who had studied Chinese in a second language program for four years but was struggling with reading and writing tasks. The author sought to check the student's current state of character knowledge by calling out a word: 澳大利亚 (Àodàlìyà, *Australia*). The author assumed the student would know the word and be able to write it in Chinese. The student made two attempts to write the word, as shown in C1 and C2, Figure 3.2. In both instances, these two learners

**FIGURE 3.1** Attempt at reproducing characters

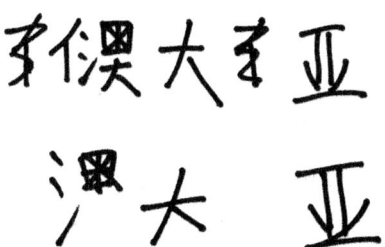

**FIGURE 3.2** Familiar characters written from memory just viewed

had received significant instruction in and experience with Chinese and it would be presumed they had developed reasonable capabilities in reading and writing Chinese characters. Despite significant input and experience with the written language, however, the outcomes in terms of character knowledge and recall were below expectations.

On another occasion, students at the end of Year 6 in primary school were asked by the author to share their views on Chinese learning. One question was: How would you describe a Chinese character? Some of the written responses were:

- *A Chinese character is really bad because it has little marks like little lines.*
- *It's a bunch of lines.*
- *A whole lot of lines going everywhere to make a word.*
- *Very difficult to write because they have lots of fiddly parts.*
- *A Chinese character uses strokes and is drawn from top to bottom and left to right.*
- *Lots of lines that started off looking like pictures but over the years has changed.*

After six years of Chinese language learning in primary school, these children had developed rather idiosyncratic views on the nature of the Chinese writing system. Some students lacked awareness of the nature of Chinese characters beyond 'a bunch of lines'. For one, the importance of stroke order and direction was significant, for another the fact that characters derived from pictures was important, but overall, their knowledge of the system remained at a very basic level.

## Reflection on the Issues

As teachers of Chinese, we have to ask why the previously described situation is this way. From the perspective of orthographic knowledge, what is it about the character system that remains so elusive to these learners? From a writing perspective, what is it about the system that makes character recall so demanding? From a pedagogical perspective, what might it be about their character learning and print processing (reading and writing) experience that leaves them with such limited capability to describe or apply their knowledge of Chinese writing? From the learners' perspective, why had these secondary students not retained their years of instruction, despite long and well-intended exposure to the character system, with a limited capability to either reproduce or recall characters in what should have been a relatively straightforward task? Why was the nature of the primary students' understanding so negative or simplistic?

### The Nature of the Second Language Learner

The possible reasons for these students' weaknesses are many and varied of course, but fundamentally the issue is simple—the secondary school learners appear to lack the ability to process the visual information in characters they had encountered in order to effectively remember, read, or reproduce those characters in a legible form. This is not just an issue of 'remembering the strokes', although that may well be a contributing factor to their inability to recall. The fundamental learning issue is their lack of orthographic awareness: the ability to identify and analyse the internal structural composition of characters, the set of components, and their structural organisation within each character.

What is seen in the writing samples in Figure 3.2 is confusion: a level of awareness that certain, more familiar or distinctive structures and features exist within the character required, but the totality of the characters, particularly their visual properties, could not be recalled or reproduced accurately. The number and arrangement of the components in the characters could not be recalled in either situation. These critical graphic features could not be retained in the short-term memory and reproduced in the first instance, nor recalled effectively from longer term memory in the second. With the primary school children, what we see is a confusion of ideas, of uncertainty as to what the system is, how to describe it, and what the information they did have might mean for their capacity to learn it.

The issues for older learners were clearly related to underdeveloped word or character processing skills, and for the younger learners to their lack of experience with characters. The nature of character instruction they had received was so limited that they lacked any real insight into the principles underlying the system, and did not own sufficient metalanguage to describe their understanding effectively

## *Information for the Second Language Learner*

At present, novice primary and secondary school-based learners are typically taught to *'remember'* characters without being provided with any deep analysis of the parts that constitute the whole, even though they may have previously encountered some the constituent components in other characters. They are seldom provided with much in the way of a) graphic deconstruction to identify components and their structural organisation, or b) any explanation of the function of the semantic or phonetic radicals that appear in each character they encounter.

For instance, if we take some high frequency compound characters that children encounter, such as 说 (*shūo, to speak*) and 踢 (*tī, to kick*), the internal component parts within each character are seldom analysed graphically. Thus, for example, students are unlikely to be assisted to deconstruct the character 说 into its component parts, or to 'spell' the entire character by components; 讠 *speech* + ⸹ *eight* + 口 *mouth* + 儿 *son*, as a way to remember the totality of the graphic information. They are unlikely to be given the opportunity to connect with similar forms such as 兄 or 总.

In the character 踢 (*tī, to kick*), students may be familiar with the physical properties of the components 足 and 日, but are unlikely to know the sound and meaning of 勿 (*wù, a pictograph of a banner, though now used as a grammatical morpheme, do not*), nor likely to learn to differentiate it from other similar forms such as 力, 刀, 刃, or the simplified component in 扬. This level of processing of the intra-character visual information typically remains the responsibility of the learner, and typically is based upon the inferences and assumptions they develop themselves as they struggle to deal with the myriad of component forms necessarily encountered as they learn to read.

Teachers often try to explain the meaning of character-components based on their form, as pictographs or ideographs. However, such form-meaning relations are typically very abstract and not immediately evident to the novice learner. For example, explaining that 讠 (*yán*) means *speech*, based on the visual properties of the component, or that 足 (*zú*) 'literally' means *foot*, can be problematic in the mind's-eye of the learner, but being able to name these basic forms, to know their sounds and meaning, does provide a foundation for identifying and processing visual information via components in compound characters encountered, and for talking about their learning in instructional settings. Without attention to explicit orthographic instruction, learners like those quoted earlier find themselves with complex and seemingly unfamiliar visual information to process in order to remember and write characters correctly. If the visual properties—the components—are not noted and recognised, there is no reading or writing ability.

If a functional analysis were undertaken, that is, if the character were analysed from a native speaker perspective, learners would be taught the usefulness of knowing the function of the two semantic radicals, the *speech* radical 讠 in 说 (*shuō, to speak*), and the *foot* radical 足 in 踢 (*tī, to kick*). In such a case, the function of the phonetic sides 兑 (*duì, to exchange*) and 易 (*yì, easy*) would appear much less logical and less useful. This lack of logical phonetic connection or relevance is especially so in the case of 兑, which learners are unlikely to encounter as a character or as a side in other characters. Too much reliance on the assumption that, as with native speaker learners, knowledge of semantic and phonetic sides is the critical information for mapping sound and meaning onto characters is unfortunately likely to lead to only more confusion for second language learners.

The reason why functional information is less useful is because, as noted earlier, these principles make little sense to the novice second language learner who lacks a well- developed spoken lexicon. This is also because of the unreliability of the information, especially when so few characters are known, and so few examples of the function of a semantic or phonetic radical are encountered. Research, however, with post-secondary learners does highlight the fact that, with sufficient input and experience, the functional properties of the sides *do* become apparent and this knowledge *does* assist learners to recall sound and meaning (Everson, 2011). But for novice primary and secondary learners, no such opportunity for input and experience exists, and simpler, more graphically oriented approaches to developing orthographic awareness are likely to be critical central for successful character learning.

The task of remembering form, however, is typically reliant on the routine practice of committing pen to paper. As a result, young, novice second language learners' broader level of orthographic awareness develops very slowly.

## The Role of Character Writing

In any language, learning to read at a young age is founded upon active reading or viewing of meaningful texts read aloud by others as the learners come to associate symbols on the page with typically known oral vocabulary. This guided reading is usually supported by rhymes, which focus on children's learning to identify the individual letters of the alphabet and to build a basic knowledge of the symbols from which the words of the language are composed. At school and at home more mechanical processes of pen and paper practice in the art of writing, creating meaningful symbols on the page in a manner legible to others, are then introduced. At the initial stages of writing practice the focus is on the basic principles of letter formation, learning the direction and sequence of individual strokes and their relation to other strokes within each letter, particularly in relation to appreciating points of intersection or connection between strokes to create letters.

Of particular importance in English writing is learning the clockwise and anticlockwise curves: the difference between writing *c* and *o* or between *d* and *b*, or *p*, for example, or where to place the horizontal stroke in *t* or the dot in *i*. They also need to learn how to connect the different strokes. The focus on stroke direction, stroke order, and stroke relationships plays a foundational role in learning any orthography, especially with very young learners engaging with pen and paper for the first time.

For novice learners of Chinese, already well-versed in writing in English, this task of returning to early learning behaviours of practicing stroke direction, sequence and relationship often seems rather mindless and even demeaning. And, indeed, it might well be so in a context where the value of learning these routines is not well explained. There is, however, little alternative to taking this path. The nature of the strokes, stroke direction and sequence, and stroke arrangements in Chinese differs substantially from the way these features present themselves in English letters; there is a preponderance of curved strokes in English, both clockwise (*p, b*) and anticlockwise (*a, c, e*), a number of vertical strokes (*l, k, h*), few horizontal strokes (*t, f*) and some diagonal stokes (such as *w, x, and k*). Then there are upper- and lowercase letters as well.

In Chinese, there are six basic strokes, and a range of additional movements (typically numbered at 24) attached to these basic forms. What is noticeable is that curves or circular shapes are largely absent and angular square-oriented shapes predominate, and the characters that these strokes create are typically much more complex than the letter graphs of English. Consequently, learning to replicate these unfamiliar and visually complex characters with an unfamiliar palette of strokes in order to create a meaningful symbol in an equally sized square space requires focussed practice and only practice will make for efficient and legible writing in Chinese. Just as correct stroke order and direction create the opportunity for fast and effective cursive writing in English, familiarity with stroke order and direction in Chinese are necessary precursors for fast and efficient writing in Chinese.

Character practice, therefore, plays an important role in developing basic writing skills, and through focussed attention on the structure and detail of the character being practised, helps instil the image of the form in the mind of the novice learner. This focussed and regular practice of characters is a tradition in Chinese that can still be seen in first and second language contexts. It remains the assumption of most Chinese teachers that de-contextualised character practice is the primary means by which the characters are to be impressed on the memory of the novice Chinese foreign language learner.

There are two major issues with this routine practice approach to memorising characters. First, learning to write in order to learn to remember is conducted at the logographic level, that is, the character is represented as an assemblage of strokes which construct the whole character (e.g. 没 = seven strokes), typically without any attention to the sub-units within the whole character, the sequence of components (氵 + 几 + 又). The second major issue with character practice as the sole means for committing character forms as 'logographic-wholes' to memory is that it leaves learners unable to describe their knowledge or understanding of characters worked on in the past, or how to use that knowledge effectively to process new characters as they are encountered.

In learning to copy characters, learners discover there are, for example, seven strokes in sequence, but they seldom learn to identify or name the sequence of components that constitute the whole character. They may have encountered these components as independent characters or in other characters, but their level of orthographic awareness; of being able to identify or name the components in particular and their sequence of writing, remains anecdotal and based on the vagaries of prior experience, at best. The learning demands of remembering the character are dependent on remembering the sum, not the parts, and the sum is often complex and the parts left unfamiliar and hard to remember, and hard to recognise (in print) or recall (to write). It is somewhat similar to learning to write words without learning the letters that constitute the word. In English we think it very important to learn how to spell, but in Chinese the priority is learning to write, without knowing how to 'spell' the character, that is, without knowing to name the individual graphemes, the components, in the sequence in which they are written.

For learning to be generative and effective in building autonomy in character learning and use, the novice learner needs to be able to talk her way through the 'spelling' of the character. Some parts of an unfamiliar character may have been encountered as a component or side in another character, but the ability to use this information effectively in learning new characters is limited by the lack of knowing what the component is and how to name it. As with the young learners' insights referred to earlier, learners' ability to describe their knowledge, and their capacity to use their knowledge to analyse and talk about any new character encountered, is restricted, and thus cannot be used to generate new knowledge.

Research into Chinese character learning among first language learners suggests that orthographic awareness is of critical importance to the native reader and in learning to read by Chinese children (Loach and Wang, 2016). There is also evidence that metalinguistic awareness among second language learners does develop once sufficient print input or exposure has occurred, even in contexts where character practice or rote methods are all that are available. Research outlined in Everson (2011) into character processing by adult (college and tertiary) learners of Chinese as a second language suggests that a level of orthographic awareness develops through experience: after a year of study it remains variable and is stronger in terms of semantic processing than phonetic processing; by second year, students who appear able to use their orthographic awareness in reading tasks perform better; and as orthographic awareness increases, students tend to become more reliant on this for character recall and character learning.

The challenge thus facing teachers of novice school-based learners is to find what can be done to build their orthographic awareness from the outset, and to build their understanding of, and ability to apply, their initial orthographic awareness of the character system throughout their character learning experiences. How can these learners be provided with a conceptual frame of reference that provides foundational orthographic awareness of the nature of the character system that will enhance their ability to acquire a working knowledge of forms, structures and properties of characters, so as to build their abilities in reading and writing efficiently in Chinese? In considering a principled approach to the introduction to the character system, an additional question arises: Is there a preferred developmental sequence of literacy learning that is likely to support both enhanced orthographic awareness and efficient print literacy development?

## Alternative Approaches to Teaching Chinese Reading and Writing Skills

Fan (2010) identifies three methods of instruction related to character learning and use in the second language classroom. The most common is rote memorisation through routine character practice and recitation of texts in characters; the second strategy is providing phonetic transcription in Pinyin to assist in accessing the sounds of new characters in texts, a scaffold which is typically withdrawn after the teacher feels sufficient viewing time has been provided; the third strategy is explicit orthographic instruction through analysis of the internal structural components in characters encountered. No matter what strategy is employed, the glossing of unfamiliar characters with Pinyin is invaluable until, through a range of means, the learners are able to read the character readily without support. Pinyin is therefore a critical factor for second language learners, who look upon it as their sole means of access to the sounds of new characters. From the author's perspective, the gradual withdrawal of Pinyin glossing isn't a positive strategy to assist character recognition. It is merely a scaffold to help in reading aloud and in vocabulary or grammar learning activities. Thus, the removal of Pinyin glossing too early does not help learners recognise the character or remember its form, it simply adds to the pressure they feel and this hinders their ability to participate in class activity. At the same time, however, providing Pinyin glossing should not be seen as an alternative to focussed writing practice and explicit orthographic instruction which are valuable strategies to help develop familiarity with the character through its form.

In his review of approaches to teaching characters in first language contexts, Lam (2011) notes two orientations towards character learning: a *character-centred* approach and a *meaning-centred* approach. In the character-centred approach the focus is on de-contextualised learning in which a focus on character forms precedes reading activities. The teaching activities, however, may vary from traditional recitation and mechanical memorisation through to the analysis of character forms and their functions. The alternative meaning-centred orientation focuses on contextualised character learning through reading and listening for meaning, often with Pinyin support to assist connecting forms to sounds, in context. Lam argues that the meaning-centred approach, while inherently valuable in engaging learners with meaningful texts, lacks attention to the actual process of developing orthographic awareness of characters, a strategy that is more likely to be attended to through a character-centred approach. He suggests the communicative methods applied in second language contexts have focussed teachers' attention on a meaning-centred approach backed up by mechanical memorisation through routine character practice, with systematic introduction to and analysis of the character system seldom evident.

Textbooks also tend to focus on routine character practice and Pinyin glossing, with little in the way of explicit orthographic instruction being evident. Textbooks seldom contain anything more than 'nice to know' introductory information (Fan, 2010) about character origins, and about features which are relatively accessible and easy to explain, such as the etymological origins of some basic characters and some explanation as to the functions of semantic and phonetic radicals in small sets of characters displaying higher than average levels of reliability. Beyond this, as Li and Zhang (2016) claim, . . . 'the expression "tiger head and snake tail" (虎头蛇尾, *hǔtóu shéwěi*) can perhaps be used to characterise the dwindling amount of attention to characters beyond the initial stage. For many textbooks, character instruction starts and ends with a general introduction to the origin and evolution of characters and an explanation of the basic principles of character formation and stroke order' (2016: 157.)

## Literacy Inertia in the Classroom

Despite the good arguments for improving learner's orthographic awareness through explicit instruction, this is not yet a common practice in instructional settings. Yet if omitted, awareness of character structure and identifying components and their arrangement in characters as a cue to remembering form, meaning and sound, remains a skill that only develops implicitly though extensive input and exposure. A number of reasons for this may be considered.

One reason is simply *tradition*. Textbooks have for decades placed significant priority on routine character practice and it remains an important part of the tradition of how students learn to engage with Chinese characters and develop writing skills. Memorising the character is a desirable outcome of the practice, reinforced by the need to read and to read aloud characters in texts (as a form of input and exposure) as the units of the textbook are worked through. Thus, character learning is imposed on learners, but the extent to which this is effective in building orthographic awareness is questionable in many cases.

Another reason for the lack of attention to explicit orthographic instruction is the communicative language curriculum in which the macro skills of listening, reading, speaking and writing are treated as being of equal importance, or as integrated and interrelated in terms of the nature and pace of progress in learning and use of language. While there may be some recognition or differentiation between the receptive (listening and reading), and productive (speaking and writing) capabilities in using the target language, textbooks seldom make much distinction between the rate and nature of how learners acquire the ability to interact orally (listen and speak) and the ability to engage with print text (read and write). This is a tradition drawn from the study of European languages which share a common orthography, and from Chinese first language learning practices where children bring a well-developed oral vocabulary to their literacy learning. The result is that school-based learners learn to write characters with a focus on stroke order and direction only, and then learn to read them aloud in the context of short dialogues and narratives, which is intended also to serve to build their speaking skills. This reflects what Lam (2011) describes as a meaning centred approach, where characters are learned for their communicative value alone, which provides little opportunity for building systemic understanding of the system.

A third reason is the fact that, given the acceptance that characters are difficult and the development of reading and writing skills slow and uncertain, the number of characters students are expected to learn is kept to a minimum. Yet there are 3,500 frequently used characters, which represent over 99% of characters encountered in modern publications, that children in China are required learn in primary school. Tertiary leaners may encounter 1,000 characters in a full year of study. Second language learners are typically introduced to around 500 or so of these high frequency characters during all their years of schooling. While this may limit the memory burden for novice learners in the early stages of their study, it also significantly restricts their ability to engage with a wider range of characters and authentic texts and their ability read material in Chinese beyond those specifically designed for classroom use. A consequence of this is that learner's development of orthographic awareness is further restricted due to the limits of both input and experience with the printed word.

Finally, and equally importantly, is the realisation that teaching characters to novice learners is not something native speakers are well trained to do. Native speaker teachers' experience with the Chinese writing system and the underlying orthographic awareness gained in their own first language immersion is hardly adequate preparation for attempting to mediate the complexities of the orthography, its features and relative reliabilities, and variability, particularly in a bilingual context where learner understanding of such complexities needs to be mediated predominately through their own first language. The outcome is that teachers, therefore, often simply adopt the textbook representations of routine character practice and integrated learning of oral and written language into their classroom teaching practice for want of any better resource, and for want of a real understanding of learners' needs in the area of literacy development.

The issues for school-based learners are significant. Not only is the written language complex in its form and in its relations with sounds and meanings in the language, student access to the system itself is heavily constrained by low expectations of the number of characters they can learn by rote, and by the limited time on task available to engage meaningfully with the system. Textbooks tend to provide little in the way of awareness raising in relation to the orthography, and teachers' own experiences do not readily prepare them for engaging learners with the task in powerful ways. Clearly a review of curriculum and practice in character teaching and learning is overdue.

### Classroom Intervention to Develop Orthographic Awareness

Packard, Chen, Li, Wu, Gaffney, Li, and Anderson (2006) suggest that native speaker children's literacy learning is enhanced when they are taught ways to access the written language which do not rely solely on rote memory, with classroom instruction that supports generative learning increasing learners' opportunities to make connections and extend learning beyond the limits of classroom instruction. Nagy (2007) argues that the abilities associated with word learning and reading comprehension in a second language are primarily metalinguistic in nature and such abilities are demonstrably teachable. Learners' abilities in processing print could be enhanced by giving more attention to the language-specific demands of vocabulary learning, and by making vocabulary learning more explicitly metalinguistic in nature. Nagy argues that vocabulary instruction needs to teach about words (or characters in the Chinese case): how they are put together, how they can be learned, and how they are used. He suggests that if students are to take greater responsibility for their own vocabulary learning, they need to be able to reflect on word meanings, on sources of information about word meanings, and on processes for vocabulary learning (Nagy, 2007: 71).

In relation to classroom practice in Chinese, there is increasing recognition of the need to review the nature of character content and method in Chinese curriculum. Lam (2011) concludes there is a current overemphasis on the word as the unit of instruction and the use of meaning-centred approaches. He suggests a need to divide the curriculum into oral and written strands in which a meaning-centred approach (the word as the unit of instruction) is the basis for the oral language strand, and a character-centred approach, (the character itself as the unit of instruction), be applied in the writing strand, while not ignoring the need to develop learners' communicative potential as readers in meaningful contexts.

Everson (2007) points out that Chinese second language learners with insufficient orthographic knowledge tend to memorise each new character as a whole rather than understanding its structure and constituent components. He highlights the importance of learning to visually distinguish components in a character, as once components are identified and internalised, the need for processing and memorisation of characters encountered only as an assemblage of stokes would be reduced. Everson (2011) proposes that information about the character system must be woven into the fabric of Chinese reading classroom pedagogy in order to develop strategies that facilitate learning and use of characters in reading. Fan (2010) also recommends a teaching focus on orthographic knowledge of components and radicals to develop orthographic awareness because components represent 'chunking', which facilitates memory because there are fewer 'chunks' per character than strokes and, importantly, that the ability to name these chunks (components or radicals), or to know their meaning, facilitates memorisation.

In terms of selecting content for explicit orthographic instruction, Shen (2015) argues that literacy development needs to follow orthography-based instructional principles, from stroke to radical to character; from high to low frequency characters, from low to high density characters, to greatly reduce the cognitive load in character learning. Xu, Perfetti, and Chang (2014) suggest that perceiving characters as organised subunits of radicals and components may create units of encoding that are more efficient for processing than perceiving characters as piles of interwoven strokes. They argue that developing awareness of characters as composed sub-character components would mean that the task of memorising thousands of characters as independent units would give way to building an understanding of interrelated characters connected through a much smaller number of recurring radicals and components (p. 774).

## The Unit of Instruction

The literature suggests a structured curriculum and sustained instructional practice has the potential to enhance development of language-specific orthographic knowledge, and enhance the ability to apply such awareness in reading and vocabulary acquisition in Chinese. In relation to novice school-based learners, however, a note of caution is raised in the literature. The research focuses on learning in college and university settings. Fan (2010) suggests these adult learners tend to acquire orthographic competence more rapidly than first language children due to their conceptual sophistication and the benefit of explicit orthographic instruction (when available), despite their lack of oral language, their limited exposure to the writing system, and their alphabetic orthographic background. Xu, Perfetti, and Chang (2014) recommend explicit orthographic instruction for such adult learners, suggesting that relying on radicals as functional orthographic units in learning characters is an effective method of memory organisation. They do not, however, argue for a radical-based, character-grouping approach in teaching materials for primary school learners of Chinese. The reasons are due to the school-based learner's lack of conceptual sophistication on the one hand, and the limited range of character learning likely in such contexts. However one aspect of orthographic awareness that novice school-based learners will benefit from relates to building their knowledge of the forms that make up the system, the components, not the function of the parts that serve as particularly unreliable cues, the radicals. What they need to learn is to appreciate the value in knowing and naming as many of the components that make up the character system as possible.

Another aspect of literacy learning that has received considerable attention in the literature is whether character learning should begin at the outset, or be delayed until a sufficient grounding in the spoken language has been developed and a sufficient vocabulary acquired to ease the mental burden when learning characters associated with these words. A number of academics support the proposition of delayed character learning, or the 'Pinyin-first' approach, including Halliday (2014), Everson (2009), Dew (2007), Packard (1990). Shen (2015) notes that the proponents of delayed character introduction are typically non-native speaker teachers of Chinese, with native speaker teachers preferring an immediate introduction to characters based on their belief that characters are the key and foundation to the language. The debate over timing of introduction assumes, however, that learners will follow traditional practices in learning characters as needed for immediate communicative need, a meaning-centred approach described by Lam (2011) as failing to provide any systematic introduction to the character system. Lam's alternative is a character-first approach, where the character, rather than the word, is the unit of instruction, and particular attention is paid to building systemic understanding in principled ways. Lam's proposition still rests on a focus on the functional parts, the radicals, as well as the physical structural properties of the character.

In school-based contexts, however, with low numbers of characters encountered and limited prior vocabulary knowledge, the issue is how to begin the study of characters to build orthographic knowledge and develop orthographic awareness that can be applied later to new characters encountered incidentally in text. What is required is a module of study in the earliest stages of Chinese language learning in which the component is the unit of instruction. In such a program, character learning for communicative purposes is delayed. Instead, a Pinyin-first approach is used to build oral language skills in meaningful communicative contexts while a component-centred approach to building orthographic knowledge, and learning how to apply that knowledge to character learning takes place later. Once a sufficient grounding in components has been achieved, once learners are versed in using the strokes to create components and using components to create characters, learning to name components and to 'spell' characters in their component sequence, teachers can begin to merge the oral and literacy strands and characters can become the unit of instruction as Lam (2011) describes. There would then be an ongoing focus on building systemic understanding, in particular, learning to deal with the vagaries of the function and reliabilities of semantic and phonetic radicals as character learning proceeds in communicative contexts.

## A Literacy Curriculum for School-Based Learners

If explicit orthographic instruction is to begin with a component-centred approach, then the question arises as to what inventory of components should be introduced before learners move on to a character-centred and communication oriented curriculum. Shen (2015) suggests a sequence of introduction that follows orthography-based instructional principles, moving from simple to complex graphic information, for example, from strokes to radicals to characters; from basic characters to integral (compound) characters; from high frequency characters to low frequency characters; and from low density (few stroke) characters to higher density characters. Loach and Wang (2016) suggest the selection of characters to be learned needs to find a balance between character frequency and presenting characters in a hierarchical order, in which learning begins from components (or *primitives* as they term them) and moves to compound characters. They argue that learning characters in order of hierarchy is desirable because a learning order that explicitly reflects orthographic principles is more likely to generate accurate and productive orthographic awareness. Xu, Perfetti, and Chang (2014) suggest that grouping characters containing a common component or side (semantic or phonetic radical) helps draw learner's attention to the position and function of components, which is an effective method of memory organisation.

These propositions are still based predominately on learning the functional properties of components and radicals rather than dealing with the perceptual demands of recognising and remembering component forms. In an introductory, component-centred module to building orthographic awareness—perceptual skills and the ability to identify and name components—the challenge is: Which components to introduce, in what order, and on what basis? Certainly Shen's (2015) notion of moving from low to high density, and high to low frequency, is persuasive, given learners' unfamiliarity with the graphic details of character-components. Loach and Wang's (2016) proposition of hierarchical arrangement is also important when students first begin to engage with components in characters, and Xu, Perfetti, and Chang (2014) recommendation of grouping characters to show how components appear in characters (less so their function) is also important in terms of resourcing the move from learning individual components to exploring their use in compound characters as their orthographic awareness develops.

These variables don't necessarily predetermine a fixed selection or sequence of component introduction, but highlight the issues that need to be considered in making principled pedagogic decisions based on an understanding of learners and their current level of cognitive maturity and literacy development in their own first language.

In order for the process to empower learners to increase their abilities in reading, and writing, the approach to teaching and learning of the Chinese writing system needs to draw upon learners' prior knowledge and experience and look, initially, at the process from their perspective. That means making the challenge of character learning a conversation in the classroom, not an exercise for homework. The most important aspect of raising orthographic awareness is that it is based on explicit instruction, on classroom dialogue about character concepts and learning processes. The selection of content to be explored, and the role of the teacher in engaging learners effectively with that content and process of character learning, cannot be underestimated. This is not something that can be done in isolation by learners themselves.

Teacher mediation of character learning, of engaging learners with concepts and with inquiry processes as they begin to experience characters through components in the classroom, is central. Classroom discussion is a most powerful tool for promoting the development of metalinguistic awareness, and a powerful tool for promoting talk about the nature of words and the nature of characters. Classroom discussion is also a powerful means for encouraging learners to think in more powerful ways about language and learning beyond the first language experiences and assumptions they bring to the Chinese second language classroom.

The character system is complex for novice learners, particularly in contrast to the alphabetic system and the rules of English word formation using a discrete set of letters. In Chinese second-language classrooms, novice learners with no prior experience of the target language, learn to say '*nǐ hǎo*', then learn to write this in characters on almost the same day, without prior learning or explanation of the inherent structures and features of characters they encounter. Teachers often confuse the purposes of oral-language development and print-literacy development and assume that learners can somehow make the leap from a new utterance to a new form of print representation in one step, with only a most cursory explanation of the nature of the character system.

Teachers often face difficulties in adequately explaining the nature of the character system to novice learners, particularly when the system is introduced on the basis of examples of characters which have been introduced for an entirely different reason; that is, for immediate communicative needs. Consequently, teachers often explain the character system only as derived from a set of pictographs that really don't make much sense anymore and base learning mainly on the process of construction, on stroke order and direction, rather than explaining characters for what they really are: a sequence of graphic units, the components, which if understood make it much easier to remember the whole.

Teachers need to rethink their goals from the learners' perspective, to reflect upon the methods appropriate for learners coming to terms with the conceptually challenging task of reading and writing in characters, and develop resources that can challenge many of the misconceptions about Chinese language, about its writing system and about the processes of character learning that are currently in place. Most importantly, teachers need to have a clear differentiation between the knowledge, skills and practices in learning to engage in oral interaction, and the knowledge, skills and practices needed in learning to understand the orthography. It is a fundamental principle for success, given the limited time on task, the low expectations placed upon learners at present, and perceptions of the difficulties, bordering on impossibility, of non-Chinese-background learners in learning to read and write in Chinese. The questions for teachers to confront are: What do learners see, and what do we teachers want them to see, within the characters we put before them? If we take, for example, these two characters:

馨 癮

Do we want them to see:

1. Characters as an assemblage of strokes with no insights into their internal structures and features?
2. Characters as two sides containing semantic and phonetic cues as a native speaker might 'see' them, thus, for example, viewing the previously mentioned characters as: 殸 (*sheng, chimes*) + 香 (*xiāng, fragrant*) + 疒 (*bìng, illness*) + 隐 (*yǐn, hidden*)?
3. Characters as a sequence of accessible and meaningful, recurring components that help manage the visual, orthographic processing demands and assist recall the form of characters encountered, and learning to spell them, in English, as a means of connecting with their prior knowledge: 声 *sound* +几 *bench* +又, *hand* +禾, *crop* +曰, *sun;* 疒 *ill,* +阝 , *mound* +勹 , *horn* +彐, *hand* +心, *heart* ?

Characters broken up into their constituent parts can become more visually accessible and somewhat more meaningful to novice learners where all the graphic information available within the character is made available and explored from the learner's perspective as they make their way towards mastery. Ultimately, the process of learning to read and write in purposeful communicative contexts can be much more meaningful and efficient for learners if the foundations for orthographic awareness are effectively laid from the start.

## Note

1 The terminology in relation to the character system is not well-defined, and terms for graphic structures and features within characters—the components and radicals—are often used interchangeably. The term *radical* is used here to refer to the classification function of a particular side of a character, be it the 部首 (*bùshǒu, semantic radical*) or the 声旁 (*shēngpáng, phonetic radical*). The term *component* (部件, *bùjiàn*) is used here to refer to an independent unitary part that can be used to construct a character (Yin, 2003). These are often referred to as 字素 (*zìsù, graphemes*).

## References

Bai, Z. (2005) *Modern Chinese Writing System: Its Properties and Graphemic Principle.* Paper presented at the *International and Interdisciplinary Conference,* University of Mainz, Germersheim, Germany.

Dew, J.E. (2007) 'Language Is Primary, Script Is Secondary: The Importance of Gaining a Strong Foundation in the Language Before Devoting Major Efforts to Character Recognition', in A. Guder, X. Jiang, and Y. Wan (eds.), *The Cognition, Learning & Teaching of Chinese Characters*, 451–462. Beijing: Beijing Language & Culture University Press.

Everson, M.E. (2007) 'Developing Orthographic Awareness Among CFL Learners: What the Research Tells Us', in A. Guder, X. Jiang, and Y. Wan (eds.), *The Cognition, Learning and Teaching of Chinese Characters*, 33–50. China: Beijing Language & Culture University Press.

Everson, M.E. (2009) 'Literacy in Chinese as a Foreign Language', in M.E. Everson and Y. Xiao (eds.), *Teaching Chinese as a Foreign Language: Theories and Applications*, 97–112. Boston: Cheng & Tsui.

Everson, M.E. (2011) 'Best Practices in Teaching Logographic and Non-roman Writing Systems to L2 Learners', *Annual Review of Applied Linguistics*, 31: 249–274.

Fan, M.H. (2010) *Developing Chinese Orthographic Awareness: What Insights Into Characters Do Beginning Level Chinese as a Foreign Language Textbooks Provide?* Berlin, Germany: Lambert Academic Publishing.

Grabe, W. (2009) 'Epilogue: Reflections on Second Language Reading Research and Instruction', in Z.H. Hong and N.J. Anderson (eds.), *Second Language Reading Research and Instruction: Crossing the Boundaries*, 192–205. Ann Arbor: The University of Michigan Press.

Halliday, M.A.K. (2014) 'Notes on Teaching Chinese to Foreign Learners', *Journal of World Languages*, 1(1): 1–6.

Koda, K. (2005) *Insights Into Second Language Reading: A Cross-Linguistic Approach*. New York: Cambridge University Press.

Koda, K. (2008) 'Impacts of Prior Literacy Experience on Second Language Learning to Read', in K. Koda and A.M. Zehler (eds.), *Learning to Read Across Languages: Cross-Linguistic Relationships in First- and Second-Language Literacy Development*, 68–96. New York: Routledge.

Lam, H.C. (2011) 'A Critical Analysis of the Various Ways of Teaching Chinese Characters', *Electronic Journal of Foreign Language Teaching*, 8(1): 57–70.

Li, Y. and Zhang, Z.A. (2016) 'CFL Education at the College Level', in J.N. Ruan, J. Zhang, and C.B. Leung (eds.), *Chinese Language Education in the United States*, 141–166. Basel, Switzerland: Springer.

Loach, J.C. and Wang, J.Z. (2016) 'Optimizing the Learning Order of Chinese Characters Using a Novel Topological Sort Algorithm', *PoLS ONE*, 11(10): 1–17.

Nagy, W. (2007) 'Metalinguistic Awareness and Vocabulary-Comprehension Connection', in R. Wagner, A. Muse, and K. Tannenbaum (eds.), *Vocabulary Acquisition: Implications for Reading Comprehension*, 52–77. New York: Guildford Press.

Packard, J.L. (1990) 'Effects of Time Lag in the Introduction of Characters Into the Chinese Language Curriculum', *The Modern Language Journal*, 74: 167–175.

Packard, J.L., Chen, X., Li, W., Wu, X., Gaffney, J.S., Li, H., and Anderson, R.C. (2006) 'Explicit Instruction in Orthographic Structure and Word Morphology Helps Chinese Children Learn to Write Characters', *Reading and Writing*, 19(5): 457–487.

Shen, H.H. (2015) 'Chinese L2 Literacy Debates and Beginner Reading in the United States', in J. Ennser-Kananen and M. Bigelow (eds.), *The Routledge Handbook of Educational Linguistics*, 21: 276–288. New York: Taylor & Francis.

Shu, H., Chen, X., Anderson, R.C., Wu, N., and Xuan, Y. (2003) 'Properties of School Chinese: Implications for Learning to Read', *Child Development*, 74(1): 27–47.

Xu, Y., Perfetti, C.A., and Chang, L.Y. (2014) 'The Effect of Radical-based Grouping in Character Learning in Chinese as a Foreign Language', *The Modern Language Journal*, 98(3): 773–793.

Yin, H.X. (2003) 'Preface', in H.Q. Zhou (ed.), *A Practical Dictionary of Chinese in Graphic Components*, 7–8. China: Beijing Language and Culture University Press.

Zhou, H.Q. (ed.). (2003) *A Practical Dictionary of Chinese in Graphic Components*. China: Beijing Language and Culture University Press.

费锦昌 (Fei, J.) (1996) '现代汉字部件探究 [Exploring Components in Modern Chiense)', 语言文字应用 [Using Language], 2: 20–26.

# 4

# GENERATING GRAMMAR AND VOCABULARY

## Introduction

The structures of a language reflect its spirit, wrote Caleb Gattegno (1972), creator of *The Silent Way*, and the Chinese linguist, Shen Xiaolong, also wrote of the spirit of a language being found in its discourse structures. Both Gattegno and Shen name the verb as the central part of English grammar, and Shen claims that it is because the English verb is the focus that it is comparatively heavily marked compared to other parts of speech (Shen, 1988, trans. Gao, 1997). By contrast, Shen says, the spirit of Chinese grammar is diffuse, with chunks of text arranged according to logical development, ordered chronologically. The concept of grammar as spirit is a particularly positive one with which to approach the learner's path to mastery of the structures of their new language. It suggests that in tackling grammar, the learner is not setting out to trudge through long lists of new structures, as often seems the case, but is really getting to the heart of things and will find it empowering to have an increasing control over how the language is created.

As with other aspects of language learning considered in this book, successful learning of grammar is expected to come about partly as the result of metalinguistic dialogue between teacher and students over grammar in general, as well as over the particularities of Chinese grammar in contrast to that of English; and partly as the result of immersion activities and exercises directed at acquisition of the fundamental structures of the language from the perspective of the learner on the starting line. The metalinguistic dialogue is essential for building the learner's grasp of meaning making in their second language and their understanding of how it may differ from meaning making in their first language. A feature taken as the base of this work is that, at its heart, grammar is understood to be a particular language community's way of grappling with the fundamental, universal communication issues of expressing, in as specific or non-specific ways as needed, *who did what to whom, when, where, why,* and *how,* and *how a series of such statements is linked to create discourse.* A feature of the acquisition task is that, while we can know objective rules and use them to create something we want to say or to check something we have written, the mastery of fundamental structures that the learner is seeking has to be developed in their ears: when native speakers want to check the correctness of something grammatically, they say it out loud and listen, and then decide, 'That sounds right' or, 'That sounds funny'. Both knowledge of the rules and the inner criteria of what sounds right need to be an explicit part of second language grammar learning.

In textbooks, chapters are typically organised to present one or more new grammatical structures and a list of new vocabulary related to a topic presumed to be of interest to or needed by the learners. Both structures and vocabulary are usually met in texts and then extracted and listed separately. A set of exercises then provides some opportunities for practice with both so they can begin to be internalised. These two aspects are also considered here in the same chapter. However, for the sake of clarity, grammar will be addressed directly first and then vocabulary, and the two brought together in the concluding section.

## Getting Started in Grammar

Early grammars of a language were based on analysis of the basic sentences of the written language. More recently, textbooks have centred their linguistic development around presumed communicative needs of learners: greetings, self-introductions, descriptions of the world around them, combined with contrasting descriptions of the lives of people of a similar age living in the target language country. Textbooks for school learners are often based on events in the lives of a group of children who appear throughout the book. In Content and Language Integrated Learning (CLIL), where students learn their second language through the study of a regular curriculum subject, topics are scheduled as required by the wider curriculum and students can find themselves starting out learning the language for growing plants from seed or providing information about early civilisations, with the grammatical forms to be learned those essential to identifying parts and processes of the topic content and commenting on them.

### Phrases and Simple Sentences

Whatever the guiding line for development of the content, there is a generally recognised common fundamental developmental sequence of grammar that beginner and intermediate learners need to master, although they may appear at very different points in a course. These primarily include the formation of phrases and the basics of sentence formation and sentence joining. Sample lists of these in Chinese are set out in Table 4.1. The learning challenges of these

**TABLE 4.1** Constructing phrases and simple sentences

| Class | Learning Point | Example |
|---|---|---|
| **Nouns** | No articles<br>No plurals<br>Measure words/classifiers | 我有 笔<br>蓝的是我的<br>这支笔是我的，那支是他的<br>我有一支笔， 他有两支 |
| | Pluralising | 这两支笔是你的<br>这些笔是我的<br>我的笔都是红的 |
| | Qualified | 我的笔<br>蓝的笔<br>我蓝的笔<br>他买的笔<br>他买给我的笔<br>他买给我的那两支蓝的笔 |
| **Verbs** | Not marked for person | 我来他来你们来 |
| | Not marked for tense | 他昨天来 他今天来 他明天来 |
| | Negated | 不来 没来 |
| | Modified | 他还给我一个苹果<br>他只给我一个苹果<br>他还没给我一个苹果 |
| | With a co-verb | 他要吃饭<br>他会说汉语<br>我可以喝水吗?<br>我应该走了 |
| | Combined adverb and co-verb | 他只会说汉语<br>只有他会说汉语<br>只有他不会说汉语 |
| | Verb complements | 他说得太快<br>他把书打开<br>他站起来<br>她来得及<br>我买不到 |
| | Verb particles | 来了<br>他还没来呢<br>你去吧！<br>法国我来过<br>他一边吃着午饭一边打字<br>门上挂着画是她画的 |
| **Structures** | Interrogative | 你要喝水吗?<br>你要不要喝水?<br>他来了没有?<br>他是中国人, 对不对? |
| | Comparative | 她比你高<br>他没有你高 |
| | Topic Sentence | 水果你买了没有?<br>我买的水果很好吃<br>我买水果, 你买了没有? |

Chinese grammatical forms are then identified and discussed in detail and key teaching techniques for targeting the challenges they present are provided. It should be noted that items in the lists are indicative only, intended to allow consideration of the foreign learners' tasks in acquiring Chinese grammar. For display and discussion of a comprehensive set of Chinese grammatical structures, any of the many research grammars now available should be referred to (e.g. Li and Thompson, 2003; 杨 (Yang), 2013; Jiao, He, and Livaccari, 2010–2012).

In terms of the degree to which the learner's knowledge of grammar from their first language has to be disturbed, the Chinese grammar points displayed in Table 4.1 present the English speaker with quite a number of easily assimilated forms as well as some strange new structures. The former is the result of two factors: to a large extent, Chinese word order is the same as English word order, and there are none of the features such as inflected endings on extensive declensions of articles, nouns and adjectives, or multiple endings and complex moods and tenses in the verb system, which make other European languages time and labour consuming for English speakers to learn. The latter for the English speaker in learning Chinese grammar are the specifically different features: measure words; *de*-segments instead of relative clauses; no articles, tenses or word for 'yes'; verb complements; and verb and sentence particles. Of these, it is particularly structures relating to the Chinese verb that often remain the least well internalised even after some years of study. This may well be because of the learners' sensitivity to the verb phrase due to its importance in their own language, combined with the fact that it is in certain parts of the verb phrase that Chinese grammar most especially expresses a different spirit from that of English, focussed only on outcomes of the action and aspect (I am doing X now, I have done X), not tense.

## Sentence Joining

In addition to creating phrases and single sentences, the developmental task for learners is to expand their capability to handle complex spoken and written texts. Too many textbooks and curricula leave the intermediate school, and even undergraduate students, still using only a small group of connectors in spoken and written language and creating texts which have a juvenile ring to them, and often also a noticeably English construction base.

There are seven essential relationships that are created by linking two or more sentences:

A number of different parts of speech can be used to make links between sentences. Table 4.3 displays some of the conjunctions, pronouns and adverbs most commonly used in Chinese to join two or more phrases and clauses.

**TABLE 4.2** Logical connections

| Relationship | Sample Conjunctions |
|---|---|
| Addition | 和，也，还，而且 |
| Contrast | 但是，可是， |
| Sequence | 就，才，再，以后／前 |
| Cause | 因为 |
| Consequence | 所以，因此，由于 |
| Purpose | 去...,要... |
| Means | 用...去... |

**TABLE 4.3** Sentence links

### Common conjunctions

| | |
|---|---|
| 因为...所以... | because/therefore |
| 不但...而且... | not only/but also |
| 虽然...但是... | although/(but) |
| 如果...就... | if/then |
| 只要...就... | only if/then |
| 只要...才... | not until/then |
| ...还是... | [x] or [y] |
| 或者...或者... | either/or |
| 可是／但是... | but/but |
| 由于...因此... | owing to/so |
| 并不...其实... | not ... (but) actually |
| ...却是... | Nevertheless |

### Pronouns and adverb links

| | |
|---|---|
| 一方面...另一方面... | on the one hand/on the other hand |
| 有时...有时... | sometimes/sometimes |
| 有的...有的... | some/some |
| 一...就... | once [verb]/then |
| 一...就... | as [verb]/[verb]] = simultaneously |
| 一...就... | first/after that/then/finally |
| 又...又... | both/and |
| 除了...外，...还... | except for |
| 无论...都... | regardless of/(all) |

It is essential that students get to the stage of extending and linking sentences early because language beyond the single sentence behaves in new ways, and in Chinese, it introduces three features, which will be challenging to foreign learners: topic sentences, topic chains which frequently use zero noun phrases in the subject position, and peculiarly Chinese punctuation. For example:

A.  昨天晚上我看电视，也做作业。 (*yesterday evening I watched TV, also did homework*)
B.  我去法国，还去荷兰。 (*I am going to France, also going to Finland*)
C.  她学习德语，而且学得很努力。 (*she is studying German, moreover studies very diligently*)
D.  她学数学，学得很努力。 (*she is studying mathematics, studies very diligently*)
E.  你走路去，那要怎么回来? (*you walk there, in that way how will come back*)
F.  早晨六点我起床、洗澡、穿衣服、吃早饭。 (*I get up at 6.00 a.m., shower, dress, eat breakfast*)

The basic forms for constructing these linked sentences coherently involve (i) *juxtaposition*, where two clauses are linked without any conjunction (sentences D and F); (ii) *coordination*, where two clauses are linked by a coordinating conjunction, such as *and*, and/or by deictic forms (*this, that, here, there, this/that way*) (这、这儿、这么、这样、这会儿、那、那儿、那么、那样、那会) (sentence E); and, (iii) *co-subordination*, where two clauses are linked by a subordinating or non-subordinating conjunction with a finite verb in the conjunct clause (sentences A, B, and C) (Serra, 2007: 593–594).

The norms of punctuation vary according to the genre the writing occurs in and the subjective view of the author. This is especially true of narratives in Chinese literary texts, where commas and full stops are less systematically used than in science reports. This phenomenon needs to be introduced and students guided to notice it, particularly when reading, and then gradually taught to incorporate into their own expressive writing what may be a looser punctuation system than they use in English.

While the new forms of discourse creation found in Chinese are usually left for advanced learners to tackle, Liu (2015: 15–19), for example, finds that 'early stage L1 English learners of L2 Chinese are able to build new structures in L2, of the type that goes beyond the subject-predicate structure'. They will also encounter these structures in all authentic children's reading material no matter how young it is intended for. The essential to understanding and using these novel structures is to know that, even in sentences without an explicit referent or conjunction showing the relationship between the two parts, in Chinese subordinate clauses normally appear before the main clause, and actions appear in chronological order. The key to student acquisition of these forms is their being worked into language lessons gradually and in a well scaffolded way from quite early on.

## Learning Chinese Grammar

The structures listed in Table 4.1 show creating phrases and basic sentences in Chinese comprise three forms of difference for English speakers:

1. Insertions—adding words that do not occur in English, e.g. obligatory measure words/classifiers
2. Omissions—no articles, plurals, tenses, 'missing *Yes*'
3. New concepts—*de*-segments, resultative verb compounds (来到; 打开), 把 construction.

1. Insertions: In terms of learning economics, insertions such as classifiers and certain fixed word order patterns such as *subject-time-place* are not intellectually challenging: they can be explained and understood without difficulty. The learners' task is simply to remember them. The key to achieving this is auditory memory—developing an inner sense of what sounds right. This sense includes a prosodic factor—a feeling that there are enough beats (syllables) in the utterance to sound normal—plus aural habit: there is a growing automaticity in the learner's collocating of nouns and their classifiers, or elements such as subject, time and place, because, for example, 一张桌子 (one *classifier zhang* table) or 我昨天八点钟 (I yesterday eight o'clock) just 'sound right'. As has been said already in this book, one of the key roles of the teacher is to help students understand how to learn Chinese effectively. Once the concept of insertions such as classifiers has been raised and their meaning considered in relation to their first language, the teacher needs to keep reminding students that the key to learning the new forms is for them to embed the phrases in their auditory memory by listening to the pattern of beats as well as to the actual words: 一支笔 dadaDA, *yī zhī bǐ* (one *classifier zhi* pen); and then they will need practice, which requires them to engage with using the noun and its specific classifier, e.g. T: '你有几支笔?' S: '三支'. T: '他有几本书?' S: '一本'. (T: How many (*classifier zhi*) pens have you got? S: Three *zhi*. T: How many (*classifier ben*) books has he got? S: One *ben*)

2. Omissions: Omissions in a second language of words in the learners' L1 usage are among the most neglected area of learning, possibly because native speaking teachers of their L1 have no sense of there being anything missing. They do not understand the need to help their students change an old habit and learn to say what they want to say in a new way. English learners have grown up using 'Yes' to answer a question about anything and it is common to find them substituting '对' (*correct*) in Chinese for 'Yes', rather than extracting the specific verb used in the Chinese question to form their answer: 你**要不要** . . . ? 你 **知道** . . . 吗? 他 **来了**没有? 你们**去过** . . . 吗? (*Do you want . . . ? Do you know . . . ? Has he come? Have you been to . . . ?*) To answer a question correctly in Chinese takes two acts of learner attention. The first is comprehending the

thrust of the question, the second is noticing the verb used which is the key to the answer. These two steps may be separated initially, the learner first absorbing the information that she is being asked, for example, if she knows that China has more than 50 minority groups, and only then, after momentarily 'reaching for' Chinese *yes* in her mind, scanning back through the question uttered to find the verb 知道 (*know*) in order to answer. Initially the wording of the question may not have been held in short term memory and so she will be unable to answer, or will resort to saying '对' (*correct*). Unless the learners' sense of 'mentally scrabbling for something missing' is understood, their teacher will not be able to assist them in creating *a Chinese way* to answer questions. To be effective, all exercises aimed at tackling learning challenges must target the point of challenge as experienced by the learner. In the case of omissions, learners need practice in attending to the Chinese form for handling the message. Hence, for the apparently 'missing' *yes*, learners need practice in attending to the verb in the questions addressed to them. The most direct way to do this is to have them as a group answer questions using only the verb in a long and ever more quickly presented string of Questions and Answer exchanges such as:

T:  你喜欢踢足球吗? (*do you like football?*)
Ss:  喜欢。 (*like*)
T:  你要不要喝水? (*do you want a drink of water*)
Ss:  不要. (*don't want*)
T:  你会滑雪吗? (*can you ski?*)
Ss:  会。 (*can*)
T:  她是不是你的数学老师? (*is she or isn't she your mathematics teacher?*)
Ss:  不是。 (*isn't*)

And so on。

After practising there can be reflection on the form, contrasting it with English.

Learners adjust quite quickly to the omission of plural markers and articles in Chinese language addressed to them in speech or writing, although the greater non-specificity of Chinese (e.g. 街上有狗 (*in the street there is dog/s*) needs discussion, and discussion not just about form but, especially, about the thrust of a message where actual quantity isn't important. Productively they need regular, carefully designed exercises where they must choose to be more or less specific and to explore the use of pluralising terms like 一些 (*a few*), specific numbers, and the demonstratives 这 (*this*) and 那 (*that*).

English speakers have little difficulty understanding second language speaker English used without tense markers, provided adverbs of time are included. If the time of the action has been made clear by use of terms such as 'yesterday' or 'last year', learners have little difficulty translating unmarked Chinese verbs correctly into English using verbs marked for tense. With some practice, they can express simple past action in Chinese in similar style. Handling what in English would be the future tense and, especially, the future perfective (e.g. I will have finished) and other aspect markers (experiential—e.g. he will have been studying Latin for five years by then—and continuing—e.g. I will be living in London by then) in Chinese, however, are areas often poorly mastered, ever.

3.  New concepts: The fundamental learning issue with Chinese structures which are new and different from those of English is the need for deep exploration of *meaning* not just form. In the resources designed for school and undergraduate learners, there is a noticeable paucity of empathy with the learning issues of these forms, with explanations that are often incomplete and scarcely meaningful for those new to grammatical distinctions, and far too little work provided at manipulating the new concepts to show how the language actually constructs the meaning. While they give a few definite rules (e.g. using the verb particle 了 in sentences such as 他买了三本书 [*he bought three books*] and 现在下雨了 [*now it's raining*]), grammatical notes often just involve descriptions of permissible forms but no explication of what communicative difference it makes if one form or another is used. Exercises in form construction using single sentences are unable to show thrust of message because there is no development showing how the use of one option or another directs the interlocutor's attention to different intentions expressed by a speaker's use of one form or another. For example, in English 'I'm living in Melbourne' and 'I live in Melbourne' are both grammatically correct, but as one suggests impermanence and the other permanence, which one I use will suggest different lines of conversation to the person I am speaking to.

These points of grammar are complex matters to discuss with school students, and metalinguistic dialogue that not only describes Chinese but engages them to become aware of how these issues exist and are managed in their own language is essential. In addition, students need accompanying tightly structured exercises which demonstrate and force them to engage with the essential point about *meaning* in the options available to them, and frequent encounters with the same structures in listening and reading texts, to help them expand their attention and begin to grasp the intent expressed in the new forms. A tightly structured exercise would need to include a response not just a single utterance, as without the response there is no way to discern the significance of a choice, for example, to include a particle or not. In the two sample dialogues that follow, it would only be if we saw B's and D's responses that we could perceive the communicative significance of A and C inserting 呢 or not, and even then, we may need more contextual information—who '他' is and what is he expected to do when he does arrive—to really get their messages.

**A:** 他还没来呢. (*he still isn't here* + particle *ne* = he should be here)
**B:** 别着急，他一定会来！(*don't get alarmed, he'll be here for sure*)
**C:** 他还没来. (*he still isn't here* = fact)
**D:** 没关系，我自己来唱歌。(*it doesn't matter, I'll sing the song*)

The significance of options is found in Xing (2006), where quite exhaustive lists are provided across a full range of usage showing the subtle changes of meaning involved in shifting from one form to another. While much of what is provided goes beyond the usual level of school learners, the information is valuable for teachers. In fact, unless they have studied Chinese grammar and grammatical pedagogy, most native speaking language teachers will find they can quite quickly become uncertain as to usage and, especially, as to the rules and guidelines for usage. These days there are exhaustive lists and commentary on Chinese grammatical forms available online and in print in contemporary textbooks, grammars and manuals for teachers, such as those noted earlier. These provide a treasury for teachers, who should have easy access to them and be familiar enough with them to be able to check usage and rules quickly when needed. Even novice teachers can be confident in their grasp of the obligatory rules, options, and the significance of options as a result of this extensive scholarship.

## Teaching Grammar

### Giving Entry to the Spirit

Whatever the content framework used in a program, the essential to teaching grammar well is that the language is natural and usable by the students, and builds an ever-expanding capacity to realise expressive needs and understand language used by others. The critical point to consider is what acquiring the grammar of their new language demands of the student in light of their first language features, and how that can best be taught and learned. Four matters are essential in this endeavor.

1.  Despite some similarities in the arrangement of words in a sentence, from the simplest beginnings (你好, 我叫 李碧明, 我十岁), to be successful, the learners must grasp the concept that the words of their new language have a particular relationship to those of their first language: they are *equivalent in meaning* to them (in the above example: *Hello, my name's Li Biming, I'm ten*), but they do not necessarily literally *mean the same thing* (literally: *you good, I call Li Biming, I ten years*). While this may be fairly obvious to adults, children need to begin their language study aware that this is a whole new arrangement by a different society for dealing with the communication issues that are common to all societies. It can be a great boost to the enjoyment of the density that a new piece of grammar confronts learners

with if, in addition to trying to internalise its form and function, they are also engaged by the syntactic system as a whole and able to contrast it with that of their own language. This suggests immediately that in at least a fortnightly schedule, there be some time allocated to discussing in the students' mother tongue how the two languages are constructed so as to create meaning, and how, as they become users of both, they might think about them.

2. Activities involving new language structures need to be engaged in if grammar is to be internalised to the point where students can feel something sounds right or it doesn't. Whole phrases and even sentences at all levels of complexity can be repeated as single items when they are introduced and learned to be said fluently: '你要几个苹果?' (*how many* classifier gen *apples do you want*), '他比你高' (*he is taller than you*), '把他送给你的书放在桌子上*' (*put the book he gave you on the table*). Said with correct phrasing, rhythmic stress and intonation, learning whole chunks of utterances in this way, and reading them regularly, can build auditory memory of their prosodic patterns, which will assist with retention and prompt their re-use in correct form, just as humming the tune elicits the words of a half-forgotten song.

3. Building the cognitive skill to create novel utterances that are grammatically correct and accurately express what the speaker intends to say takes time, especially where they involve strong differences from mother tongue forms. It is in this area—and it is the heart of much language teaching—that differences in teachers' beliefs about learning result in different, even contradictory, teaching practices. Teachers who believe the student must first memorise the form in order to be able to use it, tend to concentrate on saying the correct thing often themselves, and believe they are assisting a student who has been unable to finish or get a sentence right by completing it for the student. These teachers often finish an intervention by repeating the correct thing two or three more times before moving on to work with another student, and they may even translate the sentence into English. The authors of this book believe that this is not an effective way to teach students to acquire Chinese structures and, indeed, that it is likely to be counter-effective and actually cause more learning problems for the students. Teachers who complain that their students find some point of grammar or another very 'difficult' need to consider whether they are not part of the cause of this problem and whether working in a different way, more patiently and giving students more opportunities to work things out for themselves, might not actually solve the apparent problem. To do this with confidence, teachers need to really understand the learning issues involved for the student, and see them as they see them, not simply know the correct language wanted at the time.

4. The use of scaffolding is based on the Vygotskian notion of giving assistance to the learner to move a step further into as yet unmastered territory. To achieve this with a new structure, the teaching needs to be based on a *theory*

*of variation:* 'In order to grasp the meaning of something you must notice how it differs from other things' (Chik and Marton, 2010: 10). Thus, introduction of the new must lead out of language already known and initially be the only difference from that already known. This allows the new to be both noticed and within the context provided, understood.

The authors of this book believe that students acquire competence with grammatical structures by having to work on them, gradually becoming more and more accurate and fluent; that is, that learning the language is the result of using the language (and reflecting on that use). *Working in this way does not mean that errors are condoned or ignored,* just that they are accepted as a natural part of learning something complex—like falling over when learning to ski or ride a bicycle—and should be used as guides as to what needs further work. Furthermore, just as a teacher cannot ride a bicycle for a novice rider, while a student is actively still engaged in putting together an utterance, hesitations and pauses mean the teacher must wait quietly, not jump in to take over and say it for them. The attention needs to be on the learner not the language, that is, the teacher should be seeking to identify what the learner has mastered and what is still causing the learner difficulty. Normally, learners will be slower to create an utterance than teachers just because they are having to work much harder to speak, but if it is clear the student has stalled—or the time really is longer than can be afforded—the teacher would indicate to the student to listen and turn to the rest of the class and ask them to say what the student needs to say. Then the teacher would turn back to the original student and see if s/he can now say what s/he was trying to say before. If this still results in failure, the teacher would indicate that the student should listen and the class again be invited to provide the right thing. At this point, the teacher must judge whether the student is still capable of listening and getting help or has become embarrassed and is not able to continue. If the latter is the case, the teacher would go on to another student or other work. But the difficulty would be noted and work done on it individually, or at the next class when the student is once again open to trying.

There are two ways that learners' difficulties with grammatical structures are often taken care of: firstly, after a night's sleep it is common to find on the following day that students are much surer and quicker about what they know and what they have still to learn in the unit being studied; and, secondly, to have them observe another student and the teacher working together. By just listening to the perfect model from the teacher it is hard for students to realise their own errors and it only gets harder if they have to produce language at the same time. It is often easier to perceive differences in features such as word order, vocabulary, and pronunciation when there are two points of reference: the teacher's model and a classmate's efforts. Then the observing students can use that perception to correct their own errors.

Even in lessons where the focus is on grammar, as soon as a line has been uttered by a student with the correct words in the correct order, attention should be paid to the quality of the utterance and, if necessary, the student should be asked to say it again with correct chunking, rhythm and intonation. Apart from it making greater sense when the utterance is said naturally, adding the correct prosodic pattern will assist the short-term memory to hold the line and for it to be available in future.

A further way to build memory of what is said is to encounter the structure regularly in listening and reading texts. Finding texts which permit solid, wider practice in reading within limited character boundaries and yet have content that is worth reading is not a simple task. L2 Chinese is still poorly served in this area and teachers often have to write, or at least assemble, reading texts for their students.

## Reflection and Translanguaging

In addition to grappling with their new language in exercises and using it for real or realistic purposes, throughout their study students need to reflect on their new language in relation to their first language. This is both a means of learning Chinese and of developing an educated bilingual understanding of the nature of human language and the specific forms of the two languages they themselves now use. Comparative study of grammar and translating are ways to support acquisition and permit students to recognise the source of difficulties they are experiencing, which can then be addressed. It is not suggested that this work, which would be conducted largely in English, be allowed to interrupt work in Chinese, but that regular time be allocated weekly or fortnightly for work directly on this aspect of learning.

## Practice

A central point about learning grammar is that to be internalised it needs to be used often. There are already scores of grammatical exercises at all levels available to teachers and students and these will not be reproduced here. Instead, just a couple of points will be made. The first is that digital technology can provide the means of creating a virtually endless set of exercises and activities that are always freshly challenging because their content can be arranged to fit current units of work; they can be constantly reshuffled and varied; and they can be made sensitive to individual and group levels of proficiency and weakness. In designing practice activities and exercises, these factors should be taken into account and challenges kept sharp by always requiring students to pause and think, and not be able to get the right answer by simply copying language provided. Examples of such quiz-like exercises, whether done electronically or on paper, would include tasks such as those shown in the components of Tables 4.4 and 4.5.

Note: the instructions given for the exercises here are for the readers of this book. While the goal is to have instructions given to students using Chinese, in the

**TABLE 4.4** Tasks which challenge

| Match text and visuals | |
|---|---|
| 她们都有几只猫；只有我只有一只 | |
| 他有四只猫，我只有一只 | |
| 她有狗，也有猫；我只有猫,没有狗 | |
| 她们都有狗；只有我有猫 | |

(Continued)

**TABLE 4.4** (Continued)

| 我们不都有宠物 | |
| --- | --- |
| 我们都没有宠物 | |
| 我们都有宠物 | |

beginning, if English is to be avoided, most would also require one or more models to be shown to the class so that they understand what is being asked. For example:

照例子用'只有/除了 . . . 以外，. . . 都 . . .'改写句子 (Instructions)
例如：A. 除了钦明以外，其他人都来学校了。(Examples A and B)
    只有钦明没来学校。
    B. 学生中只有菲菲和航航是女生。
    学生中除了菲菲和航航以外，所有学生都是男生。
1. 除了菲菲以外，其他人都是中国人。('Student A' first task)

Once sentences like these have been joined, students can be asked to read them and say who is doing what. They can also be asked to make the link between the two actions explicit: is it addition, contrast, sequence, consequence, purpose, or means? Other tasks can test students' understanding of Chinese discourse structure, especially the underlying rule that Chinese-linked sentences are sequenced in time. More advanced students can be asked to connect more sentences to form a paragraph, which will open up other features of Chinese discourse.

**TABLE 4.5** 对或错 *(true/false)* for story/factual text, e.g. CLIL Chinese science 物质的粒子 *(particles of matter)*

---

**对或错 (*true/false*)? (Here CLIL Chinese science 物质的粒子 (*particles*)**

液体有固定的体积，没有固定的形状

液体的粒子在固定的位置上振动

固体粒子间的吸引力比气体的大

气体粒子间的距离最小

**Fill in the blanks with one of the following classifiers: 支 本 个 只 件**

我的朋友有一 . . . 小狗。

我想买一 . . . 蓝的笔

老师给我一 . . . 书

我有一 . . . 事要告诉你

**Create a sentence with the words in each line.**

打期五们每球网我星

晨起们天六早钟起点我昨床

户关把上门窗和

**Create sentences that sequence the activities in each line of Column 1.**

| | |
|---|---|
| 洗澡 拖睡衣 穿衣服 | 先 . . . 然后 . . . 最后 . . . 。 |
| 等五分钟 加茶 喝茶 开水 | 先 . . . 然后 . . . 才 . . . 。 |

**Join the two sentences on each line by using a 的 segment.**

| | |
|---|---|
| 昨天来了一个人。是她爸爸。 | 昨天来的人是她爸爸 |
| 我昨天买了一本书。书很贵。 | 我昨天买的书很贵。 |
| 他送给她一只猫。很可爱。 | |
| 小孩给你打电话。是谁？ | |

**Create a sentence using the phrases given in both columns.**

| | |
|---|---|
| 她每天 | 没有？ |
| 在我的学校 | 六点半起床。 |
| 下课以后我们常常 | 有很多电脑。 |
| 她吃了 | 去游泳。 |
| 因为 . . . 。 | 那么她一定不来。 |
| 如果 . . . 。 | 所以我们不能打网求。 |
| 虽然 . . . | 而且都很努力。 |
| 她们 . . . 。 | 但是还在小学。 |

**Create a sentence by linking the phrase given and one of your own.**

他用红的笔

要暖和一点

我们用毛笔

**TABLE 4.6** Discourse structures

**Join the sentences on each line.**

我知道你来墨尔本。我很高兴。

她拿了书。她上课去了。

我们吃完晚饭。我们请你唱歌。

他们很累。他们找个地方休息。

我要去悉尼。我要看我住悉尼的老朋友。

他买了一公斤牛肉。他想使炖。

赵老走路。她上班。

我切肉。我用小刀。

他们决定。他们坐汽车。 他们去天坛。

我听你明天来。我很高兴。

老王昨天发烧。医生来了。

她要给孩子几块钱。孩子买水果。

**TABLE 4.7** Topic chain construction and deconstruction

Provided: 我叫她。 她去。 (*I tell her she goes*)

Students write/say: 我叫她去。 (*I tell her to go*)

Provided: 我看报纸发现广告说新字典出版了 (*reading the paper, I find an ad that says a new dictionary has been published*)

Students write/say: 我看报纸。我发现广告。广告说新字典出版了。

(*I read paper I find ad ad says new dictionary published.*)

Students need a lot of practice manipulating forms and functions. Practice by making a coherent class narrative to which everyone adds a sentence that includes one of a set of given phrases (such as from the list in Table 4.1) is a quintessential way to practise sentence joining, think with Chinese grammar, and work on prosodic patterns, as well as offering the chance to engage humour and ingenuity.

## Vocabulary

### Introduction

*One cannot help but be struck by the alarmingly poor retention of vocabulary by students over time. How can this be?*

(Li and Zhang, 2016: 154).

The previous quote is a cry not confined to CSL teachers. Vocabulary is an area that receives comparatively less attention in most second language studies (Milton and Alexiou, 2012), and yet it forms a central piece of the base on which language is developed. However, compared to another European language, developing this base in Chinese for English speakers is always tempered by two considerable challenges. Firstly, there is a great deal more vocabulary to be learned from scratch in Chinese as, unlike many other languages, there are virtually no words in common (e.g. French *télévision, computer, football*) or even cognates (e.g. *scienza, ciencia* in Italian and Spanish for *science*); and the volume of what needs to be learned is significantly increased when the demand is to remember both how it sounds and how it is written, as is the case with characters. A second difficulty is that Chinese vocabulary is not easy to learn. Quite aside from characters, the words themselves, written in Pinyin, are hard to absorb because they look very unfamiliar and also very alike: short, two- and three- letter words, some 24% of which begin with X, Y, or Z (*xú xí xià, yí, yú, zú zài, zì*) (compared to some 0.06% of English words), composed of a very limited number of sounds, with a great many homophones and words that sound similarly (是, 事, 市 *shí, shí, shí*; 十, 时 *shì, shì*). Together these features, and the energy needed to deal with them, make acquiring Chinese vocabulary one of the major challenges to success in learning the language and to a large degree these challenges remain largely unaddressed. What research there has been on vocabulary in CSL has tended to centre on the quantity and kind of words (and characters) students should learn, with only a small amount of attention also paid to the depth of vocabulary they need and their grasp on the development of word formation. Vocabulary is an area which needs a great deal more attention than it generally receives.

## Selecting Vocabulary

### Quantity

Scans of Chinese written material have long revealed that all non-specialist texts make very high use of quite a small number of characters and words. Today's dictionary and learner vocabulary and character lists are selected on the basis of their frequency from the *Guóbiāo* (国标), the national standards issued by the Standardization Administration of China. The *Guóbiāo* (GB) publishes a first level set of 3,754 most commonly used characters. *Clavis Sinica* at the University of Michigan has published a number of internationally recognised analyses of the GB lists. Of particular relevance to teachers is their dictionary, which provides 25,000 separate vocabulary entries generated from 4,000 characters made up of the GB's first level set plus an additional 250 from the GB's second level set. They find these characters will cover 98 per cent of characters found in newspapers and 100 per cent of characters found in college-level Chinese textbooks.

This is valuable information for teachers wanting to minimise the effort required of their students to learn characters and to maximise the dividend they reap from the investment they have made in those they do acquire.

The *Clavis Sinica* figures indicate a potential overall ratio for vocabulary to character of approximately 6:1, that is, that on average each character can generate up to six words in combination with other characters. This ratio is not constant, of course, because fewer characters will generate fewer words and at the outset the ratio is 1:1. It is also the case that students do not learn—and do not need to learn—all the possible vocabulary items that might be generated by combining all the characters they already know with each of the new characters they learn. One guide to character-vocabulary ratios in learner material can be found in Xing (2006: 130), who presents researched ratios for tertiary level study. They show, for example, that the three levels of the originally very popular Chinese readers in the DeFrancis series present a total of 1,200 new characters and some 7,000 compounds, a ratio very close to 6:1. Little data is available to guide those teaching school children, but Wu and Bai's (2012) school learners' dictionary, 汉语 800 字 *Essential Chinese Dictionary for Australian Students*, presents 930 characters, which the compilers estimate would yield some 2,500 useful Chinese words. Not an exhaustive total of all possibilities, this is only a yield of 2.7:1, but it represents a usable set for the target learners to aim for as it amounts to about half the volume of vocabulary that an L1 adult might typically make use of in speech. Wu and Bai's characters comprise the same 800 characters found in the *Essential Chinese Dictionary* published by China's Foreign Language Teaching and Research Press, with an additional 130 frequently used terms that are specifically Australian, such as the names of Australian states and words for *surfboard* and *wombat*. These additions serve to remind us that the vocabulary that learners need to talk about their lives will not ever be entirely found in lists based on common use by Chinese native speakers.

Probably the best known Chinese learner vocabulary lists of their kind are published by the Hanban (2018a) (*Office of Chinese Language Council International*) for their proficiency level tests, the *Hànyǔ Shuǐpíng Kǎoshì* (HSK, *Chinese test levels*), which have also been based on the GB lists. At the top end, the HSK *Chinese Proficiency Test Vocabulary Guideline* (Hanban, 2018b) presents 8,822 words that contain all the vocabulary in HSK tests up to and including the advanced level. The HSK lists for school learners of Chinese increase steadily for the first four levels, with Levels 1 and 2 each comprising 150 words, 200 more to reach Level 3, and a further 500 to be acquired in each of Levels 4 and 5, giving a total of 1,500 words. These totals seem ambitious in light of a total of only some 800+ items of core vocabulary taught in a successful 50–50 English-Chinese immersion program in Portland, Oregon (Woodstock, 2009), or the UK Independent Schools

Board's (2018) target of some 300 words and 100 characters to have been learned by the end of the primary years. In Australia, one 60–40 English-Chinese instruction program expects to have students graduating at the end of Year 6 with approximately 1,000 characters (private correspondence), which should mean a much higher vocabulary yield. In any case, however the current targets are set, the range of useful words that could be generated by the characters learned in writing whatever desirable core vocabulary is set for any given age group is important knowledge not yet available.

## Kind

Teachers generally leave it up to textbook publishers which vocabulary and characters they teach. Publishers most often cite the HSK Levels as the source of their selections and beyond that focus the content of their products on children's daily life and some information on China. As a result, a large proportion of the topics in beginner and intermediate textbooks for school learners are common, although the order of their appearance can vary considerably. Furthermore, within these topic areas teachers will still find a wide variation in vocabulary items and hence characters. Nevertheless, given the generally low vocabulary and character counts achieved by school learners, as claimed in the textbooks, all that are offered there are likely to fall within the lower levels of the HSK lists and, as such, be of high frequency.

**TABLE 4.8** Topics presented in the commonly used school textbooks *Nǐ Hǎo* 你好, *Easy Steps to Chinese* 轻松学中文, *Chinese Made Easy* 轻松学汉语, *Happy Chinese* 快乐汉语

Greetings

Numbers

Who is he/she, age

Stationary

Family, occupation

Pets, animals

Countries, languages

Sports

Body parts, appearance

Food, fruit, vegetables, health

(Continued)

**TABLE 4.8** (Continued)

| |
|---|
| Dates, birthdays |
| Daily routine, time |
| House, furniture, locations |
| Clothing, colours |
| Prices, shopping |
| Making a telephone call |
| Weather |
| School subjects |
| School life |
| Transport, neighbourhood, directions |
| Hobbies, leisure activities, entertainment |
| Traveling, life adaptation, holidays |
| Sickness |
| Part-time job |
| Internet, modern technology |
| Personality, friendship |
| City, environment |
| Young people's world |
| Future plans, aspirations |
| Culture and literature |
| Household chores |
| Festivals |
| Accidents |

## Learning Vocabulary

There are no clear guidelines as to how many items of Chinese vocabulary might be learned in any given space of time, or by learners of any particular age, and virtually no research published on this, either. Even figures for the tertiary level are only desirable estimates, as frequency of encounter and method of teaching will both be important factors in creating what is possible. Suggested figures for school age learner reading material made by educators and publishing companies in Chinese speaking societies such as Hong Kong and Singapore, as well as in Taiwan and Mainland China, are always greatly in excess of what second language learners in regular programs in English speaking countries can manage. This is mostly due to a lack of awareness of just how much exposure to characters and spoken language there is around school students in those Chinese societies, the frequency and meaningfulness of which constitute a great support for memory. Yet, mindful of the minimum of 3,500–4,000 characters needed to read a newspaper, school teachers often feel an urgency about drumming in the characters and lament their students' resistance and poor efforts to remember more than a handful every week. This is often encouraged by examination guidelines which list characters to be known, but it is a generally misguided path to take because it neglects giving students entry to the word generation possibilities of new characters that would increase their vocabulary not just their set of known characters. Even by the end of primary school, therefore, students fall a long way short of being able to tackle reading material for the lowest L1 levels in Chinese schools, let alone something suitable for their age. This is dispiriting, especially when compared to what can be achieved in another European language. Students in Content and Language Integrated Learning and Content Based Teaching Chinese programs often fare better as their language topics are drawn from normal school-based curriculum areas in fields such as Science, Mathematics and Social Studies and hence involve learning about something more age appropriate.

The weakness of second language learners in remembering Chinese vocabulary is often due to memorising not being recognised as a skill that improves with practice. Many Chinese teachers do not realise their own formidable powers of memorisation are the result of years of very heavy practice. They are inclined to claim their students who are very poor at memorising are lazy, but this usually is not the source of the problem. While earlier generations of students in Western countries memorised spelling lists, times tables, poetry, prayers, Shakespearean soliloquys, and the occasional piece of oratory, these days Western students in primary and secondary schools learn to recite very little, so memorisation remains a very underdeveloped learning tool for them. In addition, good contemporary teaching methods in the West more often require cognitive skills and judgement, so memorising is rarely experienced as an interesting or particularly meaningful activity. It is, of course, necessary for students to memorise the words of their second language, but it is suggested here that there are more effective ways of achieving that than simply allocating lists of words on paper or screen to be remembered for a test. They include work based in an understanding of the fundamental learning issues inherent in the language and reliance on the learning styles familiar to students and respected by educators, as well as simple techniques such as increased listening opportunities as a way of keeping vocabulary in mind.

## Teaching Vocabulary

Given the enabling role of vocabulary in language acquisition, it is important to appreciate there is a great deal more to teaching it well than simply providing a word and its meaning. In fact, there is a series of scaffolded phases in vocabulary teaching and the better each is carried through, the deeper and stronger the students' learning of vocabulary will be. These are the basic processes:

1.  Sound vocabulary teaching begins before the new language is introduced, with a link made between the topic and context of the new language, students' existing language, and their own experience (Shen and Xu, 2015). This primes them to expect to add to their power to express themselves in a certain area and gives a defined purpose to acquiring the new words.

2.  The new vocabulary should be introduced in groups of words that form a linked set, e.g. *face, forehead, eyes, ears, nose, mouth, chin*. This helps to create a memory chain, where recall of one word will trigger others. A clear meaning for each new term must be provided. The use of accompanying visual representation of meaning (diagram, picture) and physical representations (the actual thing, gesture, mime, action) as part of the introduction have been shown to support the three factors of acquisition: comprehension/recognition, retention, and speed of retrieval. (Cutica and Bucciarelli, 2008; Macedonia and von Kriegstein, 2012; Tellier, 2008).

3.  Contextualisation further strengthens comprehension and acquisition. This is because it provides greater depth to word meaning.

4.  Students' use of the new items is essential for internalising them. Acquisition is also reinforced if at the same time as they speak, students act out, or manipulate illustrations or objects, real or toy, of what they are saying, or create congruent iconic or metaphoric gestures to match speech.

5.  Once met, vocabulary needs to be practised. Shen and Xu (2015) divide vocabulary practice activities into three: (i) de-contextualised practice, which involves concentrating on just the items themselves, for example by using flash cards, matching exercises, and word games; (ii) semi-contextualised practice, which involves using the new words in pieces of text, for example, to fill in blanks, complete sentences, and as substitutes for other words; and, (iii) contextualised activities, which involve using the words to carry out realistic communicative tasks.

6.  A final practice stage involves integrating the new language into language already known.

7.  Once learned, vocabulary needs to be maintained and developed through on-going encounters. What is important at this stage is not just that words are met frequently, but that they are also met in different settings from the original encounter, which both keeps attention on them alert, which assists memory, and helps to expand and establish the boundaries of their meaning, which provides deeper understanding of them and wider possibilities for their use. It is also essential that in these encounters the vocabulary continues to be used actively and passively by the learners across the four skills.

8.  In an ongoing process from the introduction of an item, vocabulary should be developed through work on register and studied through exploration and analysis of word formation.

## Register

Not only in Chinese, but across many languages, teachers of more advanced levels lament the paucity of their students' vocabulary and the often rather juvenile tone of words used instead of a more adult or academic register. Students need to realise early on that language exists at different levels (register) and begin gradually to acquire some options for being more and less formal—for example, not just 和 (*and*) but also 与 (*formal 'and'*) and 而且 (*moreover*); not just 所以 (*so*) but also 由于 (*consequently*). This applies to lexical forms as well, hence they gradually need to learn 赤 (*scarlet*) and 丹 (*brick red*), in addition to knowing the basic 红 (*red*). While formal language, functional or lexical, may seem unnecessary, even extravagant, for beginner-intermediate learners, the right word should never be avoided, whatever its level of formality; nor should something like an important poem, for example, not be taught just because it would introduce a few formal words. The gradual acquisition of less common words over time is an easier way to learn them than later meeting great lists of new and relatively rare terms that will be naturally recycled only very occasionally.

## Word Formation

Vocabulary can be developed not just by adding new words, but by having learners study Chinese morphology, the characteristics of the formation and compounding of basis units of meaning, *morphemes* (each of which is written with its own character) (Li and Zhang, 2016). Thus students can learn how compounds are made and related, for example: 火车, 火山, 火锅 (*huǒchē, huǒshān, huǒguō (train, volcano, hotpot)*); 红色, 橘红色, 粉红色 (*hóngsè, júhóngsè, fěnhóngsè (red, orange, pink)*); and other common compounding forms using affixes such as 性 (*xing(abstract nominalising suffix)*), 化 (*huà (transforming suffix)*), and 子 (*zi (concrete nominalising suffix)*); duplicating: 星星, 看一看 (*xīngxing, kànyīkàn*); and contrasting opposites: 多少, 长短, 大小, 矛盾 (*many few, long short, big little,*). Most teachers and many textbooks do show examples of compounding, but this tends not to be taken far. Writers like Mickel (1996) suggested that learners would gain a deeper grasp of how the language functions and remember words better if vocabulary lists were designed with recurrent morphemes highlighted and cross-referenced to relate a partially new word to an old word, instead of treating it as a completely new item. So, when meeting a term such as 明亮 (*míngliàng*), for example, students would be reminded of known words 明白 (*míngbái*) and 聪明 (*cōngmíng*). These links and generative possibilities can be shown to them and can also be asked of them. For example: 'What other words might you be able to make now that you have learned with the word *dēng (light)*?' In this exercise it is important to realise that good results do not always have to be actual Chinese words! To have grasped the strategy of forming words in Chinese by compounding morphemes is to have entered quite deeply into the spirit of the language, even if the results are only good possibilities not yet realised in the actual language. Other scholars, especially those teaching at tertiary level, have shown that the study of morphology has some benefits in assisting students to tackle reading unfamiliar texts (e.g. Everson, 2009).

For the most part research into the value of teaching word formation has been related to extending reading skills. It is estimated it may take a 95% recognition rate for a text to be independently readable (e.g. Nation, 2001). A typical Chinese book page contains 600 characters, which means even with 95% recognition, every page is still going to leave the learner some 30 characters to look up, which adds a minimum of 30 half-minute interruptions to the flow of reading a single page. In this situation, any strategies which assist students to gain better access to a text must be considered useful. To date far less is known about how students might make use of an understanding of Chinese word formation to do this, let alone how it might improve their own writing.

## Conclusion

The study of vocabulary in terms of word formation and register blends naturally into the study of the functional language which carries them. It merges also with exercises and activities designed to develop reading and writing skills and increase knowledge of characters, and with the teaching of set phrases, idioms and four-character expressions. This allows the serious work on language to have deeper rewards in expanding the learners' appreciation of the nature of language and of Chinese. At all levels there is ample room for large-and small-scale individual research projects into the language itself, which can be shared across the class. While this may seem like a diversion, in fact work on the nature of the language gives learners a sense of getting a grip on the whole system and appreciating it as a system. This adds meaning to the activity, which, in turn, increases the likelihood of the content under scrutiny being remembered.

## References

Chik, P. and Marton, F. (2010) 'Chinese Pedagogy and a Pedagogy for Learning Chinese', in F. Marton, S.K. Tse, and W.M. Cheung (eds.), *On the Learning of Chinese*, 9–30. Rotterdam, Boston, and Taipei: Sense Publishers.

Cutica, I. and Bucciarelli, M. (2008) 'The Deep Versus the Shallow: Effects of Co-Speech Gestures in Learning From Discourse', *Cognitive Science*, 32: 921–935. doi:10.1080/03640210802222039

Everson, M.E. (2009) 'Literacy in Chinese as a Foreign Language', in M.E. Everson and Y. Xiao (eds.), *Teaching Chinese as a Foreign Language: Theories and Applications*, 97–112. Boston: Cheng & Tsui.

Gattegno, C. (1972) *Teaching Foreign Languages in Schools the Silent Way*. 2nd edition. New York: Educational Solutions, Inc.

Hanban. (2018a) *Hànyǔ kǎoshì xué píng* (HSK). Retrieved 27 September 2018 from http://english.hanban.org/node_8002.htm

Hanban. (2018b) *HSK 6 Vocabulary List*. Retrieved 14 February 2018 from http://english.hanban.org/node_8002.htm

Jiao, D., He, W.W., and Livaccari, C.M. (2010–2012) *Structures of Mandarin Chinese for Speakers of English, 1 and 2*. Beijing: Peking University Press.

Li, C. and Thompson, S. (2003) *Mandarin Chinese: A Functional Reference Grammar*. Taipei: Crane Publishing Company.

Li, Y. and Zhang, Z. (2016) 'CFL Education at the College Level', in J. Ruan, J. Zhang, and C.B. Leung (eds.), *Chinese Language Education in the United States*, 141–166. Heidelberg, New York, Dordrecht, and London: Springer.

Liu, F. (2015) 'Acquiring Topic Structures in Mandarin Chinese', *CASLAR*, 4(1): 1–21.

Liu, L.L., Jiang, D.W., and Zhang, K. (2000) *Chinese Proficiency Test Vocabulary Guideline a Dictionary of Chinese Usage: 8000 Words*. Beijing: Beijing Language and Culture University Press.

Macedonia, M. and von Kriegstein, K. (2012) 'Gestures Enhance Foreign Language Learning', *Biolinguistics*, 6(3–4): 393–416. Retrieved 27 September 2018 from www.biolinguistics.eu

Mickel, S. (1996) *Reading Chinese Newspapers: Tactics and Skills: Student Workbook* (Far Eastern Publications Series). New Haven: Yale University Press.

Milton, J. and Alexiou, T. (2012) 'Vocabulary Input, Vocabulary Uptake and Approaches to Language Teaching', Guest Editorial, *The Language Learning Journal*, 40(1): 1–5.

Nation, I.S.P. (2001) *Learning Vocabulary in Another Language*. Cambridge: Cambridge University Press.

Serra, C. (2007) 'Assessing CLIL at Primary School: A Longitudinal Study', *International Journal of Bilingual Education and Bilingualism*, 10(5): 582–602.

Shen, H. and Xu, W. (2015) 'Active Learning: Qualitative Inquiries Into Vocabulary Instruction in Chinese L2 Classrooms', *Foreign Language Annals*, 48(1): 82–99.

Shen, X.L. (1988/1997) 'Bright Hope for the Future: Chinese Cultural Linguistics', in Y. Gao (ed.), *Collected Essays of Shen Xiaolong on Chinese Cultural Linguistics*, 35–43. Changchun: Northeast Normal University Press.

Tellier, M. (2008) 'The Effects of Gestures on Second Language Memorisation by Young Children', *Gesture*, 8(2): 219–235.

UK Independent Schools Examination Board. (2018) *Common Entrance Examination at 11+ and 13+ Mandarin Chinese*. Retrieved 14 February 2018 from www.primaryschoolchinese.com/Mandarin_Chinese_Common_Entrance_Level_1_and_2_word_and_character_list.pdf

Woodstock. (2009) *MIP K-5th Core Vocabulary*. Retrieved 27 September 2018 from www.google.com/search?q=woodstock+mip+K-5th+Core+Vocabulary&ie=utf-8&oe=utf-8&client=firefox-b

Wu, J. and Bai, L. (2012) 汉语 800 字 *Essential Chinese Dictionary for Australian Students*. Singapore: Cengage Learning Asia Pte Ltd.

Xing, J.Z. (2006) *Teaching and Learning Chinese as a Foreign Language: A Pedagogical Grammar.* Hong Kong: Hong Kong University Press.

杨玉玲 (Yang Yuling). (2013) 国际汉语教师语法教学手册 (Handbook of Grammatical Pedagogy for International Teachers of Chinese). 北京: 高等教育出版社.

# 5
# ADAPTING CURRICULUM

## Introduction

The challenges for learners of Chinese are well understood: the character based orthography, the tonal nature of the spoken language, the often unfamiliar sounds attached to Pinyin letters, unfamiliar letter clusters in words such as *zhéxué* and *qīzhì*, and the differences between English grammar rules and the unfamiliar word order and grammar rules in Chinese. The challenges for novice teachers of Chinese are also significant. Not only are they new to the languages classroom, but they are often learning to familiarise themselves with policies and practices in languages education, and with national or state curriculum frameworks or guidelines that are designed to inform their planning and their teaching. Native speaker teachers may also be unfamiliar with teaching their mother tongue, Chinese, to non-Chinese learners.

One of the greatest challenges for the novice teacher of Chinese, indeed of any language, is deciding what needs to be done in the classroom, year by year, unit by unit, term by term and lesson by lesson. This challenge involves not only deciding what needs to be done in the short term and over time, but also determining how a learner's achievements within the program should be assessed and reported on at key stages in their learning. These challenges relate essentially to determining the what, the why, the when, and the how of curriculum, challenges that teachers continue to face throughout their career. For all of these reasons, developing curriculum for a Chinese language program in a particular school site, for a specific group of learners, represents a most significant challenge.

One simple solution might be to let the current textbook determine what is to be taught, in what order, and then to relate learners' achievements in the local context to generalised curriculum outcomes frameworks, achievement standards or proficiency guidelines. However, it is becoming increasingly clear that textbooks are insufficient as guides to planning contemporary curriculum. The dynamics within the broader language education field are demanding more learner-centred and context-sensitive responses from teachers in planning the teaching and learning of their particular language. It is these ongoing demands on the experienced and less experienced teacher of Chinese that are discussed in this chapter. The key questions explored are:

- What curriculum construct is best able to respond to both the distinctiveness of the task of teaching and learning Chinese language and culture, and to reflect current understandings of what goals teachers should set for learners in Chinese language and culture learning?
- What content areas or subject matter, and what processes of engagement in learning about and learning to use Chinese, are likely to lead to both active participation and meaningful learning outcomes for learners of diverse background at different phases of schooling?

While still acknowledging the important role that national and state curriculum documents serve in providing for consistency and commonality across languages and contexts within educational jurisdictions, the key point of this chapter is to step away from these broader, languages-generic models of curriculum, be they content frameworks or proficiency standards, and to consider local, contextual, and learner-focussed issues in the teaching and learning of Chinese in school-based settings.

## Influences on Teacher Planning

Determining what language content to teach, what subject matter to engage learners in using the language, and how to organise that content and activity into a meaningful sequence is a critical component of teachers work. Richards (2013: 6) describes curriculum as the overall plan or design for a course, how content is transformed into a blueprint for teaching and learning which enables desired outcomes to be achieved. Curriculum planning typically involves a series of phases, including setting goals, determining content, planning delivery, and monitoring outcomes (Nation and Macalister, 2010), but these phases of curriculum development are typically interrelated and dynamic rather than being a simple linear process (Graves, 2008). Nevertheless, the way teachers frame learning and organise content to achieve the goals they set, to building a pathway to progress and success for learners in learning and using Chinese language, is central to teachers' work in the Chinese language classroom.

There are a number of influences or considerations which impact teachers' curriculum planning. These include the broad, external curriculum context in which teachers must work, including how generic frameworks impact on teachers' understandings of teaching Chinese as an additional language. Planning also includes local school-based contextual factors such as the textbook currently in use, the local curriculum arrangement, including time on task available for teaching Chinese, the diversity of learners in the classroom, and, of course, the language background and learning experiences of the teachers themselves.

## The Macro-Context

The macro-context, including national or regional curriculum frameworks or guidelines, such as the National Standards Framework (NSFLEP, 2015), and the ACTFL Proficiency Guidelines (ACTFL, 2012) in the United States, and the Australian Curriculum Content and Achievement Standards (ACARA, 2014), are increasingly influential in shaping teacher's understandings and expectations of language curriculum constructs and quality teaching and learning. These broad, overarching frameworks are designed to provide a sense of commonality of purpose, content and structure across languages, contexts and learners (Leung and Scarino, 2016), and thus tend to be highly generalised and open to broad interpretation. Even when produced in language-specific versions, these frameworks tend to treat the nature of language and language learning in a consistent manner across languages and contexts, meaning that the specific characteristics of, for example, the Chinese language, are often underestimated or overlooked in the desire for consistency and systematicity across the entire languages education field. Most importantly, given that these generalised frameworks focus, naturally, on communicating as the central goal of language learning, the specific challenges of learning to speak, and learning to read and write in Chinese characters, of building the knowledge and skills particular to the learning of spoken and written Chinese, are often absent or not addressed in a detailed, developmental way. As a result, despite the fact these frameworks are designed to influence both the quality of content and the quality of instruction, they seldom provide Chinese teachers with the insights and understandings of how to build a pathway to success, of understanding how to develop learner's conceptual knowledge of the Chinese language and procedural knowledge of effective strategies for learning features of the language that will engender the sorts of communicative and intercultural goals that contemporary languages curriculum expect of teachers of languages in schools.

Another feature of these broad, generic frameworks is that the attention that is paid to language in curriculum tends to be monolingual in nature. Content frameworks tend to focus on what is to be learned *about* the target language and proficiency guidelines and scales tend to outline what learners are meant to be able to do *in* that language, in nominally real-life communicative contexts. Learners' own language(s) and culture(s) are occasionally referenced in content descriptions as a point of comparison, but proficiency outcomes are perceived in essentially monolingual terms, encouraging what Cenoz and Gorter (2014) describe as a monolingual approach of language separation in curriculum planning, rather than a bilingual approach encouraging interaction between languages in the classroom. There is increasing emphasis in curriculum design in recognising second language learning and communication as being fundamentally multilingual in nature (Leung and Scarino, 2016). The limited reference to learners' own language and culture background in curriculum design and instruction, and the lack of recognition that additional language learning represents the development of a bilingual capability, tends to reinforce monolingual instructional strategies (Cummins, 2007) in which only the target language matters and learners' own linguistic and cultural identity is often ignored or undervalued. As a result, the two languages remain separated and the use of second language typically bound to the classroom context only, a form of parallel monolingualism (Heller, 2007). Learners' first language and culture is the prism through which they interpret and learn to understand the other. It is their pathway to understanding and addressing the challenges of learning to communicate in Chinese. The absence of attention to learners' own first or dominant language (assumed to be English in this instance) in curriculum and outcomes frameworks means these documents seldom provide teachers with the skills and understandings to recognise the learning demands and the skills which need to be taught explicitly, especially to young, school-based Chinese language learners.

### The Micro-Context

A second influence or consideration in curriculum planning and design is the micro-context, including the local site in which the teaching is to take place. Among the major influences at this level is, firstly, the Chinese language textbook currently in use and, secondly, the manner in which the languages program is placed within the broader curriculum offering in that site. It is not uncommon for a single textbook (typically a set of volumes) to be in use in one school site for a number of years. Naturally the textbook becomes a de-facto version of the curriculum, with the content and sequence of learning within the book imposing a significant influence on what teachers teach, how learners learn, and how learning is monitored and assessed. As outlined in Chapter One of this book, textbooks for Chinese language learning tend to provide extracts of 'pedagogically perfect' texts focussing on particular grammar structures introduced in the context of a particular topic, such as hobbies, school life, shopping, and so on. New vocabulary is usually limited to a discrete set of topical words (and characters) and texts, both oral dialogues and some written genres, seldom displaying variability in form or content beyond the new vocabulary items. Learners are unlikely to encounter unforeseen structures or vocabulary. As a model for curriculum, such resources leave teachers with some real challenges in achieving the communicative and intercultural goals that are reflected in the external frameworks and proficiency guidelines that are meant to guide teachers' curriculum development work. Sample texts in textbooks are presented as models of real language. They also represent a curriculum model of macro-skill integration in which what learners learn to read and listen to typically represents what they are then expected to learn to say and write, a model which is hardly reflective of real-world language use. Such commonality between language inputs as pedagogic texts and language production as replicas of these models seldom provides learners with the skills for dealing with the uncertainties and variabilities of the real-world language they might encounter beyond the classroom. Thus, while textbooks do remain an indispensable part of the resource base, especially in the initial stages of learning Chinese as an additional language, they are seldom a sufficient basis for curriculum planning, particularly when local curriculum needs to be referenced against external standards frameworks and proficiency guidelines.

A second component of the micro, local context are the realities of the language program: time on task (frequency and duration of lessons), the size of the class, and the diversity of learners in terms of their prior language knowledge and learning experiences. These context specific features are, alongside the specific features of the language and the challenges these create for learners of the language, site specific features that generic frameworks cannot adequately cater for, and which must therefore be addressed in localised curriculum planning. It is well understood that the time required to acquire a certain level of proficiency in Chinese is considerably more than that required for learning a European language. It is also well understood that one main reason for this is the time required to develop a working knowledge of a sufficient number of Chinese characters to be able to read and write efficiently and effectively. Where time on task is limited, the rate of acquisition of the knowledge and skills to communicate effectively is even further restricted. Curriculum development in Chinese, therefore, needs to determine how the limited time available is best committed to the diverse tasks of vocabulary acquisition, grammar development, character learning and to communicative activities that give context and meaning to the learning of these language resources. In terms of class member diversity, it is now common to find learners who speak Chinese at home, learners with some Chinese heritage but little active use of Chinese, as well as new learners with no prior identification or experience with Chinese, sitting side by side in the one classroom, undertaking the same curriculum journey. Such context sensitive features need to be addressed in curriculum design as much as in classroom practice, in selection of texts, in task design, in determining how classroom interactions and tasks can be scaffolded or learning activities differentiated to ensure all learners, of whatever background, have opportunities to participate and achieve their best with the resources and within the time available in the local classroom context.

## Teacher Values and Beliefs

A third influence or consideration in curriculum planning and design are the teachers themselves. The traditions under which teachers learned or studied Chinese as their first language as children or as an additional language as young adults, and the methods that were used in teaching them Chinese and English as either a first or as an additional language, will influence teachers' understandings of what they believe must be taught and how they might best engage learners in activity to build mastery in the language. The consequent expectations about teaching the language, about engaging younger learners in particular, and addressing the specific challenges of learning Chinese in classroom settings, are often challenges new teachers feel ill-prepared for. New teachers have often struggled to find ways of adapting to the realities of the foreign, classroom-based context for Chinese teaching and learning (Hanson, 2013; Liao, Yuan, and Zhang, 2017; Scrimgeour, 2014). Conceptions of curriculum for such teachers, and the representations of language and subsequent teaching methods and learning tasks they plan, often derive from their own first language learning experience as young children, or from their experiences with Chinese language textbooks designed originally for adults learning in-country. Such learners are typically committed to learning the language, and to the demands on time and memory that Chinese requires. Strategies for engaging and empowering younger learners in classroom settings whose engagement with Chinese seldom extends beyond the classroom are not a natural part of the novice teacher's learning experiences or teaching repertoire and take some time to develop in practice. Generic curriculum frameworks, proficiency guidelines, even textbooks, are seldom sufficient in providing insights into addressing these challenges at the local, language specific level.

Overall, teaching practices, and textbook representations of learning and using Chinese tend to reinforce the notion that addressing the learning demands of Chinese language requires a significant amount of repetition and memorisation. Approaches to teaching Chinese to new learners, in particular, tend to overlook the important role of focussed analysis and attention to building a broad conceptual understanding of the Chinese language as a system and of its challenges, especially in contrast to English. Curriculum development for effective Chinese learning requires teachers to develop a deeper understanding and an expanded perspective of the challenges learners of Chinese face, in order to better inform their planned instruction and their spontaneous classroom artistry of recognising the learning opportunities that result from learners' contributions, and to build on learners' ideas, understandings and interpretations, which in fact represent the best foundation for effective Chinese language learning in the longer term.

## Approaches to Curriculum Planning

The key phases in curriculum planning, including goal setting, content selection, planning learning activity and task selection, and monitoring outcomes, are interrelated and dynamic rather than representing a simple linear process (Graves, 2008). Richards (2013), for example, identifies three common approaches to curriculum planning: forward, central or backward design. Forward design takes content (or syllabus) as the key organising feature, central design takes process or method as the key organiser, and backward design focuses on the target or learning outcomes as the key organising principle. *Backward design* (Wiggins and McTighe, 2006) is a well-recognised tool for curriculum planning. Backward design views the desired results of learning, what students should be able to do at the end of a learning sequence, as the key focus in planning curriculum and determining instructional activity. These backwards design principles are reflected in contemporary standards-referenced approaches to planning. The CELIN *Brief on Designing a Chinese Program* (Chao, Hakam, and Lin, 2016) argues that backward design (using the ACTFL proficiency guidelines) provides for clear expectations and measured progress; and that determining one's end goals (what learners can do with language) should be the precursor to the design of instructional activity. Wen (2015) also argues for a backward design approach, suggesting that identifying the desired evidence of learning or end results is necessary prior to planning instruction. In a contemporary communicative- or proficiency- oriented curriculum, these learning outcomes which act as the drivers of curriculum planning, focus on what learners can do in or with language as a result of the learning experiences. Leung and Scarino (2016) argue these outcomes tend to be monolingual in nature and tend to make little reference to the bilingual nature of student learning and outcomes in learning an additional language. As outcomes frameworks tend to be generic, they also tend to overlook the challenges inherent in the process of becoming proficient both orally and in writing in a language such as Chinese. Using outcomes frameworks such as the ACTFL proficiency guidelines for planning tends to conceal or underestimate the issues of addressing the uniqueness of Chinese in curriculum planning (Luo, 2015). Given the challenges in learning Chinese characters, for example, Luo (2015) suggests setting the ACTFL proficiency goal for writing at one level below that for listening, speaking and reading. Setting the goal one level lower acknowledges the challenges in writing in Chinese. However, setting the goal lower provides no further insight or advice for teachers on how the issues of learning to read and write should be addressed in planning. It also assumes that reading skills will develop at the same rate, and be at an equivalent level to listening and speaking skills, despite the time on task and effort required in learning to recognise characters and read for meaning in everyday contexts, when related oral vocabulary (acquired with the assistance of Pinyin) may be more easily acquired through active classroom oral interaction. While there is much support for backward design models using outcomes as the determiners for curriculum planning, teachers still must determine not only to what learners will be able to do in Chinese as a result of their learning experiences, but how to build learners' conceptual understandings of the structures and features of spoken and written Chinese and, as a result, how that might impact on the development of learners' oral language and print-literacy-based outcomes.

*Forward design* represents a more traditional approach to curriculum design (Richards, 2013). In this approach to curriculum planning, the process begins with a mandated textbook or with a topic to be taught, such as might be found in a mandated syllabus or curriculum document. Teachers perceive little flexibility in determining what to teach, or in what sequence, or what resources to use. Teachers subsequently plan their program around delivering the predetermined content in the best way they can. For many teachers who have grown up in societies where mandated curriculum is the norm, or where using a common set of textbooks is expected, such planning processes would seem quite natural, and the planning process quite straightforward. Even where some flexibility in planning is possible, forward design can also be seen as a desirable process, particularly in introductory language programs. In such contexts the preferred sequence of grammar learning and vocabulary development through topics related to learners' immediate environment, are largely organised in a predetermined sequence (simple verb structures, adjectival phrases, possessive pronouns, numbers and measures, etc.) and accepted as the natural 'curriculum' for beginner learners. Such forward planning orientations are, as Richards (2013) suggests, typical of introductory language programs where learners are expected to build a repertoire of grammar and vocabulary before they begin to feel they have the resources for personal meaning making in more everyday communicative contexts. These approaches, however, can be very limiting, especially where the modes of delivery are routinised into a monolingual '3P's methodology' of presentation, practice and production with a monolingual (target language focussed) orientation, in which relating learning to learners' own language and identifying subsequent learning needs is seldom addressed effectively. As a result, learners are seldom empowered in gaining a clear insight into the challenges they face in learning Chinese, or developing the skills to become more autonomous in learning, and more flexible in applying their knowledge of their new language across a range of communicative contexts.

The third type of curriculum planning process outlined by Richards (2013) is *central design*. In central design, curriculum planning is understood as being more learner focused and learning oriented (Leung, 2012), with 'what happens in the classroom' (Graves, 2008) being the driving force behind curriculum planning. One example of a central design orientation discussed in Richards (2013) is Gattegno's 'Silent Way' (1972) approach, in which the planning process focuses on designing problem solving activities which aim to activate learners' powers of awareness of features of language as they engage in tasks involving language use. Another example of central design is Kumaravadivelu's 'Postmethod' (1994) approach, in which experienced teachers prefer an idiosyncratic response to curriculum planning and delivery that is based on their professional knowledge of what works and why, and of how their own group of learners learn the language best in their particular site or situation. A central design orientation reflects a teacher's well-developed sense of what works in a particular setting, with an emphasis on the known classroom context, on the particular group of learners and the learning community. Planning learning is therefore viewed as planning ways in which learners themselves will construct new knowledge through participation in the planned interactions and activities that the teacher facilitates in that specific classroom context.

Each of these three orientations towards curriculum planning has merit in particular contexts of Chinese language learning. The *forward design* orientation is particularly relevant in contexts where learners are new to the language, where linguistic content, as new knowledge of the structures and features of an unfamiliar language, is delivered in a fixed developmental sequence through modules related to learner's everyday knowledge and experience. For new learners this would necessarily include modules designed to introduce them to concepts related to understanding the system of a tonal phonology and the sound values attached to Pinyin Romanisation. It also requires modules that introduce them to the structures and features of the character system and the challenges of not only learning to write, but also learning how to recognise character forms and ways to attach meanings (and sounds) to each character encountered. Much of this learning is entirely novel and not easily related to learners' first language. As such it is necessary that it be taught explicitly as the teacher helps learners to build the foundations to understand the learning demands of Chinese, foundations necessary for more exploratory and communicatively oriented learning experiences in the future. In forward design there is the risk of over-prescription; that teachers may accept, for example, the textbook as a de-facto model of what should be taught and the means by which it should engage with new learning. Such a reliance often lacks adequate consideration of the particular learning needs and interests of their particular group of learners who are encountering Chinese for the first time. Many textbooks, as discussed earlier, are a useful resource, but do not necessarily reflect contemporary understandings of learners and learning, particularly in the context of learning Chinese as a foreign language. Textbooks are therefore not sufficient to represent the curriculum itself. If new learners are to feel more empowered in their learning of Chinese, planning curriculum for Chinese needs to find ways to take learners beyond the textbook and engage them more holistically and conceptually with the systems of the target language and with their own language by comparison.

The *backward design* approach, now regularly promoted as the preferred approach to planning (Chao, Hakam, and Lin, 2016), has its merits in setting common and agreed targets for learning, which are fundamentally proficiency-oriented and aligned to goals which are purposeful in nature. By providing clear targets and a common set of goals, backward design offers a framework for organising instruction clearly aligned to communicative uses of language, giving teachers a sense of structure, purpose and direction that is undoubtedly valuable in achieving a higher degree of consistency and quality across languages and school contexts. However, for teachers still developing their skills in planning and delivering effective classroom instruction, knowing the goal may be little help in establishing valid and reliable processes for achieving that goal. The danger may be that teachers focus more on the outcome, on what learners should be able to do at the end, rather than on the process, the classroom experiences learners have, and the underlying knowledge and skills learners should develop as they work towards that goal.

The *central design* approach, with its focus on learners, learning and the classroom experience, has merit in its attention to not just engaging learners with the language and content, or to achieving the desired communicative outcomes, but in its attention to the actual teaching and learning experience: the ways in which the teacher and the learning group interact in the classroom in the process of exploring, interpreting, applying and reflecting on their experiences of communicating in Chinese. Of course, teacher experience plays a key role in the extent to which teachers feel comfortable about planning *for* learning that is primarily on planning *how* learners will learn, rather than on *what* content learners will encounter or what performances they will be expected to display as a consequence of their learning.

Contemporary intercultural orientations to language learning (Liddicoat and Scarino, 2013) highlight the centrality of understanding the learners and their experiences in the process of building a successful language program. In the context of Chinese teaching with an intercultural orientation, learners' own language and culture are viewed as the foundation upon which understanding and ability to use Chinese, and develop an intercultural capability in communication, are based. Thus for the teacher, using a central design approach, understanding the challenges and planning for experiences with learners that not only draw attention to these challenges, but also to the processes by which learners can overcome them, are necessarily a major feature in this form of curriculum design.

Curriculum planning is an interrelated and dynamic process (Graves, 2008). It may not be as simple as selecting one approach over another. It does necessarily involve a degree of content-driven forward planning, especially with beginner learners. Understanding the particular features of the Chinese language and the challenges learners face, predetermining linguistic content based on a well-recognised developmental sequence, and prioritising oral language skills that are capable of more rapid progress than reading and writing skills, are all important considerations in forward design planning. Good curriculum design also involves an element of backward design principles: a focus on outcomes-oriented planning, and the setting of clear and measurable targets related to external, proficiency related frameworks as a measure of accountability and a tool for consistency across school sites. But central planning, planning for the classroom interactions with learners, the conversations that facilitate collaborative exploration of concepts about language and culture, about learning to learn Chinese as an additional language, is also essential. The focus of such planning is to empower young learners to recognise the challenges, and build the skills to overcome them on their pathway to communicative and intercultural capabilities in Chinese. Teachers need to ensure their curriculum planning is undertaken in a way that recognises the specific demands learners of Chinese will face and addresses them in a coherent, longitudinal fashion.

Teachers do need to follow guidelines for curriculum planning that are out-lined in national or state-based frameworks. However, for teachers developing Chinese specific and context sensitive curriculum, as set out earlier, a number of Chinese-specific issues arise, including, primarily, how to build learners' capabilities in all four macro-skills in order to engage with every day, authentic texts and to communicate purposefully in a language that is very different from the students' first language. A second issue to consider is how to build learners' understanding of the features of the Chinese language, particularly oral language development and print literacy development, in a holistic, developmental manner. A third issue is how to incorporate the study of culture in the context of language learning, with an intercultural orientation. A final issue is to relate to the role of learner's own languages, specifically English, into a communicatively oriented curriculum that prioritises target language use as the key goal of language learning.

## Addressing the Macroskills in a Communicative Curriculum

Developing a communicative capability is clearly a priority in the broader cur-riculum guidelines and proficiency frameworks in use around the world. In the Australian Curriculum for Languages (ACARA, 2014), and in the National Standards Framework in the USA (NSFLEP, 2015), the communication goal is central to both the curriculum construct and the outcomes to be achieved. By US Standards, the communication goal is represented in three modes of use; the *interpersonal, interpretive* and *presentational* modes. In the Australian Curriculum the Communicating strand comprises a number of dimensions, including *social-ising, informing, creating* and *translating*. In both these instances, the aim of the constructs is to provide some framework for integrating the four macroskills of listening, speaking, reading, and writing in a more practical or purposeful construct. In the American Standards model, the interpersonal standard focuses largely on face-to-face oral interaction involving listening and speaking; that is, using spoken language both receptively (listening) and productively (speaking) in interaction with others. The interpreting standard focuses predominately on receptive language, that is, reading or listening, and the presentational standard on the productive skills of speaking or writing. While the purposeful, com-municative orientation is appropriate, there is no clear differentiation or rec-ognition of the different skills and capabilities likely to be required by learners in developing receptive and productive oral language skills and capabilities in both reading and writing in Chinese. Luo (2015) and Chao, Hakam, and Lin (2016) both acknowledge that the proficiency outcomes in writing expected of Chinese learners are likely to be lower on the ACTFL proficiency scale than for listening, speaking, and reading. But how teachers are expected to reach a common standard in both listening and reading where authenticity of text is a priority, and how teachers are to plan for and develop the particular knowledge and skills required to engage meaningfully with each of these macroskills, is not clearly identified. In the Australian Curriculum: Languages (ACARA, 2014), the dimensions of use within the communicating strand include separate content descriptions for both oral and written modes in the Chinese curriculum for each two-year band of schooling. The achievement standard which students should meet after each two-year band of schooling, however, tends to merge achievements across all four macroskills into one overarching statement of achievement of what learners can do as a result of their learning.

Both models of curriculum encourage the use of authentic materials as sources for reading and listening in meeting the relevant standards. However, the teaching demands in building learners' skills in engaging with everyday spoken and written texts would be quantitatively and qualitatively different, each demanding a specific set of knowledge, skills, and resources to comprehend and process information from spoken or written texts, as the case may be. The nature of the standard likely to be achieved is not at the same level, and would require a different set of scaffolds or resources to assist learners in comprehending and processing information which could be expected to extend beyond their textbook. Similarly, in terms of language production, engaging in social oral interaction or preparing and presenting information orally to an audience would require different skills from producing a personal social or informative text in Chinese characters. These are challenges of not only identifying at what standard learners should be at a certain stage in their learning journey; of what learners are able to do with the language when the source of input is oral or written; or in the language when learners communicate their own meanings in speech or writing. It is also the challenge of determining what knowledge and skills would need to be taught in order for learners to achieve these communicative goals.

## Addressing the Challenges of Learning to Understand the Features of Chinese

While the curriculum frameworks provide a useful common construct to guide all language teachers' planning and teaching towards locally accepted proficiency or achievement standards, the challenges of building learners' knowledge and skills to engage in the recommended communicative activity in Chinese is particularly complex. As previously noted, curriculum design must include planning the scope and sequence of building learners' knowledge and skills of the key features of Chinese that will underpin their developing communicative capability in Chinese. The two curriculum frameworks discussed here both prioritise communication as the goal of language learning, but also recognise the need for additional goals considered essential to support communicative language development. In the Standards Framework in the USA (NSFLEP, 2015), the communication goal is underpinned by the interrelated goals of *Culture, Comparisons, Connections* and *Communities*. The Comparison's goal includes Standard 4.1, Language Comparisons: *Learners use the language to investigate, explain, and reflect on the nature of language through comparisons of the language studied and their own.* Within this standard, sample progress indicators include references to aspects of Chinese grammar, phonology, and the writing system that should be studied at different phases of schooling, for example, *recognising the unique function of Chinese time indicators; demonstrating awareness of distinctive sounds and/or tones that must be mastered; recognising the relative lack of parsing* (word separation) and so on. Within the Australian Curriculum (2014), an additional goal (or strand), *Understanding Language* is included, which contains two relevant sub-strands: *Systems of language*, and *Language variation and change*. The *Systems of language* sub-strand contains content descriptions related to learning the Chinese spoken language system (phonology), the writing system (orthography), to grammar, and to texts for each two-year phase of learning. For example, elaborations for each content description for new learners in early secondary include: *exploring features of phonology; examining the range of sounds andrecognising how spoken syllables and tones are represented in Pinyin; learning the origins and features of components encountered in characters;* and *analysing the formation of characters, including recognising the frequency and positioning of common components; analysing the variety of verb types found in Chinese;* and *exploring features and conventions of Chinese texts, including lack of word spacing, and punctuation.* Both these constructs aim to assist teachers of Chinese to attend to important, language-specific features of the target language, and their own by comparison, as they work with the broader, overarching communication standards. Each framework emphasises the importance of planning not just for communicative outcomes, but also for building understanding of key features of the target language system, and of their own language(s) by comparison. The Australian version provides a more explicit, systemic, and developmental pathway through the key aspects of phonology, orthography, grammar and text than in the American model, while reference to these features in the Comparisons goal of the American framework is more incidental in nature, and how these might be incorporated into teaching and learning within curriculum planning is less explicit.

## Attending to Culture in Developing Communicative Capabilities

Another feature that is addressed in the American and Australian curriculum frameworks is the place of culture in the construct, and the nature of cultural knowledge that is to be learned, at different stages of their learning pathway. In the American Standards Framework, culture is represented in the Culture goal with two standards, Standard 2.1: *demonstrate an understanding of the relationship between the practices and perspectives of the cultures of the Chinese speaking world*, and Standard 2.2: *demonstrate an understanding of the relationship between the products and perspectives of the cultures of the Chinese speaking world.* These standards are elaborated in sample progress indicators such as *observing and describing culturally appropriate behaviours, learning and participating in age appropriate cultural practices* in Standard 2.1; and *identifying and learning about expressive products of Chinese culture (stories etc.), and exploring and identifying the function of utilitarian products (household items, clothes etc.)* in Standard 2.2. These standards focus specifically on learning about the target language culture, conceived largely by its products and practices, which are assumed to provide insights into the values and beliefs (perspectives) of members of Chinese communities. In the Comparisons goal, Standard 4.2, learners' own culture is included as students are encouraged *to compare and contrast languages and cultures. They discover patterns, make predictions, and analyse similarities and differences across languages and cultures.*

In the Australian Curriculum: *Languages,* a sub-strand within the *Understanding Language* strand, proposes learners analyse and understand the role of language and culture in the exchange of meaning. This sub-strand is represented by content descriptions such as discussing how language choices reflect cultural practices, including clarifying roles and relationships between participants in interactions. Chinese-specific elaborations encompass discussing cultural values expressed in language use, including comparing how such meanings are expressed in other (Australian) cultures, and identifying aspects taken for granted in communication and comparing ways people interact across cultures (e.g. use of gesture, nonverbal cues).

Thus while both frameworks include culture as an important component in a communicative curriculum, the emphasis on the role of culture in communication appears more explicit in the Australian model, and the importance of understanding how products and practices reflect perspectives is a central aspect of the American model. Nevertheless, both frameworks make it very clear that understanding the role of culture in societies, of the histories and traditions that shape contemporary products and practices, and, most importantly, of understanding how culture is represented in language and how culture influences communication practices across cultures, is a central component of language learning and therefore of sound curriculum planning.

### Reflecting on the Role of English in Learning to Learn Chinese

One final feature to consider in curriculum planning is the role that learners' own first or dominant language, English, may play in learning about, and in communicating understanding of features of Chinese language and culture, and in reflecting on the experience of communicating across cultural boundaries. The American Standards Framework makes clear its preference for linguistic and cultural knowledge and skills to be displayed through communicating in Chinese, a view in which the outcomes valued most are those related to target language use at different stages of learning. The recommendation that 90 per cent of teaching time be dedicated to target language use (Bai, Lien, and Spring, 2016) is often referred to, but while proficiency in the target language is clearly an essential goal, and is the fundamental rationale behind learning an additional language, planning for learning about, as much as learning to communicate in, the target language must necessarily take into account and draw upon learner's prior knowledge and skills in English and additional languages.

The Australian Curriculum states explicitly that learning to communicate

> involves reflection and analysis, as students move between the new language being learnt and their own existing language(s). . . . It is not a 'one plus one' relationship between two languages and cultures, where each language and culture stays separate and self-contained. Comparison and referencing between (at least) two languages and cultures build understanding of how languages 'work', how they relate to each other and how language and culture shape and reflect experience; that is, the experience of language using and language learning
>
> (ACARA, 2014, Introduction)

In this model the emphasis on the important role of a learner's first language and culture in the process of learning to both understand the second language and communicate effectively in it across linguistic and cultural boundaries, is foregrounded. The role of English finds further elaboration in a range of content standards where students are encouraged to make comparisons between language systems, to notice, compare, and reflect on the nature of the target language, as well as on aspects of culture viewed or experienced in the context of communication. This important role for English in analysing and comparing language, and expressing deeper conceptual understandings that cannot yet be conveyed in the target language, finds some place in the US model, where, in the Comparisons goal, for example, students are to demonstrate understanding of the nature of language through comparisons of the Chinese language with their own.

The implications of this for planning are significant. Learners' own language (or the societal language) must necessarily be given a voice in the curriculum planning for language learning, in order to build their bilingual or multilingual capabilities that will make it possible for them to move between languages and communicate effectively across these new linguistic and cultural boundaries. The challenge in planning for teachers is to decide when and where knowledge and use of English language are useful, and how to incorporate exploration of language and culture as comparative systems into planning. If curriculum planning is viewed too narrowly through planning for target language use alone, the importance of comparison and reflection on language, culture, and learning through English, and the value in learning to mediate messages across language and cultural boundaries, may well be underestimated, even neglected.

## Some Principles for Developing Chinese Curriculum in the Local Context

Teachers must take account of the principles and goals outlined in the broad curriculum frameworks for languages (and the language specific versions of those frameworks) that are applied in their educational districts. Yet, whilst recognising the value of these overarching frameworks, teachers of Chinese also need to develop their own teaching program in a manner that is responsive to their local context, their specific group of learners, and, most importantly, to the well-recognised challenges for students learning to learn and use Chinese as a foreign language. There are many recommendations available for teachers to guide their curriculum planning. Wen (2015) suggests that the most important principles to apply in local planning are: (i) to be theme based, and therefore to provide some longitudinal continuity of content across year levels; (ii) to be communication focussed, which is clearly aligned with the overarching goal of building proficiency in the target language; (iii) to be cross-cultural, which implies some degree of comparative analysis between the target culture and learners own; and, (iv) to be cognitively appropriate for learners at that age level, which is naturally important if learners are to be able to engage with new concepts and ideas relating to language learning. These principles, however, are generic in nature and do not explicitly address the challenges for teaching Chinese. Leung and Scarino (2016) argue for a reconceptualising of goals and outcomes and propose four key principles in curriculum development. Firstly, a curriculum has clear purposes, including setting short—and long-term goals in developing learners' capability to empathise, understand and communicate meanings interculturally. In this instance, the focus extends beyond proficiency itself to a more intercultural capability in communicating across cultural boundaries. Secondly, that a curriculum reflects the nature of language learning as a multilingual experience focussed on understanding communication as the interpretation, creation, and exchange of meaning; in this principle the focus shifts to the multilingual nature of language learning, including recognising the important role of English in building understandings of the nature of language and culture and their relationship. Thirdly, that curriculum planning is recognised as localised, collaborative, and dynamic; and, finally, that curriculum is designed to be enacted by teachers and should therefore have an impact on teacher practice and learner experience. In these last two principles, the importance of recognising curriculum as a design which organises teaching with a focus on students' background and learning experiences, rather than simply on the best way to structure content and outcomes, is emphasised. This reinforces the importance of planning for Chinese learning from the perspective of the new learner, and to plan ways in which the challenges inherent in learning to understand and communicate in Chinese, both orally and in writing, are foregrounded and made central to the design and delivery of curriculum.

## Orientations Toward Chinese Curriculum Planning

In tackling local level planning of Chinese, one consideration is the process of curriculum *development*. As outlined in Richards (2013), curriculum planning may take a forward, central or backward design approach. These three approaches all play a role in a dynamic and recursive process of developing a language sensitive, learner oriented and proficiency directed curriculum.

### Starting From Where the Learners Are

Given the priority to developing learner's communicative capability in Chinese in the national curriculum documents, it is important to set communicative goals or tasks for learners which provide opportunities for personal meaning making, and reflect learners' interests and aspirations in communicating with others. Using these tasks, or related proficiency targets, as the focus for curriculum planning represents a backwards design orientation. However, in the initial stages of learning Chinese, learners' knowledge of the system of the Chinese language is limited. They also lack the skills in learning, for example, to pronounce unfamiliar tone-syllables, to string a sequence of syllables together with correct phrasing, to recall characters readily and write legibly and effectively over an extended set of ideas, or to understand and apply Chinese word order consistently. Consequently, teachers also need to plan how to engage learners in thinking about, and in comparing and talking about, systems of sound, writing and meaning-making across languages, and about how to overcome the particular challenges learners perceive as they struggle to become confident and capable learners and users of Chinese. In addressing this feature of teaching in the planning process a learner-centred, central design orientation is of evident value. Finally, there are stages where the focus of planning is on developing initial understandings of the nature of Chinese in contrast to English. For example, where a deliberate focus of teaching and learning is on building conceptual understandings of the system of sounds (tone-syllables) and Pinyin representations, or of the composition of Chinese characters and systems of strokes and components from which characters are constructed, then a forward design orientation in which content selection for building conceptual understanding is clearly appropriate.

### Planning to Achieve the Core Goals of Curriculum

Curriculum design for Chinese teaching and learning must structure planning towards a set of goals that prioritise purposeful communication, alongside enhanced intercultural understanding, and develop in learners the ability to move comfortably across language and culture systems. It must also incorporate processes for both classroom-based experiential learning, and focussed analysis and reflection on language and culture systems, to build learners skills in being able to take control of their learning, to engage readily in analysis of language and cultural features, and to use resources autonomously to support their meaning making in communicative contexts they see as purposeful and relevant. Finally, it must establish, at least initially, a coherent, developmental sequence of linguistic content that builds or scaffolds learners' capabilities in comprehending and communicating meanings in Chinese.

## Addressing the Macroskills in a Communicative Curriculum

In planning for the development of the knowledge, skills and understandings that will underpin meaningful or real-life communicative capability in Chinese, it is important to differentiate between the receptive and the productive, between the oral and the written; that is, to acknowledge that the challenges learners face in comprehending texts in authentic/real life spoken or written Chinese, are qualitatively different to the challenges they face in creating their own meanings, either orally or in print, in Chinese.

A further consideration is the construct used to organise communicative activity and to ensure balance and value in the types of communicative activities learners are encouraged to engage in. Curriculum constructs which focus on developing communicative capabilities tend to look beyond the four macroskills and organise curriculum into modes or dimensions of use, such as the interpersonal, interpretive, and presentational modes. However, in Chinese, the knowledge and skills in learning to interact orally, to listen and to speak, and to read for meaning and write effectively are substantially different and deserve some degree of individual attention, not just in proficiency outcomes, but in the planning and delivery of learning opportunities. As a result, a curriculum structure which differentiates not just the mode of communicating, but also whether the task is oral language or print-based focussed, is essential for Chinese.

In simple terms, a curriculum design for learning to communicate in Chinese should differentiate between the types of texts and communicative activities which are essentially oral in nature, and those which involve reading or writing. Given the broader languages curriculum priority in building students' capabilities not just in communicating in Chinese, but in being able to do so in everyday or real-world contexts, structuring curriculum to ensure learners have the opportunity to engage receptively with texts from the everyday life of Chinese speakers should be a consideration from the outset. The challenges of engaging learners with authenticity are acknowledged and need to be addressed. Planning for the provision of relevant supports, considering the types of interactions which are planned around such texts to make them accessible, and determining what level of comprehension and interpretation that might be expected of learners, are important factors in bringing more authenticity into the classroom.

From the learner's own personal meaning making perspective, authenticity in text and task does not necessarily require contexts or activities that extend beyond the classroom. Learning to use Chinese to socialise with others, to build friendships, and get things done may well lend itself to real world settings such as building connections with Chinese speaking peers in Chinese communities overseas using, for example, video streaming software to take students beyond their classroom and into immediate contact with other young people to share knowledge and experiences bilingually in real time exchanges. However, real-life classroom experiences—undertaking mathematical calculations, reporting on a research task or science experiment, describing a procedure for downloading a program online—also engage learners within their own peer group in meaningful communicative exchanges.

Engaging with texts from the world of the Chinese native speaker, on the other hand, bring insights into Chinese culture and society that are central to promoting intercultural enquiry and building intercultural understandings in learners. Learning to listen to authentic, everyday spoken texts (be they video snapshots from everyday life, TV dramas, films, TV entertainment for children and young adults, and so on), or viewing short samples of environmental print (things seen on the street and in everyday life such as signs, notices, advertisements, etc.) provide the stimulus for building skills in interpreting linguistic and cultural meanings. Such a focus on culture in language, rather than simply focussing on language as a communicative resource, provides an ideal context for developing intercultural understandings through comparisons across cultures.

## *Developing Understanding of the Chinese Writing System*

Engaging with the Chinese writing system is one of the more challenging aspects of designing a meaningful and communicatively oriented curriculum for Chinese. Providing for meaningful, personal communication in Chinese characters may initially be restricted to the limited vocabulary learners encounter in the classroom. Though demanding of learners, the ability to write from memory by hand heavily restricts their meaning making capabilities, and demanding memorisation typically demotivates learners from undertaking meaningful writing tasks. Access to character lists, to digital dictionaries, and other supports are a typical part of the non-native speakers' repertoire of skills and should be actively supported from the start in the second language classroom. The provision of character lists, Pinyin glossing and other forms of support, moves the focus from memory to meaning making and has the potential to engage more learners in personal meaning making through writing. Such scaffolded learning needs consideration in curriculum planning if the learning is to be effective in the early stages of learning Chinese.

Producing and presenting text in hand-written characters, while increasingly a less common practice in the real world, still has merit in focussing learners' attention on the structure and features of character form and formation in the process of personal meaning making, a focussed attention that will assist them in character recognition and recall in the longer run. There is also research evidence to show that the physical involvement of the hand is a strong support to memory creation (e.g. Minogue and Jones, 2006). The prevalence of social media applications and the ready availability of online dictionaries and translation tools have somewhat blurred the lines between oral and written language social interaction tasks and the skills required to produce texts in Chinese. Using Pinyin effectively as a digital input method to engage in online social interaction, for example, is a skill essential in a contemporary classroom and involves capacity in character identification that needs to be taught from the outset.

Receptive engagement with authentic texts in characters, either glossed in Pinyin, or supported by word lists, is also desirable from the earliest stages of learning. Access to and engagement with print resources, be they related to learners' other subject areas or from native speaker contexts, brings learners into contact with the realities of unfamiliar characters, lack of word spacing and text formalities that are not evident in spoken language. Reading authentic texts designed for Chinese communities also brings learners into contact with information framed within a cultural context, providing opportunities for intercultural learning, though character knowledge and overall text comprehensibility may be limited and need explicit support. Everyday environmental print texts (such as public signs, notices, advertisements, calendars, and shop signs) provide meaningful input in text types that learners would recognise but would not be expected to produce. Learning how to deal with unfamiliar characters, how to access character meanings via digital dictionaries, and address the challenges of online translation tools, are knowledge and skills that will benefit learners throughout their learning journey and need to find a place in curriculum planning.

## Incorporating Intercultural Learning Into Curriculum

A further feature of curriculum often overlooked is how to plan for the development of an intercultural capability in communicating, through the development of students' broader intercultural understanding of how their own culture influences communication practices, and how that impacts on their abilities to interpret meanings and communicate effectively in Chinese. Too often, culture is seen as an add on, the priority remains a focus on the linguistic forms in Chinese rather than the subtle cultural messages that are implicit in communication, between native speakers in particular. It is not sufficient to plan for cultural content, learning how to explore culture in language and explain values systems underpinning communication needs to be explicitly planned and incorporated into analysis of language, interpersonal interactions, texts and contexts; and this must be based on learners' own cultural identities as the starting point for building understanding of otherness. The issues in planning for intercultural learning relate to both how content is understood, and how teachers plan for learner's engagement with that content. While there is still a need to introduce learners to facts about the country (China and the broader collective of Chinese speaking communities around the world), such content is not the stimulus for intercultural understanding or an intercultural capability in communication.

An interculturally oriented curriculum must necessarily focus on cultural concepts related to communicating, such as politeness, respect, formality, how to express disagreement or disapproval, and so on, which find direct expression through language, and can be compared directly across languages. At a deeper and more cognitively demanding level, concepts such as individualism, a sense of community, a sense of personal space, concepts of time, of faith, of personal and group identity, can find expression in all sorts of texts and contexts, and cannot readily be planned in a developmental sequence. As such, these broader conceptual learnings need to be addressed in curriculum in a more longitudinal fashion, allowing for a process of exploration of different cultural concepts and ideas as and when they are encountered in text. It should be noted that these may occur in quite early forms of the language encountered, such as 你 and 您 (two forms of the pronoun 'you'), 张先生 and 张老师 (title of personal address). The fundamental aspect of planning required here is being alert to the opportunity for intercultural exploration embedded in texts and situations, and empowering learners with the skills to undertake such analysis and have the confidence to share their own insights and understandings.

## Developing Understanding of the System of the Target Language

Finally, but fundamentally, developing an understanding of the target language system is a foundation for any Chinese language program. Representing the language as code is necessary, but this needs to be done in the context in which learners build their understanding of the nature of the system more generally. Too often learners are introduced to key aspects of the grammatical system of Chinese as isolated vocabulary items, rather than as representations of a systemic feature of the grammar of Chinese. For example, interrogative pronouns are introduced one by one across a number of units, but there is seldom a conversation about how questions are formed in Chinese and how this relates to English question formation. Similarly, the preposition 根 (*with*) is introduced early in textbooks, but the nature and function and positioning of prepositions in Chinese and in English by comparison is seldom addressed in a holistic or conceptual manner. Such atomised and unanalysed approaches to grammar introduction and learning create cross-language confusion in learners' minds and fail to build learners' control of and ability to use essential rules for word order. Learners are often left lacking the abilities to see systems emerging and so fail to become capable of transferring knowledge from one context to another. A more holistic, conceptual framing of the Chinese grammar system, including addressing cross-linguistic features which do *not* appear in Chinese, such as conjugation, plurality, verb tense, are essential if learners are to be empowered to grasp the challenges of learning across linguistic codes and with the skills to apply that knowledge to their own communication practices.

## A Suggested Format for Planning Chinese Curriculum

The challenge of applying a principled approach as discussed by Wen (2015) and Leung and Scarino (2016), as well as attempting to address Chinese specific features that need individual attention, is significant, and no one model can do real justice to the complexities discussed in this chapter. However, three key features of planning are central to all such designs:

- content is viewed longitudinally and conceptually; as a long-term curriculum design, the focus is on the systemic understanding that develops from the individual instances of topics or grammar that are encountered at different points in the program;
- features of oral and written language development, both understanding the oral language system, and engaging in oral communicative activity and exploring the Chinese writing system and engaging with written communicative activity, are addressed separately;
- consideration of how learners will be engaged in thinking about and talking about the concepts they encounter, concepts related to content, to language and to culture, in particular are the primary focus of planning;
- the orientation to learning is essentially bilingual and intercultural: learners are encouraged to relate their own language(s) and culture(s) to the new concepts and communication experiences they encounter in the Chinese classroom, and English is used purposively to explore concepts and ideas related to language and culture and their experiences in learning and using Chinese that extend beyond their current communicative capability in Chinese.

A simple representation of how these Chinese specific issues of curriculum design are exemplified in the curriculum structure is provided as an appendix to this chapter. The sample represents a longer-term curriculum plan for an extended period of learning at beginner level. It does not define the sequence in which engagement with content, or the day-to-day experiences of learning to interpret exchange or create meaning, will take place. Nor does it determine when the focus will be on communicating in Chinese, and when the focus will be on analysis and reflection in English. These are decisions best determined by the actual realities of the classroom interactions.

The principle that learners need focussed and sustained periods of time immersed in the target language is central to achieving the ultimate goal of communicative capability in the target language. As shown in the plan, through the section on classroom interactions and experiences, periods of focussed attention to developing skills in pronunciation and tone, on the skills in understanding features of character form and function, or on bringing the structures and features of Chinese and its cultural context of use into comparative perspective with the features of English language and local cultural practices and beliefs, are included. Whether these moments of analysis and reflection occur as brief sessions at the end of a lesson, or as a dedicated lesson at regular intervals in the teaching cycle, is a decision for teachers themselves. What matters most is the need to provide students with the opportunity to focus sufficiently on these underlying skills and understandings that will make their learning more sustainable, more deeply personal, and more intercultural, than might otherwise be the case.

## Conclusion

Chinese language teaching is distinctive, and planning for classroom learning requires a deep understanding of the challenges that learners face, and the ways these may be addressed in a contemporary, communicatively and interculturally oriented curriculum context. Second language learners bring few useful prior understandings and skills to the study of Chinese. The 'distance' between Chinese and European languages, in terms of the nature of the spoken language, the written language and the grammar system, is significant; new knowledge and skills need to be made available, discussed, and tested out so new learners can begin to both recognise the challenges they face and be willing to adapt their understandings and skills to meet these challenges in a sustained and effective manner. Curriculum planning in Chinese must address these needs in the scope and sequence for learning they develop; and take a broader, conceptual view of what these challenges are, how they may be introduced and addressed, and how long that might take, alongside all the other content demands that also need to be met.

In Chinese language learning, building learners' deeper understanding of the knowledge they need and the skills to acquire that knowledge does not happen in isolation. Students still view their world and their learning experiences through the prism of their own first language(s) and culture(s). Curriculum also needs to acknowledge this framework of prior knowledge and find ways to plan to bring prior language knowledge and experience into comparative perspective with new language knowledge and communicative activity in the new language. Contemporary curriculum also reinforces the importance of viewing the acquisition of a second or additional language as a process of developing a bilingual capability in communication, building in learners the skills to move competently and appropriately between languages and learn to communicate with others in an increasingly diverse and interconnected world. All of these challenges, and priorities need to be foregrounded by teachers as they develop their skills in planning, resourcing and presenting a curriculum that also addresses the particular needs of learners of Chinese in their own, local context.

# Appendix

**TABLE 5.1** Exemplar of a Chinese curriculum scope of learning for a long-term introductory unit (middle school focussed)

| | Key content areas | Key concepts | Key inquiry questions | Key interactions and classroom experiences |
|---|---|---|---|---|
| Explanation of each column and row | A structure to focus on the specific challenges of learning speech and writing, the system of grammar, and contemporary cultural practices which impact on communication in Chinese | Broader concepts to be explored within the content areas in the module | Holistic and recurring (**sample**) questions related to the key concepts which engage learners in meaningful intercultural enquiry | Activities to engage students with Chinese language and culture, directed towards building opportunities to discuss key concepts as they engage with key content areas |
| **Topic**<br>– Represents the key content focus for the module (including comparisons across cultures/societies) | E.g. **Self and family**, school life, my community, an active and healthy lifestyle, keeping a budget (incomes and expenses), contemporary trends in youth culture | **E.g. Self and family;**<br>– Key family relationships<br>– Key personal data; naming practices, age and date of birth, ethnicity/nationality, gender terms | – How do we create a family tree? How do we refer to members of our family?<br>– What personal information would you like to share with others? When and where do you share personal information? | – Discuss how family and personal information is presented in English and compare how these ideas are expressed in Chinese (with a focus on word order)<br>– Participate in classroom exchanges to share basic personal data |
| **Language concepts**<br>– specific language structures and features to be introduced | Language structures and word order (across languages), questioning, nouns, personal and possessive pronouns, adjective phrases (with adverbs of degree), numbers and measure words, prepositional phrases etc. | **Key verb structures**<br>– Verb types; verbs of identification, existence<br>– Verbs used in talking about identity; naming, residence<br>– Verbs of action<br>– Verbs of emotion | – How do we use the verb 'to be' (am/is/are), and state the existence of something (there is/are) in English?<br>– What verbs do we use to describe self and family? | – Observe/listen to Chinese conversations in which the verbs 是 and 有 are used and explain how these ideas are expressed in English and Chinese |

| Language concepts | | | | |
|---|---|---|---|---|
| Language structures and word order (across languages), *e.g. questioning* | **Questioning** Word order – for yes/no questions, – when using question words (interrogative pronouns) Ways of replying yes and no in Chinese | | – How do we make questions in English and Chinese? (How does word order change when compared to statements?) | – Make a list of questions in English and determine different question types and word order in English – Translate Chinese questions into English (using pinyin vocab lists) and compare the word order between the two – Identify patterns (rules of word order) noticed in asking questions in Chinese |
| **Spoken Chinese** – Specific knowledge and skills related to areas of phonology; speech patterns and oral interaction | – Features of speech, tone, pitch and stress – The Pinyin Romanisation system – The Chinese tone system – Letter values and syllable pronunciation across languages | – Identifying rhythm in short flows of speech – Identifying tones in single syllables and in phrase level speech – Reproducing rhythms, tonal syllables and phrases – Letter sound-values in Pinyin – Mapping sounds to syllables in Pinyin – Comparing spelling and speech in diverse languages | – How do the sounds of syllables vary between English and Chinese? – What is 'tone'? How does it differ from pitch and stress in spoken language? – How do letter-sound values vary across languages (e.g. English and Chinese)? | – Participate in shared 'listen and repeat' activities – Learn and recite short rhymes and poems – Learn to understand and use common spoken classroom expressions, including courtesy phrases – Read aloud Pinyin texts with attention to pronunciation, tone and phrasing – Engage in brief dictation exercises to check ability to encode/record spoken sounds into Pinyin – Identify and compare familiar syllables in English with different pronunciation in Chinese (e.g. can, pie, sun, ran, tie etc.) |
| **Spoken Chinese** | – Engaging in dialogues to exchange personal information – Asking key questions and follow-up questions – Sharing personal information | – Features of interpersonal exchanges (greeting, bidding farewell) – Ways of showing interest/ concern for others – Asking appropriate questions | – How we greet familiar and unfamiliar people across cultures – What are features of politeness when greeting others, making new friends? – What are polite ways of greeting and farewelling/ taking leave of people? | – Observing brief conversations between native speakers and identifying ways of greeting, showing interest in others, sharing information, and leave taking – Participating in classroom interactions sharing personal information in response to questions – Comparing ways people socialise and make friends across cultures |

*(Continued)*

**TABLE 5.1** (Continued)

| | Key content areas | Key concepts | Key inquiry questions | Key interactions and classroom experiences |
|---|---|---|---|---|
| **Written Language** – *specific knowledge and skills related to areas of orthography addressed in order to engage in reading and writing* | – Stroke types, graphemes (letters or components), across languages<br>– Basic writing skills<br>– Features of words across languages | – Diverse writing systems (Roman alphabet, Chinese characters, other familiar systems)<br>– Basic writing skills (stroke types, stroke order and direction)<br>– Word forming across languages (letter strings in English, component sequences in Chinese) | – What writing systems can you read? How do they differ? What do you know about Chinese writing?<br>– How do we learn to read and write? What role does writing practice play in becoming literate? What strokes are used to make letters in English? What strokes are used to make characters?<br>– What are characters composed of? What are components? How are they related? How many are there? | – Compare samples of writing across languages<br>– Identify strokes and stroke sequences in letters, and stoke types and sequences in basic Chinese characters<br>– Identify the number and arrangement of components of compound characters<br>– Explore components in related sets (by stroke type, by meaning etc.) and identify rules for writing and links between component form and meaning |
| **Written Language** | – Generating texts using digital media | – Ways of typing or generating digital text in Chinese (Pinyin input methods and character selection)<br>– Evaluating digital translation tools | – How do we type in Chinese? What skills do we need in creating digital character texts?<br>– How effective are digital translation tools? What issues in translation can you see? | – Generate short messages online–use character lists and online dictionaries to assist in selection of characters to generate accurate texts<br>– Translate texts to/from Chinese using online translation tools, identify areas of difficulty in creating accurate translations this way |

| | | | |
|---|---|---|---|
| **Written Language** | – Features of written texts in Chinese, e.g. public signs, posters, personal ID cards | – Word direction and spacing<br>– Features of familiar text genres (signs, notices) | – How are written texts organised in Chinese? Can you see words in the text?<br>– What skills do we need to read signs and notices in Chinese? | – Translate short signs from Chinese character by character and attempt to build word meanings and text meanings using word lists. Discuss any differences noticed between spoken and written Chinese sentence patterns<br>– Complete a personal profile in Chinese |
| **The Role of Culture in Communicating**<br>*Language-related and broader cultural concepts related to how language is used in specific contexts* | Cultural concepts<br>– being polite<br>– showing respect<br>– showing degrees of relationship<br>– basic beliefs and values<br>– festivals and celebrations | – Politeness, formality, humility, humour,<br>– Importance of family, respect for elder generations<br>– The cycle of the seasons and its relationship to festival and celebrations | – How does our language change when speaking with someone older, or who we don't know?<br>– When do we need to be polite, how is this reflected in language?<br>– How is respect for elders reflected in language we use?<br>– What are important celebrations in our local culture? Why do we celebrate these events at this time? | – Discuss how people in diverse cultures interact with each other. What features of polite speech and behaviour do we have in common?<br>– View interactions between people in Chinese contexts, discuss how age, position, familiarity influence interactions<br>– Discuss situations in which formal language is expected and how this is reflected in language use<br>– Explore prior knowledge of festivals and culturally significant occasions across cultures and identify commonalities and differences in important events |

**Key communication tasks**
– *undertaken as students build knowledge and skills related to language and culture*

Task One—engage in conversation with teacher and peers (including sister school classmates, if possible) to exchange personal information (name, age, date of birth, place of residence, nationality, languages, year level, etc.

Task Two—construct a family tree in Chinese (Pinyin and characters) and use the tree to share information about family with others

Task Three—complete a personal identity card (in print/online) and describe information on the card orally with others

Task Four—maintain a journal of thoughts and reflections on experiences learning Chinese language and culture and how Chinese cultural practices in communication appear to compare to one's own communication experiences in English/other languages

## References

ACTFL (American Council for the Teaching of Foreign Languages). (2012) *ACTFL Proficiency Guidelines*. Chinese. Retrieved 14 September 2018 from www.actfl.org/publications/guidelines-and-manuals/actfl-proficiency-guidelines-2012/english

Australian Curriculum and Assessment and Reporting Authority (ACARA). (2014) *Australian Curriculum: Languages*. Retrieved from www.australiancurriculum.edu.au/f-10-curriculum/languages/

Bai, J., Lien, L., and Spring, M.K. (2016) 'Mapping Chinese Language Learning Outcomes in Grades K-12', in S.C. Wang and J.K. Peyton (eds.), *CELIN Briefs Series*. New York: Asia Society.

Cenoz, J. and Gorter, D. (2014) 'Focus on Multilingualism as an Approach in Educational Contexts', in A. Blackledge and A. Creese (eds.), *Heteroglossia as Practice and Pedagogy. Educational Linguistics*, 20(13): 239–254. Dordrecht: Springer.

Chao, D., Hakam, D.K., and Lin, Y. (2016) 'Designing and Implementing Chinese Language Programs: Preparing Students for the Real World', in S.C. Wang and J.K. Peyton (eds.), *CELIN Briefs Series*. New York: Asia Society.

Cummins, J. (2007) 'Rethinking Monolingual Instructional Strategies in Multilingual Classrooms', *Canadian Journal of Applied Linguistics*, 10(2): 221–240.

Gattegno, C. (1972) *Teaching Foreign Language in Schools: The Silent Way*. 2nd edition. New York: Educational Solutions Worldwide Inc.

Graves, K. (2008) 'The Language Curriculum: A Social Contextual Perspective', *Language Teaching*, 41(2): 147–181.

Hanson, E.C. (2013) *'To Know the System and Know the Culture Is Difficult' Understanding the Cultural Adjustment Process of Teachers From China Working in U.S. K-12 Schools*. Thesis Submitted to the Faculty of the Graduate School of the University of Minnesota.

Heller, M. (2007) 'Bilingualism as Ideology and Practice', in M. Heller (ed.), *Bilingualism: A Social Approach*. Palgrave Advances in Linguistics. London: Palgrave.

Kumaravadivelu, B. (1994) 'The Postmethod Condition: (E)merging Strategies for Second/Foreign Language Teaching', *TESOL Quarterly*, 28(1): 27–48.

Leung, C. (2012) 'English as an Additional Language Policy—Rendered Theory and Classroom Interaction', in S. Gardner and M. Martin-Jones (eds.), *Multilingualism, Discourse, and Ethnography*, 222–240. Abingdon: Routledge.

Leung, C. and Scarino, A. (2016) 'Reconceptualizing the Nature of Goals and Outcomes in Language/s Education', *The Modern Language Journal*, 100(S1): 81–95. https://doi.org/10.1111/modl.12300

Liao, W., Yuan, R., and Zhang, H. (2017) 'Chinese Language Teachers' Challenges in Teaching in U.S. Public Schools: A Dynamic Portrayal', *Asia-Pacific Education Researcher*, 26(6): 369–381.

Liddicoat, A.J. and Scarino, A. (2013) *Intercultural Language Teaching and Learning*. Chichester: Wiley-Blackwell.

Luo, H. (2015) 'Curricular Goals and Curriculum Design: The Case of a College-level Chinese Language Program', *Journal of Chinese Language Teachers Association*, 50(3): 23–44.

Minogue, J. and Jones, N.G. (2006) 'Haptics in Education: Exploring an Untapped Sensory Modality', *Review of Educational Research*, 76(3): 317–334.

Nation, I.S.P. and Macalister, J. (2010) *Language Curriculum Design*. New York and London: Routledge.

National Standards in Foreign Language Education Project (U.S.); American Council on the Teaching of Foreign Languages. (2015) *World-Readiness Standards for Learning*

*Languages*. Alexandria: National Standards in Foreign Language Education Project, American Council on the Teaching of Foreign Languages.

Richards, J.C. (2013) 'Curriculum Approaches in Language Teaching: Forward, Central, and Backward Design', *RELC Journal: A Journal of Language Teaching and Research*, 44(1): 5–33.

Scrimgeour, A. (2014) Dealing With Chinese Fever: The Challenge of Chinese Teaching in the Australian Classroom', in N. Murray and A. Scarino (eds.), *Dynamic Ecologies of Languages Education in the Asia-Pacific Region*. New York: Springer.

Wen, X.H. (ed.). (2015) *Teaching Chinese as a Second Language: Curriculum Design and Instruction*. Beijing, China: Beijing Language and Culture University Press.

Wiggins, G. and McTighe, J. (2006) *Understanding by Design*. 2nd edition. Alexandria: Association for Supervision and Curriculum Development.

# 6

# ADDRESSING DIVERSITY

## Introduction

Over the past few decades there has been a significant rise in interest in Chinese learning, with the Hanban playing a key role in assisting in the provision of Chinese language learning opportunities in schools and universities around the world (Gil, 2017). The rapid rise in Chinese teaching and learning has provided new opportunities for students around the world, but new challenges have arisen as well.

The rise in interest in Chinese learning at schools and colleges has led to the development of new curriculum and textbooks to help teachers design their programs and deliver meaningful learning opportunities for learners. These curriculum and teaching materials and the programs themselves have been largely designed for learners with no prior exposure to Chinese language and culture. The programs assume a single entry point for learners (the beginning of primary, secondary or college or university), who are also assumed to be largely monolingual English (or other national language) speakers with little or no knowledge or experience with Chinese language and culture. Curriculum documents, typically developed from generic frameworks, are also used to frame the anticipated outcomes from learning Chinese, providing a single, linear trajectory for mapping achievements for all learners, irrespective of their age, time on task, or other variables.

Chinese textbooks also assume learners to be a 'homogenous' grouping, giving little recognition of diversity in language and culture background or identity. Not only are learners 'standardised' by textbooks and curriculum pathways, the language represented in curriculum and textbooks also reinforces the notion of a standard version: Modern Standard Chinese in this instance, using Pinyin

Romanisation and simplified characters to present the language in sentences and formulaic texts, with few opportunities to explore diversity within the language itself, or for learners to experience the realities of how the language is used in everyday contexts in its own environment, in either oral or written genres. The result is a curriculum and a classroom practice that is built upon assumptions of homogeneity, where diversity in background or experience are often overlooked, resulting in a common pathway and set of aspirational goals for all (Ashton, 2017), irrespective of learners' linguistic and cultural background and experiences with Chinese.

## Acknowledging and Responding to Diversity in the CSL Classroom

Whilst in many classrooms the learner group may still be predominately second language in background, there are increasing numbers of learners who not only identify as being of Chinese heritage, but these days who may also speak Chinese at home on a regular basis. They may also speak one or more dialects of Chinese. They may only speak it at home, or also use it socially with friends. They may actively engage with Chinese language through music and film and other forms of media entertainment. They may maintain contact with their speech community via social media in Chinese. They may have attended or still attend community school. They may have been given sound initial literacy education by parents, at community school, and may be active readers for their own purposes. These variables are in each instance significant and have major implications for learners' future learning trajectories.

With the growth in provision of Chinese programs in schools and colleges, students with Chinese language background are encouraged or attracted to the chance to study their heritage language as part of their formal education. The challenges of teaching Chinese in the school classroom are thus compounded. There remains for teachers the main challenge of developing and delivering a program that empowers second language learners to understand and use it in somewhat limited social and transactional contexts. The challenges in learning to read and write in Chinese characters, to speak with a fair degree of tone and prosodic accuracy, to master its fundamental grammatical structures and features, are all addressed elsewhere in this book. The other challenge for teachers, however, although highly variable in its presence and complexity, is the diversity within the learner group itself.

The focus of this chapter is on discussing ways in which teachers can provide a meaningful classroom-based experience for Chinese heritage learners of whatever background or experience within a regular lesson with non-Chinese background classmates. The increasing presence of children who speak Chinese at home in the second language classroom has implications for all learners, and addressing their needs is a pressing concern (Orton, 2008, 2016). Their skills and capabilities are complex and variable, their potentials as learners of Chinese need to be understood in the context of their individual life experiences. It is not simply a matter of testing their current state of proficiency. Teachers need to understand these learners in terms of their own particular experiences, motivations and aspirations, in terms of their own sense of their relationship with Chinese and local languages and cultures, that is, with their bilingual experience, not just their Chinese 'self'. Such understandings are essential for teachers to fully understand the needs of these learners and help them fulfill their language learning aspirations.

Addressing Chinese heritage learner needs is broadly a curricular issue. As Orton (2008, 2016) argues, ideally, students who speak Chinese at home should be taught with a dedicated curriculum and separate teaching program. However, this is seldom viable in school-based contexts. The reality is that teachers are faced with what is best described as a 'multi-level' classroom, where 'level' relates not just to proficiency but also to identity, motivation, and aspiration. Thus, the challenge to be addressed is how teachers can address diversity primarily at the program level, in the individual classroom, with its unique set of interpersonal dynamics, and importantly also at the individual level, where each and every learner has their own particular background, identity, needs and aspirations in that particular class context.

## Defining a Chinese Heritage Learner

In reality, attempting to define learners and allocate them into separate learner categories is highly problematic. Aspects that might be pertinent to defining learner background include by generation, by ethnic or cultural affiliation, and by language proficiency. Generational definitions focus on country of birth of the child and the parents: being first generation, that is, overseas born and significantly educated before arrival; generation 1.5, that is, born overseas but arriving in early childhood; second generation; being born in the host country to parents born in the mother country; third generation: both parents born in the new host country. Naturally, proficiency typically wanes over generations, but ethnic identification with the target language community may remain strong as long as there are active links maintained with that community.

Defining learners by such ethnic or cultural affiliation focuses on the degree of participation in the cultural life of the language community in the host country, which implies a sense of connection within the community irrespective of proficiency. However, increasing enculturation into the social and cultural world of the local community through such avenues as school friends and sporting commitments will tend to diminish the sense of affiliation with the heritage community and culture over generations. Community schooling is often a means by which parents attempt to keep a sense of belonging in the next generation, but the experience of community schooling does not appeal to all young people, especially those with lower proficiency than their peers in that setting.

Finally, and most importantly, learners may be defined by their current abilities in using the target language, fostered by active use and support at home to maintain the language through social networks and sustained attendance at community school. Given the assumption that heritage leaners are by and large not educated in their parents' country of birth, it is assumed that whatever proficiency has been attained is typically oral in nature (listening and speaking), and that reading and writing skills in many instances remain at a foundational level at best.

One commonly accepted definition of a heritage language learner (Valdés, 2000, 2001) as applied to Chinese identifies a heritage learner as one who has been raised in a Chinese speaking home, who speaks or understands Chinese and is to some extent bilingual in Chinese and the local language (such as English). Carreira and Kagan (2011) recognise heritage learners' exposure to Chinese language in childhood, but highlight the fact that such learners have not learned Chinese to full capacity because another language (i.e. English) became dominant. Given the breadth of definitions often applied to such learners, Wen (2011) prefers to distinguish those learners with native speaker parents who still actively use the language as 'Chinese background learners', preferring to use the term heritage learners only for those with some (more distant) connections to the language and culture. Such terminology is common to various state Curricula in Australian. Most recently, a Background Language Learner Pathway has been developed as part of the Australian Curriculum for Chinese, designed for students who have exposure to Chinese language and culture, and who may engage in some active but predominantly receptive use of Chinese at home (ACARA, 2014).

For the purposes of this chapter the term Chinese Heritage Learner follows the definitions of Valdés (2000) and Carreira and Kagan (2011), and identifies a heritage learner as one who used Chinese regularly before attending school, and continues to use the language to some extent, although is now English dominant. Continued use of Chinese may include attending community school. As this definition highlights, what is most significant in terms of what such learners bring to the classroom is, first and foremost, a degree of proficiency in Chinese at a native speaker standard, as Chinese language was part of the world-defining learning they experienced as an infant. It is this capability that sets them apart most critically from other learners. For these groups, entering the Chinese classroom is entering a strange new world of new sounds, symbols and cultural influences on meaning making. For the heritage learner these unfamiliar elements are already part of their linguistic and cultural repertoire.

These definitions do not provide a discrete and fully inclusive category for heritage learners. Heritage learners lie somewhere between overseas-born and educated native speakers, and novice second language learners with no prior knowledge or experience of the language. In reality there are no such fixed boundaries to any of these categories and there are many variables that impact upon a learner's sense of who they are and of the opportunities to both develop and maintain an active working knowledge of the target language. At the upper limit, heritage learners may have been born overseas but migrated to the host country prior to or during early primary school, (and thus have strong oral skills but only initial literacy skills on arrival). At the lower level, heritage learners may have been born in their host country and have only one Chinese speaking parent, thus limiting the extent of exposure to oral Chinese in childhood to very a limited range of contexts. Essentially, a heritage learner began and continues to speak Chinese at home and possibly beyond, and therefore has prior knowledge of and experience using Chinese that a second language learner will never attain in the classroom.

## The Role of Heritage Learner Identity in Chinese Language Learning

The discussion on defining what constitutes a heritage language learner must not be seen as a 'title' to be bestowed or otherwise on each learner as they enter the Chinese classroom. Ultimately the potential for learning that heritage learners bring is equally determined not by proficiency but also by the learner's sense of identification with the speech community (of Modern Standard Chinese in this instance), and their attitudes and motivations to study the language in a formal school setting that result from that sense of identification. This sense of belonging, of the learner's self-identification with Chinese language and culture, is highly variable in terms of their social practices, contexts of engagement, as well as their experiences in learning as well as using the language. However, it is also clear that a learner's sense of proficiency is an important part of their sense of belonging (Carreira and Kagan, 2011), and that sense of identity is as important as their current state of proficiency in understanding their potential as learner and the likelihood of success as learner in the classroom (He, 2008). Heritage learner identity is diverse, multifaceted, evolving, contextualised and relative to others' perceptions of them, especially among their non-Chinese speaking peers (Zhu, 2016). Additional variables in a learner's identity development and sense of belonging, to both the heritage speech community and their identification as heritage learners of the language, include the extent of parental support and participation in developing their language capability, the extent of involvement and participation in the social and cultural life of the community, and importantly, their positive experiences in heritage school contexts (Zhu, 2016).

As young people engaged in education and socialisation in their host country, or country of birth, heritage learners' identity cannot be readily divorced from their sense of belonging in their local society. Developing a bilingual identity is a central part of their learning journey (García, 2009) and their sense of belonging to two linguistic worlds typically involves code switching or translanguaging at home, and especially among their Chinese peer group (Li, 2011). As such their sense of self as a speaker of Chinese and a member of both speech communities is fluid, creative, hybrid and situated (He, 2008). The role of both languages and cultures in their ongoing identity formation must be considered when addressing their learning needs in the Chinese classroom.

## Why Heritage Learners Study Chinese

Many studies have been undertaken into the motivational features and forces behind heritage learners' engagement in language learning. Significant studies were undertaken mostly at university level a decade ago (He, 2006, 2008, 2010; He and Xiao, 2008; Lu and Li, 2008) with recent studies exploring the personal experiences of Heritage learners in schools and post-secondary levels (Wen, 2011; O'Rourke and Zhou, 2016; Xiang, 2016; Zhu, 2016). Studies of heritage motivation have found inconsistent findings (Wen, 2011), with research in diverse contexts finding both instrumental and integrative orientations to be significant factors in heritage learners decisions to study and continue to study their heritage language (Comanaru and Noels, 2009; Lu and Li, 2008).

Integrative orientation, in which learners seek to further develop or maintain their language and culture links with family and the community, is closely aligned with a learner's sense of identification with the language (Hendryx, 2008), and tends to be stronger when access to speakers is readily available (Wen, 2011). Instrumental motivation, related less to a sense of self and more to the value of knowing the language, tends to become stronger as learners continue their studies and begin to realise the future social and economic benefit or utility of proficiency in Chinese (Wen, 2011). Instrumental motivation can also be evident in a learner's sense of obligation to parents to try to learn the home language; though such motivation is seldom a predictor of a learner's success in developing language proficiency (He, 2008). However, motivational orientations are highly situational or experiential: much depends on the environments in which the heritage learners currently use the language (or not), in which they engage with the community, and the impact of the experience studying the language in formal educational settings, including community school. Ultimately, family support and their own sense of self as a user of the language, and the social context and positive experiences in the learning context, remain the most significant variables to motivation and to achievement for the heritage learner, especially in the school years (Xiang, 2016).

### Demotivating Factors for Heritage Learners

Despite the significant motivating forces to study Chinese as their heritage language, classroom experiences can be and often are powerful demotivating factors for many heritage learners. Most significant is the multi-level classroom, where heritage learners find themselves in the same class with second language learners. There are multiple causes for dissatisfaction with this situation, for heritage and non-heritage learners alike. Heritage learners often have no sense of belonging with 'real beginners' for whom the program is designed. Beginner learners often feel a sense of 'unfair competition' with heritage learners who seem to be able to pass the tests with little effort, and be rewarded with grades higher than for the new learners, despite the additional effort expended by them, resulting in a damaging relationship of 'mutual negativity' (O'Rourke and Zhou, 2016). Curriculum can also be demotivating for heritage learners as they find the linguistic content, subject matter and activities designed for second language learners unrelated to their needs, interests or aspirations. The teacher can also create a negative experience for the heritage learners, especially when the teacher places demands or expectation on heritage learners in terms of effort and output which heritage learners perceive as unreasonable, or where the learner's personal language is of a non-standard variety which the teacher attempts to erase or ignore in teaching and addressing the learner's progress, resulting in a stereotyping or an alienating experience (Weger-Guntharp, 2006).

Textbooks designed for second language learners, which begin with the assumption that learners have no prior knowledge of the language and culture, and present content related to simple everyday topics, with limited grammar development and with communicative activities which expect modelled responses to pedagogic texts, are also alienating for heritage language learners as they that don't reflect their everyday experience with the language, and are limited to routine topics already familiar to them. Ultimately, there is the potential for the classroom to be a negative experience that results in little more than demotivating heritage learners, as they begin to feel a sense of alienation or lack of recognition, as they experience boring and repetitive language learning experiences that are below their current potential, and struggle to find opportunities to progress their language development. However, it is not the multi-level classroom itself, or the teacher, or the textbook that is the main problem in such contexts. The real issue lies in the manner in which heritage learners are invited to engage in constructive interaction in the classroom, with the language, with their co-learners, and with their identity, capabilities and potentials, as both Chinese heritage language learners and as developing bilinguals in their local context.

In fact, many teachers do attempt to differentiate learning and provide more challenges and a positive learning environment for both heritage learners and second language learners in the same classroom. A common approach in classrooms where a small number of heritage learners are present is to deliver the same content, instruction and activity, but to challenge the heritage learner by compacting or accelerating the program, giving them less time to complete the same tasks. This only makes the challenge one of 'competing against the clock' in simple tasks rather than developing their skills in new ways at higher levels. An alternative strategy is to remove some of the supports provided for second language learners such as word lists or dictionaries, making the challenge one of greater memory load for heritage learners to achieve the same language output. More nuanced responses may include some modification to input texts, or to outputs in response to tasks using the same content or topic area, or to vary the context, or purpose of the task to require a more complex textual response from heritage language learners than from their second language classmates.

Overall however, while teachers do recognise the need to modify their practices to attend to the needs of heritage language learners in multi-level classrooms, many simply do not do so (Bernstein, Burke, Favre, and Delcourt, 2010). The pressures of the school language classroom in particular, of delivering a coherent and interesting program to second language learners, typically remains the predominant priority of language teachers. The textbooks assume a homogenous class, with no prior knowledge, who need drip-fed access to sets of vocabulary and individual grammatical items based around familiar topics. The curriculum standards and proficiency frameworks assume learners are on a common pathway to basic proficiency. Learners are assumed to be distant from the language and the culture. Such curriculum, resources and classroom practices alienate heritage learners from the own language and culture. Changes are needed in all aspects of Chinese language teaching for heritage language learners to find their place and be given the opportunity to progress towards their own proficiency outcomes and achieve their desired personal, cultural and professional aspirations as bilingual citizens in their own social contexts.

## Identifying Heritage Language Learners' Needs

The needs of heritage language learners are diverse. Wen (2011) argues teachers need to find ways to provide heritage learners with meaningful, positive learning experiences to foster positive attitudes and impact on motivational efforts and the desire to continue to study the language. Fundamental to providing such positive experiences is to understand where learners are at in their language knowledge and use, and use that foundation to move them forward. In general, however, there are characteristics of heritage language use that are useful to know when considering what their learning needs may be, especially in their initial years of language learning in the school context. Research has identified both the strengths and limitations of heritage language proficiency, especially in the secondary and post-secondary environments. It is important to remember that individual proficiency is highly variable, complex and evolving, and not necessarily progressing at the time they enter the school language program.

Common features of heritage learners' language use typically include the strength of their oral interaction skills over their print literacy skills. However, limitations in oral vocabulary, register, genre and contexts of use are evident compared to more proficient native speakers. Comparing heritage learners to native speakers implies a deficit or inferior proficiency, which is not helpful when considering their personal context of learning and likely communicative needs and aspirations in their own environment. Heritage learners are better compared with second language learners, as they are likely to be sharing the same classroom, and the challenge for teachers is determining how to address the needs of these two groups in a coordinated manner.

Research highlights the fact that heritage language learners have more in common with second language learners due to their general lack of the age-appropriate literacy skills displayed by native speaker students (Xiao, 2010; He and Xiao, 2008; He, 2008; Wu, 2008). Compared to second language learners, heritage language learners display a wider range of vocabulary and ability to understand and use a range of grammar structures encountered in frequent natural inputs. They tend, however, to produce rather simple formulaic expressions in their own speech and to avoid complex, Chinese-specific structures in their own communication (Xiao, 2010). This is especially so for those who have not experienced extended formal instruction in Chinese speaking communities.

Research undertaken has shown that compared to beginner learners, heritage language learners do perform at significantly higher levels and differ in the nature of their performance when achievements on common tasks are assessed (Scarino, Elder, Kim, Iwashita, Kohler, and Scrimgeour, 2011; Elder, Kim, and Knoch, 2012; Scrimgeour, 2012). Once accustomed to learning within a second language context, using the same texts, tasks and instructional practices, school-based heritage language learners display differences in their knowledge and ability to understand and use a range of Chinese specific grammatical structures, and perform significantly better in the range, accuracy and appropriateness of these features in both speech and writing. Heritage language learners do also display some weaknesses in their character writing, but these weaknesses display more phonological errors (same sound, wrong character) than the orthographic errors (character written incorrectly) that are commonly displayed by second language learners (Scrimgeour, 2012).

The overall research reinforces the point that the characteristics of language learning and use by heritage learners are quite distinctive and require differentiated attention. (Scrimgeour, 2012, 2015). It is important to stress the point that heritage learner identity, motivation, attitude to the classroom context, and proficiency, both oral and in print, are highly variable and dynamic, but they are not on a common scale with second language learners, given their relatively extensive exposure to language in everyday contexts and their wider access to opportunities to use the language for personal, social and interactional purposes.

## Addressing Diversity in the Multilevel Classroom

Overall the research highlights the distinctive nature of heritage learner's knowledge, skills, identities, trajectories and motivations. The recommendations throughout the literature reinforce the point that the best approach to addressing heritage learner needs is to teach them separately using materials designed for their particular needs. However, this isn't always possible or desirable in school-based settings, where inclusive education and differentiated approaches to teaching and learning are actively applied to build a sense of community and common purpose among learners.

Before looking at ways to integrate heritage learners into the Chinese language classroom curriculum, it's important to reinforce some principles for teaching and learning that pertain to heritage learners' needs as identified in the literature. Firstly and foremost, teachers must understand what each heritage learner brings with them to the classroom in terms of their proficiency, their background and experiences with Chinese language and culture, and their current motivations or aspirations to learn and use the language now and in the future. Only by understanding what they bring can teachers consider how best to move them forward, to help them understand what they can and cannot do at present, to appreciate their strengths and identify their areas of weakness.

Secondly, by recognising their prior knowledge and experience in using and moving between two languages and cultures, teachers need to not teach them directly, or from scratch as with second language learners, but to focus on restructuring their language for new contexts and purposes and extend their usage into new content areas, including across their learning areas at school. Such content decisions clearly need to relate to the subject matter being explored by second language learners in the same learning space. For heritage learners this can include encouraging them to explore a wider range of texts or sources of new information on the topic, which they can then apply meaningfully, either by sharing their insights with their second language learning peers, or by applying their new knowledge through tasks requiring them to apply new discourse building skills, especially in writing, as they restructure their understandings of Chinese language use to include a wider range of contexts and purposes, and consequently genres and forms of discourse within them.

Thirdly, while aiming to create a sense of community among all learners irrespective of background, it's important to build group rapport among those who identify as heritage learners and as bilinguals by creating a culture of learning which acknowledges and supports their translingual, transcultural competence (MLA, 2007), and uses the classroom as a site for engaging in translanguaging (Li, 2011; He, 2013) as they search together for a deeper understanding of their multifaceted and diverse identities in their local context. Building a sense of rapport and common purpose among the heritage group has great potential to assist in maintaining motivation and creating a cooperative and collaborative dynamic learning environment for these learners with often diverse capabilities but a common sense of purpose in learning Chinese.

In sum, as learners of 'advanced' proficiency compared to their beginner second language classmates, more autonomy and responsibility should be transferred to heritage learners at an earlier point in their classroom learning journey. However, this transfer should not be individual but collective, encouraging heritage learners in their active exploration of concepts and in the personal expression of their interpretations of texts and the construction of their own ideas. However, teacher intervention is still a significant part of their learning experience, although clearly not every element of vocabulary or grammar needs to be taught or practised in modelled and routine ways as it might be with second language learners. Heritage learners may, however, need to develop their metalinguistic awareness, to learn how to understand and discuss their current set of knowledge, skills and understandings of Chinese, and the capability to compare their communication skills and experiences across their Chinese and English social contexts. Developing this understanding of the formal properties of Chinese not only facilitates their own future learning, it also provides them with the facility to share their insider knowledge of Chinese language and their experiences with Chinese culture with their second language learner peers, to become supporters and collaborators and guides for less proficient classmates as they explore new concepts and sources of information in collaborative class time.

Grammar learning, and building discourse skills in new contexts and through new genres of speech and writing might not in most cases require explicit teaching, as it may with second language learners. Rather, grammar instruction may best take place in the context of exploring texts, negotiating meanings with the teacher and other heritage learners in class, and in the preparation of responses to tasks designed to move them forward in the complexity and sophistication of their oral and written expression. As such, these grammar learning needs may not be common to the whole group, so individual attention might be needed, or more competent others may be able to identify and explain language features that are new to their peers. Grammar teaching in this instance isn't preordained or sequenced developmentally as it might be for second language learning. It is identified and discussed in the context in which it occurs, or in the context in which a learner finds a gap in their ability to express a slightly more complex idea. Such is the artistry required when teaching heritage learners in ways that move them forward which are meaningful, challenging, and importantly relevant to their immediate communicative needs.

Finally, in relation to providing heritage learners with the knowledge, understanding and skills to undertake self-managed tasks and to take greater control and responsibility for their own learning and use of Chinese, specific and explicit attention needs to be given to showing them how to become literate in Chinese. This is not a task in common with the needs of second language learners. Heritage learners have a sound foundation of vocabulary and an implicit skill in acquiring new oral vocabulary as it is encountered in meaningful contexts. What they lack are the skills in mapping familiar vocabulary onto the appropriate character form when reading texts, and in differentiating between similar characters when generating their own texts. Given their wide experience with the spoken language, characters need not be taught one by one as they might be with second language learners. What heritage learners need is a broad conceptual understanding of how characters work and how to identify the particular features of characters, the number and arrangement of components in characters encountered, and how to identify meaningful clues that will assist in mapping sounds and meanings to these characters and in recalling these characters in the future. Digital dictionaries and character input tools mean, especially for orally proficient heritage learners, that character identification and discrimination between similar characters is a fundamentally useful skill in text processing and text creation. Such a skill can be taught explicitly and at a conceptual level, so that learners build their character recognition skills through active and continuous use, not routine and meaningless practice.

## Inclusive Differentiated Instruction

Overall, the aim of teaching to the particular needs of heritage learners is essential, but the context under consideration is still one of a particular mix of both second language and heritage learners, who both require instruction, but who, in the interests of fairness and inclusion, need to be brought together as much as possible to both create and maintain a collaborative learning community where common interests are recognised and distinctive needs are met. The notion of differentiated instruction has been promoted in education for some time, in response to various types of diversity or multi-level-ness commonly found in classrooms, including academic capabilities, attitudes and motivation, extent of prior learning, diverse forms of physical disability, and composite classes containing students at different year levels. The following discussion of features of differentiation in the Chinese language classroom draws on Tomlinson (2017), who discusses differentiation based on academic capabilities, and Ashton (2017), who explores teaching responses to language classrooms containing students at different year levels.

Given a principle of inclusive teaching and learning, and recognition of difference in needs and approaches, it is important to recognise what is not appropriate as effective differentiation in the multilevel (heritage and second language) Chinese classroom. Differentiation is not treating heritage learners as advanced second language learners being taught with the same texts and context but with different expectations in terms of questions asked, supports available, or task requirements. It is not 'teaching to the middle' (Ashton, 2017) then dealing with the edges or those with difficulties or extension, that is, reacting to mismatches between general instruction and specific learner needs. It is certainly not separated streams of teaching and learning where 50 per cent or so of the teaching time dedicated to each group, with the 'away time' dedicated to deskwork or 'self-study'.

As Tomlinson (2017) proposes, effective differentiation involves providing heritage learners with multiple options and different avenues to achieve goals that learners are able to set for themselves; to explore and interpret new sources of information; and to interact and collaborate to share information, insights and experiences between themselves and with others, including their second language classmates. This opportunity, however, needs to be created while also developing and maintaining a sense of community, of shared and mutual benefit from the efforts and contributions of all member of the class. Ashton (2017) suggests a process of orderly flexibility in providing a dynamic opportunity for group work where the entire class is focused on a common topic and a common set of concepts they are keen to explore, and participate collaboratively in selecting from a range of tasks, using resources appropriate to their task and their overall proficiency level, as they work towards a nominated product which is open ended and flexible in terms of the medium in which it is presented, and the audience for whom it is intended.

Tomlinson (2017) suggests the aim of this type of classroom is to create a collaborative community working towards a mutually beneficial outcome, moving learners forward both individually and collectively through prioritising student thinking, contribution and insights as they engage with powerful ideas related to a common theme or topic. The sense of community comes from within the learners themselves, where teachers allow learners to organise themselves into groupings based on a common interest in a particular line of questioning/research task, in a particular medium for exploring and expressing new ideas (through video, animation, interview or whatever), and importantly but not specifically, on sharing a common set of language skills. Where students agree to work together, the proficiency may be less important than other prior knowledge of skills that learners bring to the group, and the potential for learning collaboration between second language and heritage learners is enhanced considerable by their common agreed goal.

The role of the teacher in creating such a dynamic workspace for learners still requires explicit if nuanced attention to the needs of both groups, as well as individuals within each group. Second language learners will still require a micro-approach to language instruction (Carreira, 2017) involving controlled sequences of vocabulary and grammar, modified texts, and text construction focused on sentence level meaning making. Heritage learners, however, will also benefit from a more macro approach, or discourse perspective (Xiang, 2016), in which instruction focuses on meaning making systems, on learning to understand discourse features of different types of authentic text and learning to apply these features in their own purposeful communication.

While this instruction may be beyond the capabilities of most second language learners in the same class, heritage learners may benefit to some extent from participation in second language micro level instruction by providing examples of modelled interactions using the new grammatical features second language learners are encountering, and engaging with them in drafting or practising new structures in controlled situations. The benefit for heritage learners lies in their deepening appreciation of the challenges second language learners face, in actually understanding how to analyse and describe features of Chinese they take for granted, and, importantly, to participate actively in overcoming the sense of mutual negativity that infects many multilevel classrooms where effective differentiation is absent.

Tomlinson (2017) identifies three qualities of a differentiated classroom, interpreted here for the multilevel Chinese classroom that takes account of the diversity of second language and heritage language learner needs. Firstly, such a classroom is proactive, pitched at groups with common interests and skills, working to develop specific knowledge and skill sets as appropriate, with teaching and tasks fine-tuned as learners progress. Secondly, teaching is qualitative in nature, providing robust challenges related to language learning, content knowledge, and communicative activity for individuals and groups, with teaching contingent on identified need and focused on providing the requisite supports for learners to move on in collaborative, supported group activity. Thirdly, and most importantly, the differentiated classroom is student-centred, with the deliberate aim of developing learner agency, the capacity to think and act both individually and collectively in new and increasingly autonomous ways. Such a student-centred orientation focuses on the classroom as a collaborative learning community, where learners become aware of each other's prior knowledge skills and potentials, and view each other not as impositions on their learning time and task, but as potential collaborators to engage in meaningful and knowledge-oriented activity that extends well beyond the simple acquisition of Chinese language in the classroom.

## The Challenges of Differentiated Instruction

This idealised notion of a well-differentiated Chinese classroom is not without its challenges. Differentiating and providing opportunity for collaborative self-selected group work is clearly a complex endeavour, especially for the novice teacher. Teaching Chinese in a multi-level classroom in a differentiated manner is a challenge simply because there are few examples of how to proceed. Resources for identifying learner background and experience are increasingly available, but there are very few resources available which imagine learners working together in multi-level groups. At present, there are also few curriculum models that provide specific content and achievement standards for heritage learners on a separate but related scale to second language learners, so there are few incentives for teachers to consider heritage learners' learning pathways differently to those of second language learners. The Australian Curriculum: Languages (ACARA, 2014) provides a useful model of heritage (or Background Language) learner curriculum through the primary and secondary years, and Scrimgeour, Foster, and Mao (2013) discuss ways in which the learners can be taught alongside second language learners using this curriculum. The greatest challenge for the teacher attempting to integrate second language and heritage language learners is finding an adequate resource set to engage all learners in active learning, and setting a suite of tasks that motivate learners of diverse proficiency to work collectively and collaboratively together. The challenge for the teacher is in setting aside teacher-directed instruction until and when it is absolutely necessary, based on the current state of understanding of different groups. Such instruction on a largely predetermined sequence of grammar and vocabulary will be more regular and consistent for second language learners, and more strategic and incidental for heritage learners, based on identified needs with a particular task or resource set. Equally importantly, allowing learners to work together is to create the interest and environment where learners begin to learn from each other as they negotiate their way through new texts and sources of information, and work together to generate new ideas through texts in Chinese.

Collaborative group work should not mean that heritage learners push second language learners beyond their current capabilities, or that heritage learners are held back by the slow progress of second language learners. Clearly, within groups, differentiated tasks and texts are required, but learners can still work together to process information and develop a common product as a result of their work, learning how to adapt diverse knowledge and skill sets in the production of new and creative ways of sharing information with others. The teacher's role as facilitator involves bringing learners together to evaluate progress, identify issues learners are facing, discuss strategies to resolve problems, and importantly, to assist second language learners to manage their learning and document new information encountered in ways that will assist access and recall in the future.

The role of the teacher in the differentiated classroom is no doubt complex. Facilitating collaborative learning means managing tasks and progress through whole class, team, and at times individual instruction. It means setting broad and challenging goals for the class and allowing learners to self-select their groupings based on common interests, goals and levels of readiness. It may be a natural part of the selection process that learners self-select into proficiency groups, based on their perception of the demands of the task. However, there will be times where interest in the task, the content, the type of format for producing a response, will stimulate learners to work across proficiency level groups, enhancing the prospect of collaborative learning and respect between groups. Contributions may differ, teacher monitoring of group dynamics and needs may be greater, but opportunities are maximised for collaborative and increasingly autonomous learning that are ultimately beneficial to those involved.

Over a unit of work teacher control and input would vary considerably. Initially, the class is largely teacher-directed, as the teacher leads discussion on a new topic, raising issues and identifying broad concepts that encourage learners to identify current understandings and knowledge gaps they would like to explore, building a sense of community towards exploring the topic in more detail, and directing learners towards possible research activities and forms of knowledge production. Two key questions can drive this class discussion:

- What do we want to find out, to know, to explore, to share about the topic?
- How can we collaborate to bring this new knowledge together to share with each other?

The class can now engage in task selection, coming together in common interest or skill groups to begin planning likely approaches to the selected task, advising the teacher on their understandings of their roles and their resources, and seeking advice and support on best ways forward. A degree of direct instruction is required for second language learners: identifying important vocabulary sets and grammatical forms that will be encountered or required as they explore new knowledge—information useful to heritage learners who can benefit from and contribute to building second language learners' understanding of new language.

Groups can then begin their task, accessing and working through texts to identify new information required for their task, with the teacher monitoring progress and contributions, regularly drawing second language learners together to clarify their understandings and challenges, and strengthening their knowledge of new language forms and content areas. Much of this reflection and analysis may occur in English to ensure deeper conceptual understanding and clarity. Heritage learners also require monitoring, but discussion with them can occur in Chinese and formulations of new learning checked for accuracy of information, and appropriateness of language addressed as it is expressed. Collaborative teamwork will continue with regular whole of class time used to share progress and ideas, and to clarify processes and expectations. The unit reaches its goals with group presentations of information in their preferred modes of delivery, leading to class discussions on new information and insights gained. The unit concludes with individual submissions as written reflections and one-on-one interviews with the teacher to reflect on achievements and assess individual progress, as a second language or heritage learner.

## A Sample Unit

A sample unit of work on the topic 'School life or routines in diverse communities' is provided in the following text as an example of the process described earlier.

### Selecting Content Relevant for All Learners

Concepts to be covered may include understandings of curriculum (subjects taught at different year levels) and the education of the whole learner (academic, physical, moral, civics education); community expectations and pressures, and opportunities provided to learners; the place of languages in curriculum; school structures and routines; as well as any other concepts raised in discussion, such as gender equality in education, extra-curricular activities available; boarding school life, etc., as appropriate to learners' interests and experiences. These concepts can be explored in both the local and the target language community, and may include information on education in other societies where learners have an interest or experience in such places.

The overall goal of the unit, in terms of content knowledge, language to be learned, and tasks to be completed are to access and process information in Chinese, and English where necessary, on education in diverse societies, on learners' experiences in such societies, and to report their findings and reflections back to the class at the conclusion of the unit. The communication objectives may include to obtain, interpret and present facts about an aspect of education in specific locations, including to translate some exemplar materials from Chinese or into Chinese to include in their task portfolio, and reflecting on challenges faced and differences apparent in translation of the text. The key domains of use are information interpretation and exchange, obtaining and sharing new knowledge and ideas through presentational modes of delivery (in speech, writing or audio-visual modes), and involving classroom interaction as ideas are explored in teacher-led discussion.

New language learning required, especially for second language learners, would include vocabulary related to curriculum (subjects), and school structures, and to activities associated with school life. Grammar required would include a focus on time and duration, on descriptive phrases related to student experience, and relative comparisons of experiences across countries and cultures. Text genres that would be encountered and need analysis may include timetables, descriptive statements (of school curriculum), personal narratives (of school experience), and comparative reports. Cultural concepts that may be raised include traditional and contemporary perspectives on the role of education in society, including the value placed on physical and moral and civics education across cultures.

The culminating range of tasks (which students may select to present) may include (at lower levels of proficiency) a simple personal narrative on 'my school day', and a factual report on a typical school day in China, with some comparison and reflection; and at higher levels of linguistic and content complexity, an account of curriculum content and timetable in two comparable school sites (such as in China and locally); and finally, a detailed report in Chinese and in English documenting specific features of school life and routine in a specific school site in China. Each of these tasks should require some verbal or visual presentation to the class (delivered in a manner comprehensible to second language learners with visual/textual supports), and some form of documentary report to the teacher reflecting the learner's advances in knowledge of abilities to communicate that in written Chinese.

## *Process*

In terms of process, the unit would begin with a class discussion on knowledge and experience of school education in diverse settings, drawing learners' attention to vocabulary already encountered that relates to the new topic (e.g. time, subjects, qualitative terms related to impressions, experiences). This exploration can become an opportunity for translanguaging, as more and more words in Chinese replace familiar words in English, with teacher questioning moving increasingly from English to Chinese. Heritage learners can also begin representing factual knowledge familiar to second language learners in Chinese in order to familiarise them with ways of expressing ideas effectively, and assisting in building a list of relevant words to be used in the upcoming activity. The primary goal of the introductory activity is to establish a common understanding of key concepts related to education and to identify knowledge gaps and areas of interest to explore further through research.

The next phase is to encourage student collaboration, refining some research areas and research questions (related to the intended task set) and identifying classmates interested and capable of leadership of groups to undertake selected research tasks. Class discussion can help clarify and confirm research areas, key questions for consideration, and likely formats for presentation. Students can then be invited to select a research area and task and join a team based on shared interests, relevant skills and common goals. Clearly, some negotiation and reorganisation will be necessary to ensure the size of groups is manageable and intentions and expectations well understood.

Teams may then begin their initial investigations, accessing information from sources, including those made available by the teacher, and planning their process of research and text creation towards their class presentation. The class can reconvene regularly to hear from groups and clarify questions of content, process and expectations. As second language learners become increasingly aware of their limitations, some teaching time will be dedicated to direct instruction, and activity to reinforce knowledge of new linguistic structures applied to the developing vocabulary set required for their task. Heritage learners on more advanced tasks may work independently during such instruction time, while heritage learners with lower skills sets can productively participate in targeted learning activity alongside their second language peers. As the unit progresses, class time is increasingly team work related, with the teacher monitoring and participating in evaluating data gathered and the process of drafting the final product, teaching to the challenges identified, and providing additional individual support to those struggling to keep up with team work, even perhaps renegotiating the role or responsibility of individuals to suit their particular skills set. Incidental reconvening of the class may be required to maintain focus and allow for cross fertilisation of ideas between teams as they refine their final products.

Finally, a significant amount of class time is dedicated to class presentations, beginning at the lower end of proficiency in presentations, allowing the second language learners to display their newly acquired knowledge and skills in highly structured and scaffolded orientations with a focus on feedback about accuracy and appropriateness of language used as a means of using the task itself to further inform their learning. Once over the pressure of presentation, the second language learners can then listen to presentations delivered by more proficient peers, providing more detailed or more complex information with a focus on delivery that is largely comprehensible in language and pace for their classmate audience. These presentations also require analysis of language accuracy and appropriateness, but more attention can also be paid to new insights and interpretations contained within them to stimulate further class discussion and learning.

Once all presentations are completed, the students can focus on compiling a folio of work undertaken for individual assessment, and the teacher can undertake one-on-one discussions to reflect on contributions and growth in knowledge and ideas with individual members of the class. Folios submitted would include samples of written work in Chinese and reflections, in English or Chinese as appropriate, about what has been learned about language, culture, and societies on the topic of education, and the learner's personal reflection on the experience of working in groups on the task selected.

## Conclusion

The skills to manage the dynamics of group work, of pushing learners towards more autonomous work in learning and using language for their own communicative purposes, of managing multiple teams at one time, of instructing second language learners and allowing heritage learners more autonomy, are challenges that require much time and experience to develop. However, the only way forward for successful and appropriate instruction in the multilevel classroom is an inclusive model of differentiation. Such a model is necessarily organic and responsive, and evolves from the dynamics of the specific class group and their degree of commitment to understanding each other and working together and to making the classroom a better more productive environment for all learners. It requires skills in planning and resourcing, and in team building, to understand how to reach each student where they are at in their learning, motivation and interest, and in their readiness to move on and improve their knowledge and skills in Chinese.

The aim of a differentiated classroom is to treat heritage learners differently, but not separately; to look beyond issues of proficiency and to address issues of identity, aspiration and motivation; to provide them with the challenges they seek, the leadership roles and responsibilities they can undertake, and the opportunities to perform at their best. Teachers must not lose sight of the fact that second language learners and heritage learners are in the same room, and both groups of learners need to learn to understand the others' needs and aspirations. Creating a dynamic community of practice involving both second language and heritage learners is essential for positive learning experiences to occur.

# Appendix

Exemplar of a Chinese Curriculum Scope of Learning for a Long-Term Introductory Unit (Middle School Focussed)

| | Key content areas | Key concepts | Key inquiry questions | Key interactions and classroom experiences |
|---|---|---|---|---|
| Explanation of each column and row | A structure to focus on the specific challenges of learning speech and writing, the system of grammar, and contemporary cultural practices which impact on communication in Chinese | Broader concepts to be explored within the content areas in the module | Holistic and recurring (**sample**) questions related to the key concepts which engage learners in meaningful intercultural enquiry | Activities to engage students with Chinese language and culture, directed towards building opportunities to discuss key concepts as they engage with key content areas |
| **Topic**<br>– Represents the key content focus for the module (including comparisons across cultures/societies) | E.g. **Self and family**, school life, my community, an active and healthy lifestyle, keeping a budget (incomes and expenses), contemporary trends in youth culture | **E.g. Self and family ;**<br>– Key family relationships<br>– Key personal data; naming practices, age and date of birth, ethnicity/nationality, gender terms | – How do we create a family tree? How do we refer to members of our family?<br>– What personal information would you like to share with others? When and where do you share personal information? | – Discuss how family and personal information is presented in English and compare how these ideas are expressed in Chinese (with a focus on word order).<br>– Participate in classroom exchanges to share basic personal data |
| **Language Concepts**<br>– specific language structures and features to be introduced | Language structures and word order (across languages), **e.g. key verb structures,** questioning, nouns, personal and possessive pronouns, adjective phrases (with adverbs of degree), numbers and measure words, prepositional phrases etc. | **Key verb structures**<br>– Verb types; verbs of identification, existence<br>– Verbs used in talking about identity; naming, residence<br>– Verbs of action<br>– Verbs of emotion | – How do we use the verb 'to be' (am/is/are), and state the existence of something (there is/are) in English?<br>– What verbs do we use to describe self and family? | – Observe/listen to Chinese conversations in which the verbs 是 and 有 are used and explain how these ideas are expressed in English and Chinese |

(Continued)

(Continued)

| | Key content areas | Key concepts | Key inquiry questions | Key interactions and classroom experiences |
|---|---|---|---|---|
| **Language Concepts** | Language structures and word order (across languages), **e.g. questioning** | **Questioning**<br>Word order<br>– for yes/no questions,<br>– when using question words (interrogative pronouns)<br>Ways of replying yes and no in Chinese. | – How do we make questions in English and Chinese? (How does word order change when compared to statements?) | – Make a list of questions in English and determine different question types and word order in English<br>– Translate Chinese questions into English (using pinyin vocab lists) and compare the word order between the two<br>– Identify patterns (rules of word order) noticed in asking questions in Chinese |
| **Spoken Chinese**<br>– Specific knowledge and skills related to areas of phonology, speech patterns and oral interaction | – Features of speech, tone, pitch and stress<br>– The Pinyin Romanisation system<br>– The Chinese tone system<br>– Letter values and syllable pronunciation across languages | – Identifying rhythm in short flows of speech<br>– Identifying tones in single syllables and in phrase level speech<br>– Reproducing rhythms, tonal syllables and phrases<br>– Letter sound-values in Pinyin<br>– Mapping sounds to syllables in Pinyin<br>– Comparing spelling and speech in diverse languages | – How do the sounds of syllables vary between English and Chinese?<br>– What is 'tone'? How does it differ from pitch and stress in spoken language?<br>– How do letter-sound values vary across languages (e.g. English & Chinese) | – Participate in shared 'listen and repeat' activities<br>– Learn and recite short rhymes and poems<br>– Learn to understand and use common spoken classroom expressions, including courtesy phrases<br>– Read aloud Pinyin texts with attention to pronunciation, tone and phrasing<br>– Engage in brief dictation exercises to check ability to encode/record spoken sounds into Pinyin<br>– Identify and compare familiar syllables in English with different pronunciation in Chinese (e.g. can, pie, sun, ran, tie etc.) |
| **Spoken Chinese** | – Engaging in dialogues to exchange personal information<br>– Asking key questions and follow-up questions<br>– Sharing personal information | – Features of interpersonal exchanges (greeting, bidding farewell)<br>– Ways of showing interest/concern for others<br>– Asking appropriate questions | – How we greet familiar and unfamiliar people across cultures<br>– What are features of politeness when greeting others, making new friends?<br>– What are polite ways of greeting and farewelling/taking leave of people? | – Observing brief conversations between native speakers and identifying ways of greeting, showing interest in others, sharing information, and leave taking<br>– Participating in classroom interactions sharing personal information in response to questions<br>– Comparing ways people socialise and make friends across cultures |

| | | | | |
|---|---|---|---|---|
| *Written Language* — specific knowledge and skills related to areas of orthography addressed in order to engage in reading and writing | – Stroke types, graphemes (letters or components), across languages<br>– Basic writing skills<br>– Features of words across languages | – Diverse writing systems (Roman alphabet, Chinese characters, other familiar systems)<br>– Basic writing skills (stroke types, stroke order and direction)<br>– Word forming across languages (letter strings in English, component sequences in Chinese) | – What writing systems can you read? How do they differ? What do you know about Chinese writing?<br>– How do we learn to read and write? What role does writing practice play in becoming literate? What strokes are used to make letters in English? What strokes are used to make characters?<br>– What are characters composed of? What are components? How are they related? How many are there? | – Compare samples of writing across languages<br>– Identify strokes and stroke sequences in letters, and stoke types and sequences in basic Chinese characters<br>– Identify the number and arrangement of components of compound characters<br>– Explore components in related sets (by stroke type, by meaning etc.) and identify rules for writing and links between component form and meaning |
| *Written Language* | – Generating texts using digital media | – Ways of typing or generating digital text in Chinese (Pinyin input methods and character selection)<br>– Evaluating digital translation tools | – How do we type in Chinese? What skills do we need in creating digital character texts?<br>– How effective are digital translation tools? What issues in translation can you see? | – Generate short messages on line—use character lists and online dictionaries to assist in selection of characters to generate accurate texts<br>– Translate texts to/from Chinese using online translation tools, identify areas of difficulty in creating accurate translations this way |
| *Written Language* | – Features of written texts in Chinese, e.g. public signs, posters, personal ID cards | – Word direction and spacing<br>– Features of familiar text genres (signs, notices) | – How are written texts organised in Chinese? Can you see words in the text?<br>– What skills do we need to read signs and notices in Chinese? | – Translate short signs from Chinese character by character and attempt to build word meanings and text meanings<br>– Complete a personal profile in Chinese using word lists. Discuss any differences noticed between spoken and written Chinese sentence patterns |

*(Continued)*

| | Key content areas | Key concepts | Key inquiry questions | Key interactions and classroom experiences |
|---|---|---|---|---|
| **The Role of Culture in Communicating** *Language-related and broader cultural concepts related to how language is used in specific contexts* | Cultural concepts: <br>– being polite <br>– showing respect <br>– showing degrees of relationship <br>– basic beliefs and values <br>– festivals and celebrations | – Politeness, formality, humility, humour, <br>– Importance of family, respect for elder generations <br>– The cycle of the seasons and its relationship to festival and celebrations | – How does our language change when speaking with someone older, or who we don't know? <br>– When do we need to be polite, how is this reflected in language? <br>– How is respect for elders reflected in language we use? <br>– What are important celebrations in our local culture? Why do we celebrate these events at this time? | – Discuss how people in diverse cultures interact with each other. What features of polite speech and behaviour do we have in common? <br>– View interactions between people in Chinese contexts, discuss how age, position, familiarity influence interactions <br>– Discuss situations in which formal language is expected and how this is reflected in language use <br>– Explore prior knowledge of festivals and culturally significant occasions across cultures and identify commonalities and differences in important events |
| **Key Communication Tasks** *– undertaken as students build knowledge and skills related to language and culture* | Task One—engage in conversation with teacher and peers (including sister school classmates, if possible) to exchange personal information (name, age, date of birth, place of residence, nationality, languages, year level, etc. <br>Task Two—construct a family tree in Chinese (Pinyin and characters) and use the tree to share information about family with others <br>Task Three—complete a personal identity card (in print/online) and describe information on the card orally with others <br>Task Four—maintain a journal of thoughts and reflections on experiences learning Chinese language and culture and how Chinese cultural practices in communication appear to compare to one's own communication experiences in English/other languages | | | |

# References

Ashton, K. (2017) 'Approaches to Teaching in the Multi-level Language Classroom', *Innovation in Language Learning and Teaching*: 1–16. doi:10.1080/17501229.2017.1397158

Australian Curriculum and Assessment and Reporting Authority (ACARA). (2014) *Australian Curriculum: Languages*. Retrieved 14 September 2018 from www.australiancurriculum.edu.au/f-10-curriculum/languages/rationale/

Bernstein, S., Burke, K., Favre, L., and Delcourt, J.P. (2010) 'Recognizing the Needs and Talents of the Heritage Language Learner', *Educator's Voice*, iii: 66–73.

Carreira, M. (2016) *Principles and Strategies for Teaching HL Learners*. Heritage Spanish Workshop: Adapting and Creating Activities for Heritage Learners of Spanish, June 10–11, 2016, COERLL: National Heritage Language Resource Center, UCLA.

Carreira, M. and Kagan, O. (2011) 'The Results of the National Heritage Language Survey: Implications for Teaching, Curriculum Design, and Professional Development', *Foreign Language Annals*, 44(1): 40–64.

Comanaru, R. and Noels, K.A. (2009) 'Self-determination, Motivation, and the Learning of Chinese as a Heritage Language', *The Canadian Modern Language Review*, 66(1): 131–158.

Elder, C., Kim, H., and Knoch, U. (2012) 'Documenting the Diversity of Learner Achievements in Asian Languages Using Common Measures', *Australian Review of Applied Linguistics*, 35(3): 251–270.

García, O. (2009) *Bilingual Education in the 21st Century: A Global Perspective*. Malden: Wiley-Blackwell.

Gil, J. (2017) 'Confucius Institutes and Classrooms Can Make the Grade—A Primer', *Asia Times*, April 4. Retrieved from www.atimes.com/harmonious-confucius-institutes-classrooms/

He, A.W. (2006) 'Toward an Identity Theory of the Development of Chinese as a Heritage Language', *Heritage Language Journal*, 4(1): 1–28.

He, A.W. (2008) 'An Identity-based Model for the Development of Chinese as a Heritage Language', in A.W. He and Y. Xiao (eds.), *Chinese as a Heritage Language: Fostering Rooted World Citizenry*, 109–124. Hawaii: National Foreign Language Resource Centre.

He, A.W. (2010) 'The Heart of Heritage: Sociocultural Dimensions of Heritage Language Learning', *Annual Review of Applied Linguistics*, 30: 66–82.

He, A.W. (2013) 'The Wor(l)d Is a Collage: Multi-performance by Chinese Heritage Language Speakers', *The Modern Language Journal*, 97: 304–317.

He, A.W. and Xiao, Y. (eds.). (2008) *Chinese as a Heritage Language: Fostering Rooted World Citizenry*. Honolulu: National Foreign Language Resource Center, University of Hawai'i at Mānoa.

Hendryx, J.D. (2008) 'The Chinese Heritage Learners' Existing Linguistic Knowledge and Abilities', in A.W. He and Y. Xiao (eds.), *Chinese as a Heritage Language: Fostering Rooted World Citizenry*, 53–66. Hawaii: National Foreign Language Resource Centre, University of Hawai'i at Mānoa.

Li, Wei (2011) 'Moment Analysis and Translanguaging Space: Discursive Construction of Identities by Multilingual Chinese Youth in Britain', *Journal of Pragmatics*, 43(5): 1222–1235.

Lu, X. and Li, G. (2008) 'Motivation and Achievement in Chinese Language Learning', in A.W. He and Y. Xiao (eds.), *Chinese as a Heritage Language: Fostering Rooted World Citizenry*, 89–108. Honolulu: National Foreign Language Resource Center, University of Hawai'i at Mānoa.

MLA AdHoc Committee on Foreign Languages. (2007) 'Foreign Languages and Higher Education: New Structures for a Changed World', *Profession*, 2007: 234–245.

O'Rourke, P. and Zhou, Q. (2016) 'Heritage and Second Language Learners: Different Perspectives on Language Learning', *International Journal of Bilingual Education and Bilingualism*. doi:10.1080/13670050.2016.1228598

Orton, J. (2008) *Chinese Language Education in Australian Schools*. Melbourne: The University of Melbourne.

Orton, J. (2016) *Building Chinese Language Capacity in Australia*. Sydney: Australia China Research Institute.

Scarino, A., Elder, C., Kim, S.H., Iwashita, N., Kohler, M., and Scrimgeour, A. (2011) *Student Achievement in Asian Languages*. Report to the Australian Government, Dept of Employment, Education & Workplace Relations, Canberra.

Scrimgeour, A. (2012) 'Understanding the Nature of Performance: The Influence of Learner Background on School-age Learner Achievement in Chinese', *Australian Review of Applied Linguistics*, 35(3): 312–338.

Scrimgeour, A. (2015) 'Responding to the Diversity of Chinese Language Learners in Australian Schools', *Babel*, 49(3): 26–37.

Scrimgeour, A., Foster, M., and Mao, W.F. (2013) 'Dealing With Distinctiveness: The Development of Chinese in the Australian Curriculum: Languages', *Babel*, 2(3): 20–30.

Tomlinson, C.A. (2017) *How to Differentiate Instruction in Academically Diverse Classrooms*. 3rd edition. Alexandria: ASCD.

Valdés, G. (2000) 'Teaching Heritage Languages: An Introduction for Slavic-language-teaching Professionals', in O. Kagan and B. Rifkin (eds.), *The Learning and Teaching of Slavic Languages and Cultures*, 375–403. Bloomington: Slavica.

Valdés, G. (2001) 'Heritage Language Students: Profiles and Possibilities', in J.K. Peyton and S. McGinnis (eds.), *Heritage Languages in America: Blueprint for the Future*, 37–77. Washington, DC: Center for Applied Linguistics and Delta Systems.

Weger-Guntharp, H. (2006) 'Voices From the Margin: Developing a Profile of Chinese Heritage Language Learners in the FL Classroom', *Heritage Language Journal*, 4(1): 29–46.

Wen, X. (2011) 'Chinese Language Learning Motivation: A Comparative Study of Heritage and Non-heritage Learners', *Heritage Language Journal*, 8(3): 41–66.

Wu, S.M. (2008) 'Robust Learning for Chinese Heritage Learners: Motivation, Linguistics and Technology', in K. Kondo-Brown and J.D. Brown (eds.), *Teaching Chinese, Japanese, and Korean Heritage Language Students: Curriculum Needs, Materials and Assessment*, 271–297. New York: Lawrence Erlbaum Associates.

Xiang, X. (2016) 'The Teaching of Chinese to Heritage Language Learners at the Post-secondary Level', in J. Ruan, J. Zhang, and C. Leung (eds.), *Chinese Language Education in the United States*. Multilingual Education, 14, Cham: Springer.

Xiao, Y. (2010) 'Discourse Features and Development in L2 Writing of Chinese', in M. Everson and H. Shen (eds.), *Research Among Learners of Chinese as a Foreign Language*, 135–153. Honolulu: University of Hawaii Press.

Zhu, B. (2016) *Teaching Chinese as a Heritage Language in an English-dominant Society*. Thesis Submitted in Partial Fulfillment of the Requirements for the Degree of Master of Education, University of Victoria, Canada. Retrieved 24 September 2018 from https://dspace.library.uvic.ca/bitstream/handle/1828/7300/Zhu_Bingxin_MEd_2016.pdf;sequence=2

# 7

# INTEGRATING CULTURE

## Introduction

Entering any Chinese language classroom, parents and students are often struck by the 'culture—rich' environment, with lanterns hanging from the ceiling, paper-cuts on windows, posters of Chinese scenic sites, children's calligraphy, delicate kites, and so on adorning the walls. All of these visual resources enrich the environment for learning and provide ample evidence of the distinctiveness of Chinese culture and its differences from learners' own cultural life worlds. However, when culture is discussed in the context of contemporary language learning, the focus is more often related to the less tangible or more invisible aspects of culture, the values and beliefs of the community that influence how they communicate, and how these messages are understood by other members of the community. The Australian Curriculum: Languages (ACARA, 2014), for example, defines culture as 'the framework in which things come to be seen as having meaning', and involves 'understandings of the norms and expectations which shape perspectives and attitudes' of a community. In Canada, the British Columbia Curriculum (2017) declares language to be 'inextricably bound to culture, as authentic communication always takes place in a cultural context'. Thus 'culture learning acts as a vehicle for the acquisition of a deeper under-standing of a language, of others and of ourselves'. In the USA, the National Standards in Foreign Language Education Project (NSFLEP) (2015) maintains that students cannot truly master a language until they have also mastered the cultural context in which the language occurs. Within the US National Stan-dards (NSFLEP, 2015), the inclusion of a Cultures goal aims to reinforce the idea that 'language and culture are connected so deeply that neither one can really be taught or learned in isolation from the other. Language exists in a cultural context, so cultural knowledge is an integral part of language proficiency' (61).

The concept of culture in the context of language learning has been debated in great detail over the past two decades. The work of Kramsch (1993) in the USA, Byram (1997, 2006, 2015) in Europe, Liddicoat and Crozet (1997, 2002), Liddicoat (1999), Lo Bianco, Liddicoat, and Crozet (1999), Liddicoat, Papademetre, Scarino, and Kohler (2003), and Liddicoat and Scarino (2013) in Australia, among others, have improved teachers' understandings of the relationships between language and culture, and the role of culture in language learning and use. Together they reinforce the contemporary view of culture as an integral part of a language, and equally that the classroom experience is essentially a process of 'learning the language of a culture' (Kramsch, 1993), as the language allows for learners to access the natural, normal space of a culture, and to have direct experience with a culture or way of life of a community, 'offering learners an engagement with difference that is best experienced through language' (Crozet and Liddicoat, 1999). So, the integral nature of the relationship between language and culture implies one cannot exist without the other, and as a result cannot be taught in isolation from each other. The common view today is that culture learning is necessary to understand the social context for communicating with native speakers, and thus to be able to use the language appropriately and effectively in such situations. Byram (2006: 91) argues culture learning is also important because it facilitates the development of positive attitudes towards the language and its speakers, the development of empathy, and the ability to see the world through the eyes of a native speaker, and therefore to gain acceptance into their world. The Australian Curriculum: Languages (ACARA, 2014) argues that the rationale for language learning in schools should extend beyond acquiring communication skills in the language to include the development of an intercultural capability, and an understanding of the role of language and culture in communication, as well as a capability for reflection on language use and language learning. With so much emphasis on culture as an integral part of language, of the importance of language learners exploring and experiencing alternative ways of viewing the world in order to become effective communicators, understanding how culture should be represented and integrated within the Chinese language curriculum needs to be explored in more detail.

## Representations of Culture in Language Learning

The representations of culture commonly found in second language textbooks and in classroom teaching practice typically vary in relation to the extent to which culture and language are integrated into teaching practice. The spectrum of cultural representations extends from culture as facts about the country to culture's relationship to daily life, and to ways in which language conveys the cultural values and beliefs that underpin effective communication in context.

In language classrooms, teachers typically wish to share with their students facts about the nation(s) in which the language is used, such as geography, main cities or regions, population, ethnicities, and perhaps some information about the political system or economy of the country, or 'informational culture'. Such country-specific studies are often enriched with interesting facts about the nation's 'achievement culture', key events in the historical and cultural development of the nation, including notable figures, inventions, cultural landmarks of historic importance, the key institutions of government, and famous works of literature, music, art, and so on. This achievement culture is often associated with the notion of 'Big-C, or high culture' (Halverson, 1985) in which the achievements and products of the nation over time are presented as evidence of the quality and exoticism of the culture, likely to attract learner's interest in the target country and enhancing the appeal of learning the language as a result. These aspects of cultural content are also often viewed as an essential adjunct to language learning as they provide learners with a better appreciation of the traditions of the society in which the language is used today.

Another aspect of culture seen in language classrooms are representations of 'daily life culture', often referred to as 'Little-C, or low culture' in which the everyday routines and social practices in contemporary society are explored. This is often represented in textbooks as 'topical culture': interesting information about daily life associated with the current topic of study in the textbook, such as, for example, clothing, shopping, education, sport and leisure. These topical studies also open up opportunities for introducing colourful customs and traditions associated with everyday life such as dietary habits, famous foods or regional cuisine, as well as community and family activities associated with festivals and celebrations. Topical studies may also find a way to introduce aspects of folk culture, the arts and crafts, music, song and dance often associated with regions or ethnic minorities within the nation, all of which add to the richness and exoticism of cultural studies. Little association with language learning and communication practices is usually evident in this view of culture, beyond the vocabulary associated with objects and activities discussed in that topical context. These representations of culture, while often reflecting some of the diversity within the target language community overall, tend to reflect a static view of culture (Liddicoat, 2002), steeped in tradition and largely unchanging, bound by national boundaries, with culture essentially represented as facts, declarative knowledge delivered by the teacher to be accepted and in a sense, celebrated by the learners.

A more contemporary view of culture associated with communicative language teaching is the study of culture as societal norms and patterns of behaviour in the context of communication. While focussing on language in context, learners are typically taught how to behave when communicating in the language; culture is present, but it remains unanalysed and stereotypical, with learners advised to practise and replicate native speaker models of practices, behaviours and certain culture-bound phrases in order to be effective and 'appropriate' in communicating with others. Culture learning in this instance is more about gaining knowledge of how to act than knowledge of what is valued. The knowledge is learned within a particular topic or situation and learners are seldom asked to apply this knowledge in new contexts. This kind of cultural knowledge thus seldom becomes generalisable, transferable and generative in building learners' understanding of broader principles and rules of interaction in a wider range of contexts.

This orientation towards otherness tends to represent culture as a distinct entity and body of knowledge based largely on generalisations and somewhat stereotypical representations of the target language community and its cultural products and practices to which is applied a binary 'us and them' comparison. Overall, as Kearney (2015) explains, these approaches to culture in the language classroom tend to reinforce dominant cultural and societal norms, constructing a sense of foreignness and celebrating difference between the target culture and the learners' own culture. Distance is both celebrated and maintained. There is seldom space to explore why this might be or analyse how 'they' might see 'us'. Comparisons tends to be superficial and learners' own cultural, communicative practices remain unanalysed; their task is to adapt or adjust to native speaker norms, in order to be 'appropriate' from a native speaker perspective. The outcomes for learners are limited to performing otherness, not necessarily understanding otherness, or themselves, any better as a result of their learning. Learners seldom learn about their own cultural values and beliefs beyond some superficial discussion of the contrasts, the key identifiable differences between themselves and the other on broad national terms: what it means to be, for example 'American' compared to what it means to be 'Chinese'. What is most striking in these constructions of culture and the associated teaching practices is the absence of attention to learners' own linguistic and cultural background and identities and how the experience of second language learning impacts on their sense of self as a communicator.

These orientations towards culture in language learning have been criticised on a number of fronts. Kramsch (1993) was critical of the manner in which it prioritised the monolingual native speaker as the norm for communicative behaviour expected of second language learners. Byram (1997) described it as an assimilationist model, in which cultural knowledge as native speaker standards of behaviour is presented prescriptively in order to be practised and performed by learners in specific communicative contexts. Kearney (2015: 9) describes this as a monolingual ideology towards culture learning with its focus on dominant societal and cultural norms, which essentialises the target culture and maintains distance, leaving the divide intact (Carr, 1999: 103) between the learner and the target language community.

## Intercultural Approaches to Teaching and Learning Culture

In the last two decades an intercultural orientation to language and culture learning has attempted to redefine the relationship between language and culture, and reconceptualise the nature of culture in language learning and use. Liddicoat and

Scarino (2013) describe culture as a shared set of cultural practices and meanings associated with language use, the cultural frame or lens which allows people to create and interpret meanings and make collective sense of their experience. Culture is described as a toolkit of symbols, stories, rituals and worldviews used to solve different kinds of social problems. They argue that in second language learning teachers need to take a broader view of culture 'directly centred on the lived experience of people'. This '21st century view of culture' (Chan, Bhatt, Nagami, and Walker, 2015: 5) represents a shift from what culture *is* to what culture *does*, with culture viewed as an active process of meaning making, as an interactive and interpretive tool for being and becoming within a society or group. Language is thus central to cultural expression, as it is through language and social interaction that relationships are built, tasks are accomplished, values and beliefs are expressed and shared amongst members of a community.

This view of culture as an active and dynamic process of meaning making, reflecting the knowledge people have about their world, has created a new discussion as to how culture is represented, interpreted and applied in second language classrooms. Culture is no longer viewed just as static, knowledge-based, as a fixed, stable set of facts and behaviours which apply across a society and across time and space, for learners to learn and apply, replicating native speaker communication practices. Culture in language learning is now understood as an invisible, symbolic system of shared understandings, enacted by individuals though language in their own social contexts. This representation of culture as enacted by individuals in their own social spaces highlights the notion that culture is dynamic, complex, and contradictory, and importantly open to interpretation. There can be no single representation or interpretation of what culture is, but there does remain a set of shared understandings of how roles and relationships should be enacted, and shared knowledge of the anticipated meanings of words and actions used in certain contexts to which teachers need to draw learners' attention. Overall, while contemporary views bring language and culture closer together, the task of culture teaching does in many ways become more challenging.

Introducing second language learners to a generalised set of national cultural characteristics or native speaker norms of behaviour continues to remain an important focus of classroom practice, but teaching learners to replicate native speaker norms is no longer a primary goal of culture learning. As non-native, second language learners, with their own cultural mindsets and expectations, learning the language and culture of a different society is necessarily intercultural in nature (Liddicoat and Scarino, 2013). It necessarily involves the interaction of two language systems and two cultural codes. From a contemporary, intercultural perspective, the second language classroom should be a site for not only engaging in alternative understandings of the world but also deepening learners' understanding of themselves as cultural beings and as communicators across cultures as a natural outcome of this process of engagement. Liddicoat, Papademetre, Scarino, and Kohler (2003) argue that a cornerstone of Intercultural

Language Learning is developing in learners the ability to recognise and reflect on their own (first language and culture) practices and perspectives as a foundation for explicit and systematic comparison between their own culture(s) and the culture of the target language. The aim of such an intercultural approach to language learning is not mastery of native speaker norms and expectations but rather, as Chan, Bhatt, Nagami, and Walker (2015) suggests, the development of learners as intercultural speakers, social actors in their own right, interacting in a way different to native speakers, but aware of the effect of their actions. Kearney (2015) emphasises the importance of developing learner's sense of self as a cultural being, aware of their own first language meaning making resources and recognising the target language meaning making resources available for their own communicative activities when engaging with native speakers of the target language. Developing intercultural understanding in learners thus represents a process of learning to move between diverse language and culture systems, and developing their own functional multilingualism (Scarino, 2014). Second language learning should be about learning to understand target language/native speaker practices, of realising the expectations of target language speakers, but also giving learners the skills and understandings to realise the implications of their own choices about how to interact, and how to interpret the meanings and intentions of others in intercultural exchanges with others.

Overall, an intercultural orientation brings a shift in focus from a traditional emphasis on simply knowledge of the target culture and society to a focus also on the skills and processes of intercultural exploration and appreciating the role cultural values and beliefs play in the exchange of meanings. Developing intercultural understanding through language learning is recognised as a key skill for the 21st century (Kearney, 2015), as it equips learners with the ability to interpret and create meaning across cultures, with a preparedness to interact with others and exercise some personal agency in using the target language to interact and exchange meanings. For teachers, this creates a different perspective on their relationship with learners, on the two languages and cultures present, and on how they engage learners in thinking about language, culture and their relationship. The challenge for teachers in the classroom is learning to understand their role not only as a model and provider of cultural knowledge and experience, but as a mediator and guide in the process of intercultural exploration (Moeller and Osborn, 2014); and of knowing when and how to draw on their knowledge and experience as they engage learners in discussion about culture in language use.

Knowledge of norms and expectations is still necessary for learners as they begin the process of learning how to 'fit in', or accommodate native speaker expectations when interacting with members of the target culture group. However, teachers need to learn when and how to subordinate presentations of their superior knowledge in order to create an intercultural space in which learners themselves can learn to identify and understand the general set of expectations representing the underlying values and beliefs that come into play when interacting within the target culture. The classroom is the safe and secure setting in which learners can begin to negotiate their way through such difference as they learn to communicate. In this sense teachers and learners need to become co-inquirers into two sets of cultural values, their own and those of the target language community. They learn to negotiate their way through their own diverse interpretations of target language texts and explore interactions between and with native speakers, collaboratively building the knowledge and skills to engage in personal and successful intercultural encounters with otherness.

## *Implications*

So, what are the implications for teachers of an enhanced intercultural orientation to learning in the Chinese second language classroom? Firstly, learners need more engagement with authentic examples of language and cultural input as a stimulus to intercultural enquiry. Secondly, and importantly, that teachers need to develop skills in providing learners with the relevant prompts to stimulate discussion, to elicit and develop learners' understanding of otherness and their own linguistic and cultural identity by comparison. Thirdly, learners need opportunities to reinforce their developing understandings of other ways of thinking and communicating in intercultural exchanges. And, finally, learners need opportunities to reflect on and to discuss how their experience with otherness is building their own sense of self as an effective intercultural communicator with members of the Chinese community.

## Teaching Culture in the CSL Classroom

Facilitating an intercultural approach to teaching culture in the Chinese second language classroom can be a challenge for teachers. Traditional practices which address Chinese culture separately to language, which view Chinese culture largely in terms of knowledge of the country (specifically the Peoples Republic of China) and its people, their traditions and their everyday lives in contemporary times, remain a common practice in many classrooms, evidenced by the visual aids commonly seen in schools, which focus on handicrafts, festivals, famous sites, and traditions, especially Spring Festival.

The reasons for this may appear obvious enough. Young, novice learners typically have little knowledge of the country or countries in which the Chinese language is used. While teaching Chinese geography, history, and social studies may not be the main role of the language teacher, teachers themselves see the need to provide some broad general knowledge of the society from which they come, or in which the Chinese language is used. Reinforcing this argument is the common expectation that discussing culture is complex, and an element of teaching which, while important, is beyond the second language capabilities of the learners, and which needs therefore to be presented in English. The result is a tacit acceptance of the separation of Chinese language from Chinese culture and a representation of culture that while valued and interesting, is limited in terms of its impact on learners' communicative abilities in Chinese.

Over the past two decades however, as Chinese language learning has become increasingly popular in schools, colleges and universities, a range of resources to assist teachers to understand relevant Chinese second language curriculum constructs, the place of culture within the curriculum, and recommendations for classroom practices, have been published. In the section which follows the representations of culture in some of the more prominent publications on teaching Chinese in foreign, second language contexts will be explored, followed by an analysis of how culture is represented in a sample of commonly used textbooks.

## Culture in Curriculum Guidelines for Teaching Chinese

References to culture teaching in some of the well-known guides for teachers typically define Chinese culture as the way language used in communication reflects the values, traditions and beliefs of the culture. The authors also reinforce the desirability of teaching achievement and informational culture alongside culture in language use, and provide some recommendations in terms of culture content areas that should be included in classroom teaching.

*The Guide for Basic Chinese Programs* (Kubler, 2006) recommends that subtle and elusive behavioural culture, knowledge of how to act appropriately, should not be taught explicitly, but should be learned implicitly, or unconsciously through a process of observation, modelling and replication of target language norms of behaviour. Background information however, achievement and informational culture, can be explicitly taught and should not be neglected. *The Guide* also recommends some contrastive study with learners' own patterns of (first language cultural) behaviour. *The Guide* lists a range of cultural topics in the 'developing learners' cultural skills' section, including family relations, personal relations, *guanxi*, and social organisation and structures, along with more subtle features of communication, such as avoiding negativity, and indirectness in making requests or refusals in interaction with others. This list of cultural topics highlights some of the values, traditions and beliefs which might appear in the texts and interactions learners engage with in the early stages of their language learning. Additional cultural content includes subtle features of communication, which may be encountered in texts, including behavioural culture; knowledge of how to act appropriately, (such as avoiding negativity, and indirectness) which Kubler (2006) argues need to be learned implicitly.

*Teaching and Learning Chinese: A Pedagogical Grammar* (Xing, 2006) also devotes a chapter to culture learning in Chinese classrooms. The author draws a distinction between big culture (achievement culture) and small culture, described as, for example, food, liquor, tea, and cuisine, and behavioural culture, described as the social norms native speakers are obliged to obey, such as protocols for politeness, respect, modesty and deference. Xing argues that teachers need to select communicative cultural information. She identifies five categories of culture (traditions, rituals, beliefs, social behaviours and attitudes) to be taught based on their uniqueness and importance to communicating in Chinese and thus critical to learning and understanding Chinese language, the people and their beliefs. Each of these is exemplified in some detail. Xing (2006) applies her 'theory of learnability', moving from simple to complex, from concrete to abstract, from common to less frequent, to both language and to culture learning, arguing that culture proficiency must progress in line with language proficiency. The implication of this approach is that the acquisition of cultural elements must be aimed solely at enhancing language proficiency, that exposure to and analysis of culture in the classroom can only occur through Chinese. The depth of analysis will therefore be naturally constrained by learners' language proficiency at that point in time. The relationship of learners' own culture to learning about the other is not discussed, and the role of learners' own language in exploring cultural concepts is not considered. On the basis of this learnability approach for culture learning at an elementary level, Xing (2006) recommends the following topics: names and family relationships, food and drink, the Chinese zodiac, the four treasures, and 'simple interpersonal relationships and habitual activities', such as greeting, praising, thanking, all of which are taught and used as key words, in line with learners' elementary stage of language proficiency. This list of cultural topics highlights a full spectrum of cultural representations, from achievement and information culture to everyday life and the way language use (as key words) reflects the values, traditions and beliefs of the culture. The level at which these topics would be addressed would be limited to key words, and the type of analysis in building learners intercultural understanding would be much restricted as a result.

*Teaching and Learning Chinese as a Foreign Language* (Everson and Xiao, 2009) includes a number of chapters that address the issue of culture in the Chinese classroom. In a chapter on the pedagogical implications of the American Advanced Placement Chinese Language and Culture course, Chi (2009) recommends maximising learners' exposure to authentic language and culture, and choosing topics that are interesting and appropriate for students. Chi's list of general cultural topics includes social customs and everyday life, traditional thought and culture, literature and art, school, sport and recreation, and significant persons and events. The list includes topics ranging from information and achievement culture to everyday practices, with little reference to their role in communication. In a chapter on 'bringing culture to the classroom', Christensen (2009) differentiates between achievement culture and behavioural culture, which he describes as the cultural code of a language as evidenced through behaviour. Christensen argues that bringing behavioural culture to the classroom involves performance, learning how to behave, how to act and get things done. He argues teachers need to go beyond thinking that culture is a separate and distinct skill and suggests that learning how to behave appropriately, to become participating members of the target culture, is essential as 'native Chinese should not have to adapt their behaviour to accommodate communicating with learners of Chinese' (2009: 23). Christensen's representation of culture as a set of native-like forms of behaviour to be learned implicitly as performances appears to leave the underlying cultural values unanalysed, with little opportunity for analysis and comparison with learners' own cultural behaviours and underlying values and beliefs.

Overall, the recommendations provided in these curriculum guidelines place significant emphasis on incorporating culture in the classroom, but emphasise a topical rather than a more generalised, and conceptual approach to determining cultural content. The guidelines recommend teaching a range of valued cultural knowledge, from information and achievement culture through to behavioural culture and the role of traditional values which continue to play an important role in familial and social relationships in Chinese society. One aim of culture learning however appears to be to acquire a general understanding of some aspects of contemporary society and some significant cultural traditions. An additional aim appears to be to learn to replicate native speaker norms of behaviour in social interaction in Chinese. Underpinning these recommendations is the assumption that culture learning should be evidenced through the target language (as an aspect of communicative capability), by using language in culturally appropriate ways. This representation appears to be predominately a monocultural view of the Chinese classroom in which learners' own culture value sets are seldom used as a reference point for understanding the intentions and implications of particular language features and paralinguistic aspects of interaction. Developing in learners a deeper understanding of the relationship between certain communication practices and the underlying values and beliefs is not foregrounded. Rather, an implicit learn-by-doing approach appears to be preferred, and the challenge of interpreting and explaining the deeper cultural values and the challenges learners may face in understanding these, and relating them to their own cultural values set remain unattended.

## Culture in Contemporary Chinese Language Textbooks

Textbooks provide a useful vehicle for introducing second language learners to Chinese language, and to Chinese culture. Textbooks play an important role in determining not only what language content should be taught in what sequence, but what culture knowledge is important and how learners are to engage with it in the process of learning to communicate in the language. The rapid rise in the study of Chinese as a second language has seen the publication of a diverse set of resources for teachers of Chinese at secondary school and college level in particular. In this section, representations of culture in a range of textbooks are explored, highlighting issues in both the representations of Chinese culture and the ways learners are expected to engage with these representations.

A number of textbooks have been produced both in China and abroad under the auspices of the Hanban (Chinese National Office for Teaching Chinese as a Foreign Language). One of the more popular of these textbook series is the *Kuàilè Hànyǔ* (Happy Chinese) series (Li, 2014). The preface to the series states its aim is to help learners improve their Chinese and thus access the key to Chinese culture. The topics covered in each chapter of Book One include introductions, family, food, school, time, work, hobbies, and transport. However, no explicit attention to cultural information associated with these topics is provided within the Student Book. In the Teacher's Book, some 'background information' associated with these topics is provided, presented in both Chinese and in English and left for the teacher to use as she or he sees fit. The Chinese language used in the culture explanations is far beyond the language level expected in the Student Book. It appears these culture data are provided in Chinese for the teacher's consumption, and presented in English for the teacher to use in delivering the cultural data to students.

In the '*Gēn wǒ xué Hànyǔ*' (Learn Chinese with Me) series (Zhu, 2004) no reference is made to culture in the preface, but within the activities section of each chapter there is a class activity in which students are invited to discuss culture topics such as costumes, zodiac animals, and paper craft, and provide activities which seek some cross cultural comparison. The Teacher's Book includes some factual information on teaching culture, including explaining family names, a popular Chinese sport (table tennis), internet use in China, the one child policy, and festivals. This factual information is provided for teachers in Chinese only, at a level well beyond students' current state of comprehension.

The introduction to *The New Practical Chinese Reader* (Liu and Schmidt, 2012) states that one of its guiding concepts is to help students to understand the culture and society of the target language in order to use the language more effectively (2012: vi). Cultural notes presented in English are provided at the end of most lessons. In Book One, these cultural notes include information on the Chinese language (spoken language, characters, Pinyin, dictionaries), Chinese opera, Chinese names, forms of address, currency, medicine, student dormitories and geography, among others.

No reference to culture is made in the preface to the *Contemporary Chinese* textbook series (Wu, 2006). Cultural notes are provided at the end of each lesson of between one sentence to more than one page in length. These notes cover a range of culture topics, including the Chinese language, names, family relationships, geography, shopping, restaurants, festivals, calendar, transport and education. A later publication, *Voyages* (中学中文) (Li, 2010) states in the 'Compilers' Words' introduction that this text 'places emphasis on its cultural contents . . . aimed at cultivating students' cultural consciousness and extending their cultural vision' (2010: v). Unit topics covered, like in other textbooks, include family and friends, food and drink, schoolmates and campus, activities and travel, entertainment and making plans. The end of each unit (after two to three chapters) features a cultural tips section (文化常识), which provides factual information in Chinese and English on topics such as the zodiac, cuisine, the four treasures, table tennis, the Forbidden City, folk music and new buildings.

Other textbook series produced overseas and commonly used in Western schools include *Chinese Made Easy* (Ma and Li, 2015), *Nǐhǎo* (Fredlein and Fredlein, 2011) and *Jìnbù* (Zhu and Bin, 2010). *Chinese Made Easy* (Ma and Li, 2015) declares it provides information on Chinese culture and traditions through texts in Chinese at the end of each chapter. These reading (阅读) texts convey factual information about topics similar to those described in mainland Chinese textbooks. The *Nihao* series (2011) provides similar cultural information as 'something to know' conclusions to most chapters. *Jinbu* (2010) contains a culture and daily life section at the end of each chapter that provides some detailed information on an aspect of life in China, such as geography, Chinese homes, birthdays, young people's hobbies (internet, TV, sport, Karaoke, eating out), schools in China, and Chinese food. Some questions are provided to encourage group discussion, or research or presentation tasks to engage them in further exploration of the topic, with cross cultural comparison sometimes evident. Culture notes are occasionally included (names, tea, etc.) within the body of each chapter.

The constructions of culture in most of these textbook series in common use in classrooms around the world continue to reflect past practices in cultural representation and sustain a number of assumptions that limit teachers' abilities in developing an intercultural orientation towards Chinese learning and limit student access to understanding culture as a critical aspect of meaning making. The textbooks typically view culture as a static representation of national history, achievements, cultural products and everyday practices, with little relationship to how language is used or to the cultural values and beliefs that underpin communication and social relations in society. Culture is separated from language, and culture is presented as facts through English, distancing the relationship even further. Learners' opportunities to engage meaningfully with culture, to compare life worlds, values and beliefs, and how these are enacted through language, are largely absent. And finally, understanding the important role learners' appreciation of their own culture and communication patterns plays as the basis for understanding of otherness is similarly absent.

While the resource base for teaching Chinese in school-based contexts provides some evidence of attempts to incorporate culture in Chinese language learning, an intercultural orientation to culture in language learning is still largely absent. The samples of texts provided in textbooks are typically pedagogic in nature, designed to provide examples of how particular grammar structures apply in relation to specific topics using a select set of vocabulary. The majority of texts in beginner textbooks, in particular, focus on short oral exchanges, extending to short written narratives designed to provide some factual information or model a way for learners to document their own ideas in writing. There is little opportunity for learners to engage with real-world examples of culture in language use, either in everyday oral interactions or in written texts designed for native speaker readers.

This review of resources allows some key generalisations to be made: that culture is still separated from language in use, and is focussed on achievement and information culture, and facts about daily life. It is seldom integrated with communication, or delivered through authentic everyday written texts and oral interactions from target communities, and is presented in English with little opportunity for application in context. One consequence of this is likely to be a lack of access to meaningful examples of culture in language use, and a lack of opportunity for meaningful comparison and reflection between cultures and communication practices. Learners are left struggling to appreciate the relationship between Chinese language and culture, with a somewhat restricted view of the Chinese cultural mindset which impacts on communication practices, and a limited awareness of their own cultural values system in communicating as a result.

## An Intercultural Orientation to Designing Curriculum for Culture Learning

The review of literature in relation to culture in language and intercultural approaches to language learning highlights a need to rethink the nature of culture in the language classroom in terms of sources of cultural input and how culture learning is best integrated into learning to be active and effective communicators in Chinese. It raises some important questions, about the role of the teacher as mediator between Chinese culture and the learners' own culture and the processes of intercultural exploration, and the opportunities for active engagement in interpretation and exchange of meanings with other (native) speakers of Chinese.

There are clearly limitations to exploring cultural values in authentic examples of communication when learner abilities in listening (and speaking) and reading (and writing) are limited. Access to authentic examples of culture in language use are also limited. Does this mean that teachers can only deal with culture and cultural values in communication at a superficial level?

Learners' current state of proficiency naturally constrains the complexity of the texts they can engage with. As noted earlier, some authors (Xing, 2006, in particular) argue that cultural proficiency should proceed in line with language proficiency, that exploration of cultural ideas or meanings should not advance beyond learner's current capabilities to both interpret *and* create messages containing such cultural meanings; that language inputs should reflect expectations in terms of learners' own productive outputs. Developing intercultural understanding and reflecting on the nature of culture and its relationship to language use can begin early and can precede language proficiency (Carr, 1999). Doing so has the potential to provide deeper insights into the culture of the language community that would become the basis for building intercultural communication skills at later stages of learning.

There is clearly a need to consider how to provide a broader range of possible sources of cultural input through language in the Chinese classroom. Authentic examples of contemporary language use in everyday contexts in Chinese society are seldom made available in textbooks, and, consequently, opportunities to explore real examples of culture in language are almost non-existent for younger learners, and learners at elementary level. Receptive culture learning, exploring authentic examples of not only how native speakers express cultural meanings in oral interaction, but also engaging with cultural messages in written texts, provides opportunities for deeper and more substantial intercultural engagement in interpretation, analysis and comparison of culture in language beyond that currently available in textbooks. Print literacy development in Chinese, learning to read and understand texts in Chinese characters, is a particularly time consuming and challenging task. However, learning to access the cultural meanings implicit in written texts represents an important insight into Chinese culture that may be quite different to the more social and interactive cultural aspects that become evident when exploring the exchange of meanings in oral communication. Interpretive, intercultural observations of authentic examples of written texts in Chinese characters provide both valuable but distinctive means by which learners will achieve the types of cultural knowledge and intercultural understanding upon which they can base their interpretations of others in interactions, be they oral or written, and in the creation of their own texts in Chinese.

Intellectual engagement with cultural concepts identified in authentic Chinese language texts has the potential to enrich the language learning experience and engage learners more meaningfully with language in the classroom. This, of course, assumes an important role for the learners' first language in the process of translation, interpretation and intercultural exploration of the cultural meanings in texts, including contrasting those meanings with how similar texts are constructed in English. The issue of learners' low proficiency in listening and reading remains: how can learners engage with authentic examples of texts which contain language (oral vocabulary, and written characters) not yet encountered in the classroom? Dealing with uncertainty and anticipating encounters with vocabulary not yet introduced is not a common feature of Chinese textbooks, but it is a reality in the world of language use. The skills needed for dealing with unfamiliar language in oral and written texts, however, are clearly different.

To engage with culture at a level consistent with learners' current levels of cognitive ability means finding ways to overcome the constraints of low proficiency and providing learners with examples of language in use that can engage them in deeper thinking and a richer understanding of themselves and others. The challenges of engaging with content in oral and written texts, and the processes of exploring such texts, are distinctive and the features of culture inherent in them likely to be substantially different. As a result, different strategies for exploring authentic examples of social interaction and texts in Chinese characters are required, and the selection of cultural concepts to be explored within them is likely to differ.

Learners undoubtedly need scaffolding to interrogate unfamiliar examples of oral language use, but dealing with non-comprehension and misunderstandings are useful skills, especially in spontaneous real-world oral interactions. However, an intercultural orientation at an elementary level is not necessarily focussed on immediate participatory interaction, but rather on helping learners to learn to observe others in interaction, to explore authentic texts, to analyse, interpret, compare, and reflect on how it is that native speakers communicate and share cultural meanings. Provision of new words, mediation of unfamiliar accents, and addressing rapid delivery of utterances, are all parts of the scaffolding teachers may need to provide. The aim of the task is not, however, full comprehension of the exchange, and certainly not learners' accurate reproduction of the same oral exchange; the focus is on the exploration of culture, and the development of a deeper, intercultural understanding of how communication takes place in the target culture and how that compares to learners' own culture and communication practices.

Identifying cultural messages and engaging in intercultural exploration of meaning making practices in authentic texts in Chinese characters requires similar scaffolding; the provision of character meanings (and how character-morphemes create word meanings) as learners attempt, first, to establish literal meanings and, secondly, to identify cultural values inherent in this meaning. Importantly, the process of intercultural learning rests in the active interpretation of meanings and values by learners themselves, with the assistance of teacher scaffolding and mediation, where learners struggle to gain insights and connections to their own life experiences in order to resolve the linguistic and cultural puzzle they are confronted with. There is no assumption that students may need to create similar texts themselves—the task is interpretation of the native speaker culture, and by comparison, better understanding of the cultural values of their own society in similar contexts.

Intercultural exploration of authentic texts will involve learners' own first language in the process of translation, interpretation and analysis of both the language used and the cultural meanings identified in such texts. Such is the nature of meaningful interrogation of authentic examples of target language use from an intercultural perspective. With a focus on learners' own language and culture in the process of interpretation, learners also develop skills in intercultural mediation, learning to both convey the surface level message of the text and, equally importantly, the cultural meanings of such Chinese texts to others, in English.

## *Authentic Sources of Cultural Content*

The world of the native speaker is filled with rich and culturally meaningful interactions and texts that can be used to engage learners with culture in language. The set of values and beliefs that influence communication in Chinese, and cultural concepts that impact on meaning making, reflect a long history of cultural ideas and their representations in text. Second language learners are never likely to be required to replicate the types of texts that contain these rich cultural messages. However, the cultural messages learners are encouraged to identify and explore in such texts have the potential to be beneficial to their longer-term intercultural understanding and ability to interpret meanings and communicate effectively in

Chinese, or with Chinese people. The argument throughout this chapter suggests that all authentic texts and all interactions contain degrees of cultural meanings, but these may not be salient, or evident to learners, nor immediately accessible in terms of learners' current state of intercultural understanding. The challenge for teachers lies in selecting the types of texts learners are able to engage with, in determining what cultural values are important and can be explored through such texts, and how to assist learners in their exploration and interpretation of those cultural meanings.

A conscious focus on culture in authentic, native speaker communication, either in oral interaction or in print text, and the intercultural exploration opportunities provided in such texts does not presuppose that learners have the current language skills to understand the full, literal message of texts or interactions they see or hear. What is important is that the classroom engagement with the text provides the space not only for discovering the literal surface level meaning of the text but also for thoughtful interpretation of the context, the purpose, the message and the intended audience, as well as the language used to achieve its essentially culturally embedded goal.

Both oral and written texts are available and potentially useful for exploring cultural values: examples of oral interactions between native speakers in diverse contexts, as well as examples of less interactive spoken texts, such as advertisements and announcements are typically short yet rich in cultural meanings in terms of how they engage or attempt to persuade their audience. The second type of texts are everyday written texts in Chinese characters, both private texts between individuals, such as social media posts, which may reflect more oral styles of language and cultural meaning making, and more public texts, such as print advertisements, public posters, billboards, signs and notices. Such texts can be short, readily translated at a surface level, with support, and yet amenable to deeper intercultural exploration in the classroom. Ultimately, the selection of texts for intercultural exploration needs to take place in a manner that ensures primarily that learners' growing, passive intercultural understanding is developed and ultimately productive intercultural communicative capability is enhanced, and that these occur in a developmentally sequenced, but not necessarily interdependent way.

Underpinning text selection are some key considerations for longer term planning for intercultural learning. These include:

- What sort of cultural concepts constitute valued knowledge at this current, elementary stage in their learning, where proficiency is low?
- What background (historical, geographic, etc.) knowledge is desirable for learners to be able to build understanding of key cultural concepts and associated traditional values and beliefs that are reflected in communication practices in Chinese communities?
- What role will knowledge of these cultural traditions and historical circumstances of Chinese speaking communities play in learners becoming effective

communicators in intercultural encounters with Chinese native speakers in the longer term?

- How important is it to understand, for example, the role of Confucian beliefs, and of the role of Confucian texts, in appreciating the deeper cultural meanings of language used in every day interactions?
- How can learners engage productively in exploring dynamism and diversity within the language and the culture, and engage with contemporary cultural values and beliefs expressed through the language used by younger members of contemporary Chinese societies?
- How are such cultural concepts and knowledge areas represented in learners' own cultural practices (in English)? How aware are they of these practices?

A number of additional practical questions require consideration, in particular, deciding how authentic, every day public texts designed for a mass audience can be used to stimulate intercultural enquiry and enhance learners' understanding of cultural values in Chinese society today. In making decisions about the selection of texts to use for such a purpose, the texts need to display features of language and culture which are accessible linguistically, and useful in building cultural knowledge. Ideally the texts should display features of Chinese as a written language, such as brevity and balance, and the use of idiom (成语) or classical allusion (古典) to help convey a deeper, cultural message. The texts also need to display a feature of Chinese culture, or reflect a deeper cultural meaning that will need to be made accessible to younger learners and amenable to intercultural exploration (comparison with learners' own culture and values). Texts need to represent or reflect something about contemporary values and beliefs or social expectations, in order to provide a deeper insight for learners into the cultural mindset of the Chinese community, as reflected in language use.

Some examples of contemporary public texts that may be useful as sources for culture learning and intercultural enquiry are provided as an appendix to this chapter. These texts reflect ways in which the Chinese written language is used to convey cultural messages, and how traditional cultural concepts are used to convey messages to a contemporary audience. Each text is chosen to exemplify the proposition that authentic texts, be they print or spoken, are invaluable in building cultural knowledge and intercultural understanding. The texts selected are examples drawn from contemporary (Mainland) Chinese society. Many alternative and equally suitable texts can be found in other Chinese speaking communities.

In Figure 7.1 (和谐社会 温馨家庭—*A harmonious society, A 'warm' family*), the language is relatively simple and accessible. The images, as Spring Festival couplets, represent a distinctive and traditional text type, commonly encountered in Chinese communities. These couplets (usually of four to six characters) typically display phrases that may not hold much clear contemporary cultural, communicative relevance to young learners. In this instance, however, the content is more contemporary, while drawing on traditional linguistic patterns of expression.

The presence of traditional characters adds a layer of additional cultural relevance and 'links with the past' to the texts.

In Figure 7.2 (和谐; 社会主义核心价值观—*Harmony; Socialist core values*), Figure 7.3 (和谐平安，警民同建，百姓同享—*Harmony & peace, a joint effort of police and people, the '100 names' will benefit*), and Figure 7.4 (祖国和谐，家家安宁—*harmonious motherland, peaceful households*), the term 和谐 (*harmony*) is central to their messages. The term can be found in any number of public texts, even on the side of high-speed trains. The traditional and contemporary significance of the term 和谐 (*harmony*) is considerable. These texts highlight the way in which the term harmony is applied in diverse contexts. The first text provides (for more advanced learners) an explanation of how the idea of harmony derives from Chinese traditions and how it applies in modern society, drawing clear links between Chinese past cultural values and those of the present. The other two texts draw connections between harmony in society and peace at home, between the collective good and the welfare of the family—with emphasis placed on the community and family more than the individual—reinforcing the key concept of the collective good inherent in Chinese society, reflected in the language of these texts. The use of terms such as motherland and family, citizens and the '100 names' are used to draw connections between state and society, and between society and family. The use of 'traditional' four-character phrases is also notable in these examples of written language.

In Figure 7.5 (中国好孩子—*Good Chinese children*), the language (for both the title and the six activities) is simple and accessible. The images facilitate understanding and draw on a traditional paper-cut art form in their representation. The text infers there are six values and practices that are representative of good behaviour among Chinese children. At a surface level, it could be said these are common and self-evident in any society, but they also say something important about Chinese traditions. The phrases 读书 (*reading*) and 孝老 (*take care of the old*) in particular provide insights into values important in Chinese society, especially in striving for a good education and showing respect for elders. The other phrases, especially 植树 (*plant trees*) and 锻炼 (*exercise*) provide evidence of a more contemporary view of good, healthy behaviour. While the poster overall may be advocating good individual habits, it is also promoting a broader social good that would result from such activity.

In Figure 7.6 (讲文明树新风—*be civilised, and establish new trends*), the title, though brief and the characters relatively familiar, is a little more challenging to interpret, especially the second phrase 树新风 (lit. *tree new wind*). It is, however, a common phrase in contemporary society as China modernises and develops its cultural identity at home and abroad. Within the body of the poster, represented by branches of the tree there are a number of negative habits that should be avoided, most of which are readily understood. The text infers there are certain practices that in this instance are not representative of civilised behaviour among Chinese citizens. It is useful to reflect on whether such campaigns and texts are evident in local society, and what those unacceptable behaviours might be.

In Figure 7.7 (感谢孝道—*be thankful for filial piety*) and Figure 7.8 (代代孝辈辈传—*filial piety passes from generation to generation*), the two texts highlight the traditional cultural practice of filial piety which is still considered important in a modernising Chinese society. Both texts are brief and the characters relatively accessible, and they project a similar message, reinforcing the important role of filial piety in both traditional and contemporary society in different ways. The heading of the first text highlights the importance of Chinese traditions to the good functioning of modern Chinese society. The literal meaning of the second is more challenging to interpret (*maintain filial piety across generations*). The texts encourage comparisons to evidence of respect and care for elders in other societies and how such values might be changing across generations. The texts encourage consideration about changes in contemporary China and why the government may be trying to reinforce such traditional behaviours today.

The process of enquiry used to explore everyday texts aims to build knowledge of Chinese culture through language. It also aims to develop in learners the skills of intercultural exploration, skills which can be applied in the future as learners begin to realise the importance and value of seeking such cultural meanings in texts they encounter. The value of exploring the literal and cultural messages rests particularly in encouraging learners themselves to provide their own interpretations of meanings and propose their own perspectives on the cultural messages, and the implications for their appreciation of the role of culture in communicating with Chinese people, and in their own social contexts as well. The teacher's role is to facilitate discussion, to fill the gaps in learner's knowledge, to pose the questions that will help the learners to make meaningful connections between the text and the cultural context of its use.

## Conclusion: Building an Intercultural Orientation to Engaging Learners With Culture

In developing an intercultural orientation towards the teaching of culture, the main challenge for teachers rests in using texts that are appropriate to the level of cognitive development, interest, experience and linguistic competence of students. It also rests in developing skills and strategies that facilitate intercultural exploration of the text. Such skills and strategies need to encourage learners to interpret meanings and explore underlying cultural values within texts for themselves. Learner's interpretations will of course be based on their own insights, assumptions and expectations about their own cultural life worlds and values to their interpretation of the cultural values of Chinese speaking communities. It is this comparative analysis that helps learners to not only better understand otherness, but as a result, also to better understand the values they implicitly believe in. This intercultural comparison is what makes these learning opportunities so powerful. There is no set formula for meaningful intercultural exploration, but the examples provided earlier attempt to show some principled ways in which culture learning with an intercultural perspective can be made more powerful in the classroom.

Opportunities for engaging with target culture in texts in everyday contexts represents a significant shift in the orientation towards culture and culture learning. This intercultural orientation towards engaging with culture is not just about the target culture and language, nor is it just about the information and achievement cultures that represent a nation's past and present, nor just about how people go about their daily lives, what they eat, what they wear, when they celebrate. Nor is it a monocultural orientation, where learning the rules and procedures of another culture is undertaken without reference to learners' own life worlds, cultures and experiences. Cultural learning in the Chinese second language classroom is all about bringing language and culture and the people who interact within and across cultural boundaries into a bilingual, intercultural perspective.

Cultural learning can be powerful when learners are given opportunities to engage with texts and to observe and engage in interactions with others with such an intercultural lens, by asking themselves in an ongoing and sustained fashion: How are these texts and interactions understood by native speakers, and by me as a second language learner? What do these texts and interactions tell me about the other, and what have I learned about culture and communication in Chinese as a result of these experiences? And finally, and perhaps most importantly in terms of learners' own intercultural development, what has my engagement with these texts and in these interactions taught me about myself?

Drawing upon Schoenfeld's (2014) five dimensions of powerful classrooms, teachers can reflect on their own intercultural practices in the Chinese second language classroom in the following ways:

- Is culture learning sufficiently conceptual and does it develop in a coherent fashion over time? Am I clear on what I value as critical cultural knowledge at each stage of learning in my program?
- Are learners provided with intercultural learning opportunities which are both challenging and meaningful to them, as developing communicators in Chinese and in English, and in developing their intercultural skills and identities as developing bilinguals?
- Are intercultural learning opportunities through text made accessible to all by providing scaffolding and supports appropriate to current levels of linguistic and cultural knowledge?
- Are learners empowered to participate in intercultural exchanges and in interpreting texts? Do I as teacher facilitate their personal meaning making and exchange of ideas in a way that facilitates meaningful learning opportunities through open exchange of ideas across cultures?
- And finally, how do I as teacher make use of learners' insights and understandings to generate new opportunities for deeper intercultural learning in the classroom?

Ultimately, each opportunity learners have to observe everyday texts or interactions within the target language community represent opportunities for powerful intercultural learning. What learners need to acquire are the skills in intercultural enquiry; to think beyond the literal meaning of the texts or interactions and to ask themselves: what are the values that matter in communication that are reflected in this text/interaction? How do these texts provide me insight into the contemporary values and communication practices between members of these speech communities? And how does this experience enhance both my understanding of and ability to understand and communicate appropriately with members of that community? This is an important goal in incorporating culture into classroom teaching.

## Appendix

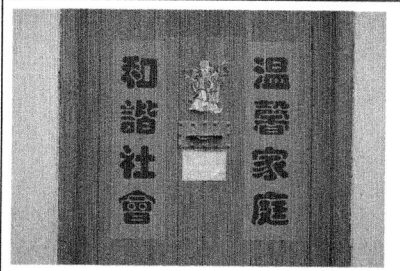

**FIGURE 7.1** 和谐社会 温馨家庭 (a harmonious society, a 'warm' family)

**FIGURE 7.2** 和谐 社会主义核心价值观 (harmony—socialist core values)

**FIGURE 7.3** 和谐平安，警民同建，百姓同享 (harmony and peace, a joint effort of police and people, the 'the 100 names' will benefit)

**FIGURE 7.4** 祖国和谐,家家安宁 (harmonious motherland, peaceful households)

**FIGURE 7.5** 中国好孩子 (good Chinese children)

**FIGURE 7.6** 讲文明树新风 (be civilised, and establish new trends)

**FIGURE 7.7** 感谢孝道 (be thankful for filial piety)

**FIGURE 7.8** 代代孝辈辈传 (filial piety passes from generation to generation)

## References

Australian Curriculum and Assessment and Reporting Authority (ACARA). (2014) *Australian Curriculum: Languages*. Retrieved 14 September 2018 from www.australian curriculum.edu.au/f-10-curriculum/languages/rationale/

Byram, M. (2015) 'Culture in Foreign Language Learning—The Implications for Teachers and Teacher Training', in W. Chan, S. Bhatt, M. Nagami, and I. Walker (eds.), *Culture and Foreign Language Education: Insights From Research and Implications for the Practice*. Berlin and Boston: De Gruyter Mouton.

Carr, J. (1999) 'From "Sympathetic" to "Dialogic" Imagination: Cultural Study in the Foreign Language Classroom', in J. Lo Bianco, A.J. Liddicoat, and C. Crozet (eds.), *Striving for the Third Place: Intercultural Competence Through Language Education*, 103–112. Melbourne: Language Australia.

Chan, W., Bhatt, S., Nagami, M., and Walker, I. (2015) 'Culture and Foreign Language Education: An Introduction', in W. Chan, S. Bhatt, M. Nagami, and I. Walker (eds.), *Culture and Foreign Language Education: Insights From Research and Implications for the Practice*, 1–34. Berlin and Boston: De Gruyter Mouton.

Chi, R. (2009) 'AP Chinese Language and Culture: Pedagogical Implications and Applications', in M.E. Everson and Y. Xiao (eds.), *Teaching Chinese as a Foreign Language: Theories and Applications*, 61–95. Boston: Cheng & Tsui.

Christensen, M.B. (2009) 'Bringing Culture Into the Chinese Language Classroom Through Contextualised Performance', in M.E. Everson and Y. Xiao (eds.), *Teaching Chinese as a Foreign Language: Theories and Applications*, 19–34. Boston: Cheng & Tsui.

Crozet, C. and Liddicoat, A.J. (1999) 'The Challenge of Intercultural Language Teaching: Engaging With Culture in the Classroom', in J. Lo Bianco, A.J. Liddicoat, and C. Crozet (eds.), *Striving for the Third Place: Intercultural Competence Through Language Education*, 113–126. Melbourne: Language Australia.

Fredlein, S. and Fredlein, P. (2011) *Ni Hao 1*. Brisbane: Chinasoft.

Halverson, R.J. (1985) 'Culture and Vocabulary Acquisition: A Proposal', *Foreign Language Annals*, 18(4): 327–332.

Kearney, E. (2015) *Intercultural Learning in Modern Language Education Expanding Meaning-Making Potentials*. Languages for Intercultural Communication and Education: 28, Bristol, UK: Multilingual Matters.

Kramsch, C. (1993) *Context and Culture in Language Education*. Oxford: Oxford University Press.

Kubler, C.C. (2006) *NFLC Guide for Basic Chinese Language Programs*. Pathways to Advanced Skills Series, 3. Columbus: Ohio State University, National East Asian Languages Resource Center.

Li, X.Q. (2010) *Voyages in Chinese*. Beijing, China: Sinolingua Co., Ltd.

Li, X.Q. (2014) *Kuaile Hanyu (Happy Chinese)*, Vol. 1. 2nd edition. Beijing: Peoples Education Press.

Liddicoat, A.J. (1997) 'Everyday Speech as Culture: Implications for Language Teaching', in A.J. Liddicoat and C. Crozet (eds.), *Teaching Language, Teaching Culture*, 55–70. Canberra: Applied Linguistics Association of Australia.

Liddicoat, A.J. (2002) 'Static and Dynamic Views of Culture and Intercultural Language Acquisition', *Babel*, 36(3): 4–11.

Liddicoat, A.J. (2009) 'Communication as Culturally Contexted Practice: A View From Intercultural Communication', *Australian Journal of Linguistics*, 29(1): 115–133.

Liddicoat, A.J. and Crozet, C. (eds.). (1997) *Teaching Languages, Teaching Cultures*. Australian Review of Applied Linguistics. Canberra: Applied Linguistics Association of Australia.

Liddicoat, A.J., Papademetre, L., Scarino, A., and Kohler, M. (2003) *Report on Intercultural Language Learning*. Canberra: Dept of Education, Science and Training.

Liddicoat, A.J. and Scarino, A. (2013) *Intercultural Language Teaching and Learning*. Chichester: Wiley-Blackwell.

Liu, X. and Schmidt, J. (2012) *New Practical Chinese Reader*. Beijing: Beijing Language & Culture University Press.

Lo Bianco, J., Liddicoat, A.J. and Crozet, C. (eds.). (1999) *Striving for the Third Place: Intercultural Competence Through Language Education*. Canberra: Language Australia.

Ma, Y.M. and Li, X.Y. (2015) *Chinese Made Easy, Textbook 1*. 3rd edition. Hong Kong: Joint Publishing Co.

Moeller, A. J. and Osborn, S.R.F. (2014) 'A Pragmatist Perspective on Building Intercultural Communicative Competency: From Theory to Classroom Practice', *Foreign Language Annals*, 47(4): 669–683.

National Standards in Foreign Language Education Project (NSFLEP). (2015) *World-Readiness Standards for Learning Languages*. Alexandria: National Standards in Foreign Language Education Project, American Council on the Teaching of Foreign Languages.

Province of British Columbia. (2017) *Mandarin Curriculum Rationale and Goals*. Retrieved 21 February 2018 from https://curriculum.gov.bc.ca/curriculum/second-languages/mandarin/goals-and-rationale

Scarino, A. (2014) 'Learning as Reciprocal, Interpretive Meaning Making', *Modern Language Journal*, 98(1): 386–401.

Schoenfeld, A.H. (2014) 'What Makes for Powerful Classrooms, and How Can We Support Teachers in Creating Them? A Story of Research and Practice, Productively Intertwined', *Educational Researcher*, 43(8): 404–412.

Wu, Z.W. (2006) *Contemporary Chinese*. Beijing: Sinoilingua.

Xing, J.Z.Q. (2006) *Teaching and Learning Chinese as a Foreign Language: A Pedagogical Grammar*. Hong Kong: Hong Kong University Press.

Zhu, X.M. and Bin, Y. (2010) *Jinbu 1*. Port Melbourne: Pearson.

Zhu, Z.P. (ed.). (2004) *Learn Chinese With Me (gen wo xue hanyu)*. Beijing: Peoples Education Press.

# 8

# WIDENING EXPERIENCE

## Introduction

Electronic technology has been a wonderful gift to those teaching in any school language course on two counts: firstly, because of its capacity to provide varied, tightly tailored learner-responsive exercises; and, secondly, because of its wealth of visual material with spoken and written language on all possible topics and in a wide range of forms about and from the country where the language is spoken: factual accounts, documentaries, cartoons, drama, news, and more. These days both these lines of electronic assistance are regularly mined by teachers from the early learning years onwards, and Internet resources have done much to expand and ground knowledge developed by international learners of Chinese from quite a young age, and help them to form an ever expanding and relatively coherent picture of the language and culture, people and society. But even in modern times, nothing can offer the same powerful awareness- and knowledge- raising experience with the language and society as time spent in China. Fortunately, as another by-product of the modern age, visiting China is an opportunity that most schools have been able to incorporate at least once into their Chinese programs for virtually all their learners.

There are two principal activities that student groups typically undertake on a short-term visit to China: a tour and a sojourn. A tour involves seeing major sites of historical and cultural significance, usually in Beijing and Xi'An, and possibly in one or two other cities, while a sojourn involves spending time in one place, usually at a school or university. These activities are sometimes arranged sequentially, or the school stay may be sandwiched in between more than one period spent travelling. Sojourning students usually live in specially built quarters and commonly have Chinese lessons in the morning and sight-seeing excursions or cultural activities in the afternoons. The visitors very often largely spend their days separate from the local students' normal daily routines of lessons and exercise and the two sets of students may only join together for a couple of designated large events, such as a school assembly, a concert, or a sports match, although they may be paired off for a one-day home visit. In some programs, they do not meet at all. Visits vary in length, but what is addressed in this chapter refers to a program lasting around two to four weeks.

There are potentially very rich learning rewards from a short school run visit to China, well worth aiming for in planning and monitoring as the visit unfolds and on return. Achieving these rewards, however, is a complex matter and by no means inevitable. Success requires there be a clear and shared vision of the possible value of the visit as a whole, sound knowledge of the various factors involved, and a lot of hard work. The multiple matters at play in a China visit, and knowledge needed for the informed planning and execution that will ensure it is an optimal learning success, are explained and discussed in this chapter.

## Learning Framework

There are four central aspects of planning a China visit which need to be integrated and congruent in values if the learning rewards are to be attained. These are:

- **Goal**: achieving experiential learning
- **Content**: seeking learning in four domains
- **Structure**: designing for learning opportunities
- **Outcomes**: recognising learning.

### Goal: Achieving Experiential Learning

The work of Pritchard (2017) on experiential learning is the overarching framework drawn on here for considering the nature of a successful visit. It, in turn, draws on a very deep study of related scholarly works about the nature of learning, such as Vygotsky (1934), Dewey (1921), Martin (1993), Herbert (1999) and Tulving (2002, 2004), among many others. In Pritchard's model, the key factors in creating experiential learning are *distinctive cognitive and memory related processes that occur as the result of experience in a particular setting* (Pritchard, 2017: 96–97). Due to the multi-sensorial input of the experience, the memory created from it is stored in episodic memory, which allows the person to retrieve it later as fully as it has been stored. Remembered in this way means it can be reflected on, and when there is perceived *cognitive dissonance* between the new experience and the person's understanding until that time, they can make the cognitive shift we call learning. Evidence that learning has taken place 'is found in the meaning constructed through reflection on experiences and behavioural changes' (Pritchard, 2017: 107).

Pritchard has identified four essential components of a student residential program that engender experiential learning. These are:

- Challenging setting
- Constructed social interaction
- Tolerance of risk
- Reflection

## Challenging Setting

Pritchard identifies the setting of the new experience as a key trigger of cognitive dissonance, and observes that the specific properties of each setting interact with learners in ways that afford specific learning opportunities. For example, while each will have its value, time spent on tour and time spent on a sojourn in one place occur in different settings and hence will provide different learning experiences.

## Constructed Social Interaction

A second strong challenge to previously held views will come from contact and interaction with a variety of new people. At the same time, individual student status and collective social structures within the home group can also be profoundly altered through the experiential settings and ruptured contact with the home community that are fundamental to the design. A great deal of the development offered by the visit experience will come from perceiving anew self and others from home in the changed environment, leading to a renegotiating of roles and status in light of individuals' responses to the new setting and daily tasks.

## Tolerance of Risk

Risk emerges as an indispensable attribute of novel experiences because, by definition, the outcome of such experiences is unknown. Acknowledging and accepting risk is a valuable learning experience in its own right. Risks can be physical, social, or cultural. In new settings they are unavoidable and must be accepted and managed within the boundaries of stakeholder expectations. This often results in 'an ongoing tension between risk and protection' for participants personally, as well as for those in charge of them (Pritchard, 2017: 97).

## Reflection

Reflection, both facilitated and non-facilitated, is the necessary means by which experiential learning is stored in episodic memory and informs the process of knowledge creation. Without reflection, experience is not likely to become learning which transforms the participant (Pritchard, 2017: 96–97).

## Content: Seeking Learning in Four Domains

Well planned, the components of a visit to China can result in the dynamic change we call experiential learning occurring in four domains:

- Personal growth
- Language proficiency
- Cultural knowledge
- Intercultural competence

(CTTC, 2011: 2).

### Personal Growth

Although the impetus for a visit is to learn about the local society and for students to use their new language, the learning available from a visit is not all about local matters. One major line of development involves students knowing more about themselves as individuals, as members of their own society, and as cultural participants. Being part of a group in challenging settings and situations, as well as the experience of living closely with other young people with whom they might not usually associate, may cause them to see people they know in a different light. The experience of being away from their usual supports may also encourage a keener and more active sense of personal and social responsibility.

### Language Proficiency

Immersion in the language environment can greatly contribute to developing language proficiency in the form of discernibly improved confidence and readiness to speak, in the acquisition of set phrases, longer utterances, better quality of rhythm and tones, and greater fluency and accuracy. Unless much of the time is spent specifically on targetted language learning, however, a short visit may not result in any dramatic increase for most students in the quantity of language they know, although it has been noticed that weaker students may get to expand their stock of vocabulary and basic structures (e.g. Orton, Pavlidis, and Cui, 2013: 6).

### Cultural Knowledge

This domain concerns knowledge of contemporary society and its issues as well as tradition and history. On a visit a significant expansion of cultural knowledge involving factual information about certain sights and events is almost inevitable, although details are also easily forgotten. Deeper knowledge can be engendered in the form of increased understanding of the significance of history on contemporary society and culture and a sharpened perception of the resulting links and differences between societies.

## Intercultural Competence

Intercultural competence is the ability to perceive situations in a new culture as they are generally understood within that culture, and to recognise the choices and consequences of ways of interacting within them. Developing intercultural competence is a long-term, uneven and iterative process divided between the initial stages of an ethnocentric perspective and the later stages of an ethno-relative perspective (e.g. Bennett, 1998). Development begins with the perception of difference and proceeds from rejection of the existence or legitimacy of difference by reactions of *denial, defence* and *minimisation* to gradual *acceptance, adaptation,* and *integration* of difference as real and reasonable within its own cultural parameters.

## Structure: Designing for Learning Opportunities

The task of designing a visit to best reap its potential educational rewards means planning the four central components of experiential learning, *challenging setting, constructed social interaction, risk,* and *reflection,* so as to activate learning in the four domains of *personal growth, language proficiency, cultural knowledge* and *intercultural competence.* Before elaborating on this, however, it is important to note that the fundamental starting factor underpinning a teacher's sound design of a visit is a realistic appreciation of their own capacities to manage aspects of the visit, and of their own need to learn as they go along. They also need to be aware of the external constraints on their ability to achieve what they want, as well as being clear what assistance will be available to them within their own group and in China. Not everything set out here may be possible to arrange or achieve, especially in the first running of a program. But no matter how small a start is made, it is highly desirable that it be congruent with an overall idea of what is being sought, so that whatever can be arranged and achieved falls within that broader frame. It can then be expanded and improved on in a scaffolded line of development as the program is repeated.

## Designing a Challenging Setting

Experiential learning programs of many kinds make primary use of a challenging setting to create a certain constant level of cognitive dissonance and they do this most commonly by choosing a location that ruptures many of the participants' usual living conditions and presents some degree of physical, social and/or cultural difference, discomfort, and risk. These conditions are naturally provided as part and parcel of a visit to China: students will be separated, perhaps for the first time for any length, from their family, their normal routines, and from many of their preferred activities and food, while spending their days in an unfamiliar environment as a member of a group of people who are also having a challenging experience, not all of whom they may know or like.

In addition to these basic challenges, as appropriate to age and the individuals, a teacher is able to design the China setting to offer further, scaffolded challenges. For example, rules about emails and phone calls home, decisions about pairing for activities and for sharing rooms, nominated restaurants for meals, can all be varied and this used to increase the degree of challenge of being there. The teacher may also be able to choose the level of comfort in travelling, living quarters, and activities that will be provided. In the latter part of a visit, after a certain acclimatisation, it may be possible to increase students' exposure to conditions that are more demanding of them, even if only briefly. Examples of this might be having them use certain forms of public transport, staying in more modest accommodation, eating in regional restaurants, or following the typical daily routine of a student at their sister school.

In addition to planning decisions which create a challenging setting for a tour or sojourn, a teacher designing a visit is able to structure activities to involve student engagement with the setting in ways likely to engender learning in all four domains of learning. Some of these activities may be set before departure, others may arise naturally from a particular situation. The guiding principle for scaffolding these activities is that the process begins by drawing students' attention to where they are, to what it is like, and how they are interacting with it. Tasks may then expand to requiring them to find out more about some aspect of setting, and finally they will need to reflect on their experiences and notice changes and uncertainties in their views and feelings.

The simplest activities will involve students having to notice aspects of their environment so as to independently manage their daily life tasks—eating, washing, sleeping, study, outings, and recreation—in accordance with the times, spaces, equipment and objects provided by their host establishment. A certain degree of learning from setting will be achieved if students are just put in charge of managing these aspects of their own day for themselves, but a further benefit can be attained by setting specific tasks which draw attention to setting, require reflective engagement with aspects of it, and even to act on it so as to change it. Typically, reflective engagement with setting may involve the use of language in order, for example, to produce a written description of where they are and what they are doing. Initially these may be simply factual descriptions, but as needed new vocabulary is learned and descriptions become easier to produce, more reflective elements in the form of noting contrasts, summing up their location and routines, and adding concluding generalisations and judgements, can be asked for. Such a task can be done by all, or only by rotating smaller groups on behalf of the whole group, with results presented and discussed before being posted on a blog shared with fellow students back home. These descriptions of their daily life and opinions expressed can be backed by evidence in the form of actual sample objects, photographs, drawings and recordings. Students may be led to notice and reflect on how aspects of the setting have appeared differently to them, or are used or related to differently as the time has gone by. This may show they have become used to certain things, or that they have come to realise why things are a certain way, and hence no longer find them as surprising as they did at first. To allow deeper thought and expression, some of these discussions may be conducted in their first language.

Another form of challenge in relation to setting may require students to use and adjust prior knowledge in new conditions, for example, taking a subway train or other public transport in a new city, going to a Chinese supermarket or department store, going to a gym or attending a class in a Chinese school. Finally, tasks may press them to consider how different Chinese people see the spaces and places they have been writing about, and to notice how they use them. This will move them beyond engaging just with setting and involve them in constructed social interaction.

In sum, just being in China will mean students being in a setting where they are constantly recognisably foreign, more often than not in large crowds, eating new foods, having to negotiate unfamiliar streets and buildings, surrounded by written Chinese, and having to use Chinese to get basic needs met. They will also have to adjust to managing their daily needs under the conditions provided by their accommodation venues. These factors alone will prompt dissonance and raise awareness of self and other, while even the sensory perception of simple objects and forms in the new environment—shapes, colours, textures, sounds, smells and tastes—will constantly be impinging on consciousness and causing disruption to habits and assumptions. These natural opportunities for multi-sensorial experience can be enhanced by a teacher's prompts and shaping in the form of tasks and explicitly reflective conversations, which can transform what is first often just called 'an amazing time' into detailed episodic memories of long-term value. On the other hand, as may be recognised, the more arrangements leave students cocooned as an undifferentiated and essentially inert member of a group on a tour or sojourn in situations which demand little more from them than their usual life, and permit few opportunities to encounter real Chinese life, the greater the reduction there will be in the potential learning benefits of a tour or sojourn.

## Designing Constructed Social Interaction

While setting is often a less well-recognised factor in creating the conditions for learning, interaction with Chinese is an expected channel of development on a visit. Plans for the tour or sojourn may include opportunities to listen to and speak to a variety of people, but to ensure the second language benefits from the opportunities available are gained, specific tasks need to be designed that require all participants to engage in some form of purposeful communication with local people. The guiding principle of such constructed interaction is gradual scaffolding: learning will be enhanced if students have the chance to repeat an experience and gradually increase their independence within the one environment. For example, students may be given the task to interview people in a public space such as a shopping mall. This will require repetition of a limited range of scripted questions, with a generally limited range of possible answers, and so they can build confidence and increase their control over the language used. Shopping, eating out, and taking public transport are all easily accessible opportunities for interaction and students should be encouraged, and coached if necessary, to take part in these transactions verbally, even where it might be possible to succeed in silence or by only using non-verbal communication such as pointing.

While on tour, it may be difficult to plan social interaction with locals, but students can be encouraged to take spontaneous opportunities that occur for interaction with guides and sales people in shops and stalls, as well as fellow pedestrians, passengers and sightseers, and to make efforts to decipher various forms of written communication around them such as signs, menus, advertisements and notices. While travelling, they can expect to be asked over and over again where they are from, what they are doing in China, how long they will be there, and how they are finding it, and much of their responses to these questions can be learned and rehearsed before departure.

A sojourn offers an excellent chance to design scaffolded local social interaction and prior to departure this can be planned not only with the students, but also with those who will be involved with them at the school in China. The most common opportunities to interact with people in their school will be:

- Receiving a formal welcome and farewell from school leaders
- Giving a self or whole group introduction to a school assembly or a class
- Taking part in lessons provided to their group
- Attending and taking some part in a regular lesson, for example, mathematics, art, or physical education, conducted in Chinese
- Incidental interaction with a few Chinese students in the playground, such as playing ping pong or kicking a football
- Visiting local shops
- Spending the day and even a night with a local student and his/her family on a weekend.

Constructed social interactions such as those listed are important not only for language use and improvement, but also as the fabric of impression formation which will be the basis of the relationships which can develop. It is therefore essential that students have the competence to perform what is required of them at least to a minimum standard. Before going to China, students need to have clear expectations of what might be asked of them and a small repertoire of set phrases to help them cope, even if it is only to say that they are not able to respond or are not clear what is being asked of them.

During a sojourn, the pairing up with a student from the sister school (a 'buddy') is a chance for students to begin to develop an independent relationship with a Chinese person. Due to the usually superior English skills of students in China compared to the Chinese skills of visitors, however, this relationship is often conducted in English. If well-prepared, however, time spent together offers the visiting student particularly rich opportunities for constructed interaction in Chinese with a genuine communicative purpose. At the same time, while arranged for practical purposes, as they engage with one another in purposeful activity that in content opens each of them up to the other, such joint exercises offer the chance for a relationship to be created by the pair. Just being together, however, is not necessarily going to result in a good relationship. Instead, it is critical that interactions between visiting students and host students are designed while keeping in mind what Weekes, Pedersen, and Brislin (1977) identify as the 'especially favourable conditions' for maximising productive outcomes in intercultural relationships. Chief among these are:

- Equal status: Visiting and host student are each a first language speaker of the second language the other is learning and this bestows a certain amount of 'being power' or natural status, on each. Coming from overseas is also a mark of status, although having local knowledge can provide a counterbalance for this. Tasks set for the two need to allow each to exercise their being power at some point.

- Shared superordinate goals: Objectives for students' joint work should provide benefits for more than just themselves. Tasks undertaken by a pair, for example, might form part of a whole group project of value to both broader groups, or the two are at least required to share what they produce with others.

- Intimate rather than superficial or formal contact: This is most generally not difficult to arrange through a 'buddy' system, which pairs each visiting student with a local student and provides opportunities for them to meet together outside school hours.

- The candid treatment of difficulties by both parties: Intercultural relationships, like any other, are particularly subject to stress from unanticipated differences. The most painful are usually deep value clashes, but there are also some surface social practices that may be extremely confronting. Intercultural briefing and training in the communication of negative feelings is essential if the handling of such incidents is not to be counterproductive and lead to bad feeling.

Three examples of the many activities which could meet these conditions are set out in the following text. As the language used by the visitor can be prepared and to some degree rehearsed prior to departure, they are tasks that have every chance of being carried out successfully in Chinese, which would be a great boost to learner confidence. The nature and process of the activities also allow the host student independent authority, which means they can assist development of an equitable relationship between the two students.

1.  The first activity is a self-introduction by the visiting student, whether presented as a single monologue or in stages as part of a conversation with the host student and his/her family, possibly accompanied by photographs. The content can be prepared over time before leaving for China, with greater detail added gradually. In terms of meaningful interaction, the most important thing about a self-introduction is that students are able to say what they personally need to say in order to share genuine information about their family, their school, where they live, and what they like to do. This means, for example, that a student who wishes to explain a complex blended family structure that might include step-siblings and half-siblings can do so; or that they can all relate significant information describing some very particular geographical features of their region or city, or the details of a person or event that their school or where they live is famous for; or that they can explain a code of football or other sport that is not well known in China that they play or like to watch. Host students can use this information to introduce their visiting buddies in speech or writing to their classmates, perhaps even doing so in English.

2.  A second activity is a recorded interview of the host student by the visitor about the host's daily life at home, in the street, and at school. This will involve language that is largely well known to the visitor and so even a quite long conversation can be accomplished with low stress, while the information opens up to the visitor both the particular life of the host student and matters of local life more generally. Either on a blog at the time or on return, the student can provide an introduction of the host student to others studying Chinese at their school.

3.  A third activity is a more formal school style project to be jointly undertaken by the visitor and host student involving a piece of Chinese history or culture. The focus might be some area of common study, or it could be a local person or event that is publicly marked by a street name, plaque, statue or named space, or involve gathering the names and explaining the deeds of the Chinese and international heroes displayed around the school. To do a project, the visiting student needs to have the language to ask questions and record answers, while the host student needs to be able to obtain the factual information to fill out the content. While the content would inform the visitor about some aspect Chinese history or culture, the activity allows both students another form of equal status in their separate but complementary roles of inquirer and information provider. The outcome would be a presentation that the two of them prepare in the form of a simple electronic display accompanied by spoken explanations. Working together to add visuals, sound, and animation would be a fruitful extension of this joint undertaking.

It is common for visiting students to be offered Chinese lessons as part of their daily routine at their sojourn school. Yet unless language lessons are tightly tailored to diagnosed need, sitting in a classroom with a teacher and a book does not usually provide students with much that cannot be provided in their home country and makes poor use of the opportunities that being in China can offer. If there are to be language lessons, the most effective for a short period is in the form of concentrated work on just one thing, for example the formation and use of verb complements, or the particle 了 (le), rather than just working through a story or textbook, which tend to be vocabulary and character heavy and hence not lead to greater development in control. Lessons which introduce places students will visit later in the day and allow some practice in language they might need while on the excursion can be useful, especially if there is a high proportion of recycled vocabulary and structures over the course. In any case, an emphasis on opportunities to practise listening and speaking every day will be most beneficial while on a short sojourn in country. As at home, lessons will be best when they allow individual work using short texts, recycled vocabulary, and dialogue that is supported by physical movement, all underpinned by a communicative need to learn the language for a real and immediate purpose.

One opportunity that being in China offers in abundance but is not often taken advantage of is having students listen to whole flows of Chinese without being required to respond. This is an exercise that reduces learners' anxiety and they can often find they can hear a great deal more than they could if they were also having to formulate a response. To be at least partly understood, students need some access to the content listened to, which may be provided by prior knowledge, or by context and action. Thus, for example, observing a kindergarten classroom or watching a televised quiz show are likely to be more accessible and hence productive than observing a senior History class or watching much of the news. There is also benefit in surrender listening, in which the goal is not comprehension but the perception of rhythmic and intonational flow over extended speech samples, but this cannot go on for more than a few minutes at a time.

Another common form of instruction offered by sister schools is lessons on cultural topics. However, too often these involve crafts such as paper-cutting, knot tying, and calligraphy, all traditional and mostly activities already introduced to students during Chinese study at home. Much more useful and interesting activities that could be suggested for such periods are modern cultural arts such as texting and using phone and computer applications; learning pop songs; viewing and reading cartoons and comics; learning how to play games and sports; cooking; or watching and analysing selected clips from contemporary TV dramas. Most emphatically, whatever the content, these lessons should always be conducted in Chinese. Not only is the language of such practical, concrete activities easily comprehended, but as discussed in Chapter 3, speaking language while performing the actions or pointing out the objects being said is the way to maximise its comprehension, acquisition and retention.

Finally, to gain the greatest benefit for their Chinese language development, learners need opportunities to practise using it in unobserved interactions, away from more competent peers and teachers. Unaccompanied tasks to practise language—e.g. going to shops, mixing with local students, taking a taxi—should be programmed into the schedule.

## Designing for Risk

There are inevitable risks in taking a group of students to a foreign country and the key to making the inherent risks beneficial for learning lies in ensuring that those running the visit are informed, understand and agree on safety procedures, and are well supported should something untoward arise. Achieving these conditions requires excellent communication between the teacher in charge and the students, and among the adults in the group, about the realities of their situation and a shared acknowledgement of the boundaries. Provided there are certain tight regulations in place about limits and expectations, and good emergency strategies have been established, risks can be accepted. Most school groups are financially insured against obvious sources of physical risk, but unless there has been a thorough discussion of risks prior to the visit, teachers whose own education has not involved a positive view of risk taking may find themselves needing encouragement and training if they are to allow students the independence to risk even minor error and inconvenience in order to achieve the benefits of initiating and managing various interactions involved in intra-city travel, exploring, eating, and shopping.

In keeping with the notion of allowing students to engage directly with their own learning activities, it is warmly recommended that there be times and even whole days for which students choose the location to be visited and for which they are required to provide a plan of how best to get there, where the group will eat, and what the costs of the outing will be. This may require reading guidebooks, using Internet information, checking with their hosts, and doing a trial run of the excursion themselves to check the viability of their plans. This kind of activity poses particular risks as it may mean mistakes will be made so that not everything planned is accomplished, or that the costs in time, money or energy required turn out to be much higher than anticipated. If students are to experience ownership of being in China, however, they need to have to take charge of reading maps, choosing routes, dealing with money, and so on, and the risk of inconvenience from error and the time needed to recover from error must be permitted. Even if there is some anxiety for students at the moment a mistake occurs, successfully managing the unexpected generates confidence to undertake further explorations. Mistakes can be reduced, although never ruled out, by scaffolded practice starting with very modest excursions to local shops and using nearby public transport that is already familiar. Student growth in competence can also be scaffolded by gradually allowing them to find their own way to tourist sites, rather than always travelling as a group on a tour bus. Finally, if an error really needs to be corrected, a teacher may prompt rather than simply take over. This would include withholding their expert language unless absolutely essential.

## Designing Reflection

Reflection in experiential learning is 'an explicit form of cognitive activity focused on making meaning from past experience. It is closely associated with memory function, and the extent to which an experience is retained in detail in the memory of the participant, it informs action' (Pritchard, 2017: 199). There are two modes of reflection useful for experiential learning: *deferred emergent-implicit* reflection and *guided-explicit* reflection. The former is an internal process in the mind of the participant over time, while the latter is a deliberative, often quite structured process that occurs soon after an event (2017: 200).

Proponents of each form put forward good arguments for their views. Those who believe that the experience will work its own transformation cite in particular that students' perceptions change even during the time away and again on their return home, and they also claim that most school students lack the cognitive capacity to reflect well, so that if required to make public statements about the meaningfulness of events they may just invent perceptions they think will meet their teacher's expectations. Those in favour of structured reflection believe it contributes to students appreciating what is happening in their lives, not just on a particular day but also more generally, leading to greater understanding of who they are and how they live their life. Structured reflection can happen informally, through one-to-one or small group conversation on a bus or walking along a street, or it can be undertaken formally, by all, at a set time in the one place. The critical factor in the quality of guided reflection for learning, its proponents warn, is the nature of the guidance and the wisdom of the person guiding the activity. There can be no right or wrong answer to how a student perceived an event or is feeling about the program or their own actions. Whether the transformative power of the experience is left to the individual to process over months, or is guided at the time by a teacher or peers, all educators involved in experiential learning believe the transformation process goes on over years, and that evidence of learning will be manifest in a participant's language and action.

There are various forms of guided reflection. A weak form is to set a regular period of quiet time each evening, or every couple of days, during which students are expected to write in a private journal or in emails to family and friends so as to consolidate learning from the day. This is an activity which advocates an explicit reflective process but does not intervene with the content. A public form of indirect reflection is enabling students to post accounts of events, comments, photos and videos on a website to store and share their experience. The focus of attention, choice of objects to highlight, and particular words used, can be taken as a rough guide to their stage of orientation to events, and teachers can do an analysis without mentioning what they perceive. In short programs a typical participant focus at the start is on self and how they are managing, with others largely spoken of with respect to their support or lack of support in assisting the participant to cope, i.e. locals may be described as *friendly, helpful, rude,* and so on. As the participant settles, these terms may shift to more objectively descriptive terms, albeit attributed to all locals as a single set, such as *hard-working, good humoured, serious.* Some participants may eventually shift to using terms which differentiate locals, modifying expressions like *they are serious* to *some are serious,* or saying *they are different,* or just *complex* (Orton, 1998).

## Outcomes: Recognising Learning

Learning outcomes may be evident in the four dimensions of personal growth, language proficiency, cultural knowledge and intercultural competence.

### Personal Growth

Personal growth is an individual matter which may manifest with respect to taking responsibility for self about health, money, clothes, etc.; emotional maturity in coping with being outside the familiar and supportive home environment, daring to eat new things, and persevering in the face of difficulty; and/or social maturity by getting on with other students with whom they don't usually associate. Personal development may also be reflected in a greater tolerance of uncertainty and the unfamiliar, and a preparedness to take more risks in interactions, and increasingly to look outside of themselves and beyond their immediate concerns (Orton and Mansell, 2011: 19).

### Language Proficiency

Development in language will typically be manifest in the student's increased capacity to comprehend, readiness to use Chinese, increased repertoire of set phrases and the names of objects in modern society, as well as in fluency. Another aspect of learning and interacting in language is having established some contact and essential communication with those in their environment, such as sojourn school teachers, students, and office staff, and being accepted by them. In conjunction with other aspects of learning, their use of Chinese language could show influences of a more Chinese meaning base. This might be manifest in deferential terms or more accommodating ways of putting forward their own ideas.

## Cultural Knowledge

Increased cultural knowledge and understanding will firstly be reflected in the acquisition of formal factual information about the cities and sights visited. As well there will be an accumulation of knowledge about contemporary urban Chinese society and issues, and enormous gains in the practical skills of how to live and get around in at least one or two of the places where they have been. Over their time in China and afterwards, there may be evidence of understanding China and Chinese people in gradually more complex ways.

## Intercultural Competence

Growth in intercultural competence will be evident in a student becoming increasingly aware of the role of culture in the shaping of identity, including their own, as well as differentiating among local people rather than seeing them as a single, uniform block. There may also be a sharpened perception of links and differences between societies and development in self-knowledge, both personal and cultural, as they begin to see anew parts of their own society and themselves and start a critical appraisal of their own cultural shaping (Gochen-our and Janeway (1993: 2–4). Over even a short visit, learning in intercultural competence may be evidenced by a lessening of stereotyping, a preparedness to take risks in interactions, and persistence in developing skill in dialogue over differences (Brislin, 1993: 208).

At the start of a visit, students may well express a strong ethnocentricity, which according to Bennett's (1998) intercultural learning path, most commonly begins with Defense, where the existence of different beliefs, values and ways of living are acknowledged, but denied the same value given to their own. The defender's position is that when differences occur, one side must be right, and, so it always seems to the ethnocentric, that right side is clearly our side! In the next stage, Minimisation, the existence of difference is acknowledged, but its significance is played down. 'Deep down, we are all really the same', the minimisers say. In the development of intercultural competence beyond ethnocentrism lie the three stages of ethnorelativism: acceptance, adaptation and integration, in which cultures can only be understood relative to one another and particular behaviour can only be understood within a cultural context (Bennett, 1998: 26–30). Progression through the stages is not guaranteed and is, anyway, a slow movement achieved only through deep contact over time. Not a great deal will be accomplished on a short visit beyond beginning to move, and even what is accomplished may include retreat as well as sudden insight and positive shift.

A sojourn allows for greater exposure to difference and greater opportunity to engage with the dynamics of intercultural development than does a tour. As a result, it also runs greater risk than a tour of reinforcing or even exacerbating stereotypes and ethnocentrism. While the tourist may come back saying 'They're lovely' about people they observed largely from behind the windows of their coach, the sojourner may come back saying 'They're awful' about people they have been quite closely engaged with, unless there has been guidance for the learner in anticipating, recognising, and working through sudden confrontations to their values and habits. This is particularly so for teenagers, who are often only beginning to perceive what their values and habits are as a consequence of these being challenged. Discovery of their own cultural inclinations is one of the most valuable and predictable outcomes of a student sojourn, and a necessary component of becoming interculturally competent and more genuinely bilingual. Gaining insight and knowledge into intercultural development is often a noisy and somewhat shocking, even painful, process. Supervising teachers need to monitor the students and recognise when they are reaching the edge of their cultural competence.

## Practical Matters

Detailed suggestions for establishing school-to-school relationships and for running sojourns are available from, for example, Asia Society publications (Wang, 2009, 2010) and CTTC reports (Orton and Mansell, 2011; CTTC, 2011), so only a few salient matters will be addressed here.

### *Touring*

While students would no doubt gain something just from visiting China as a tourist on a commercial trip, time in China organised by their school can offer a great deal more. However, reaping these rewards is often made difficult to achieve by the sheer weight of practical responsibility loaded onto the Chinese teacher. Bowed down by the pressures of travel arrangements, visas, health insurance, and individual medical requirements, it is not surprising that many Chinese teachers turn to commercial companies, and in many ways, it is a sensible decision. However, tour companies everywhere in the world are in business, and even China educational tours are pressed to keep groups moving within and between venues, and most have an understanding with certain shops and restaurants that they will bring in clientele. Few guides have any deep understanding of the educational experience the foreign teacher and their school want for the students. Finding the right company may therefore take some research.

In terms of the learning rewards possible from a tour, beyond getting to the cities and sights desired, there are three critically important matters to ensure any contracted company can provide: firstly, that the time spent at tourist venues is long enough to see and enjoy the main sights, and does not use excessive time bussing students about or taking them to souvenir shops; secondly, that there is some free time each day for the group to spend together; and, thirdly, that there is time on at least some of the days for students to get out locally in small groups by themselves. Stipulating these requirements will necessitate seeking a travel company which is interested in the experience the school wants to provide.

## Sojourn School Partners

The benefit of a sojourn, Byram (1997: 2) states, is that it is undertaken for a reason and hence, 'Where the tourist remains essentially unchanged, the sojourner has the opportunity to learn and be educated, acquiring the capacity to critique and improve their own and others' conditions'. It is important to aim to attain these benefits. A student sojourn in China may be undertaken on a simple fee-paying basis, but more typically occurs at a Chinese sister school, or a potential sister school. Because students move through their school each year, it falls to staff to create and maintain a sister school relationship from year to year. This is best achieved when there is a genuine desire on the part of the school leadership on both sides to establish and develop a successful and sustained relationship on a scale and of a nature that both can manage. A well-functioning relationship also needs enough staff, including school leaders, teachers from other departments than Chinese, and parents, to participate in and share the workload in various roles as host as well as visitor.

## Conclusion

The knowledge, skills, effort and patience required of a Chinese teacher who aims to plan for, mediate and support experiential learning from a visit to China are considerable. Self-knowledge is also essential, so that what is attempted is manageable and allows for the teacher to grow from the experience and be even better able to lead the next time.

Teachers need to recognise from the start that experiential learning requires engagement and discovery, hence the most effective experience will not necessarily be the most efficient experience; and allowing for active student engagement will take longer than simply making arrangements for them, and at times may be frustrating for all concerned. The distant and novel setting will create challenges and will most likely result in quite disrupted intra-group relationships among students at times. Unless on the watch for such developments, it can be disconcerting for a teacher to find that instead of being open to the wonders of some key destination of the tour, the students are instead hotly engaged by interpersonal issues within their group. The teacher needs to be ready and able to diffuse tensions and help turn difficulties into learning experiences.

Monitoring and assisting students in local interactions can also be very demanding, firstly because the teacher is usually also trying to manage their own relationship with the same people, which may not always be smooth; and, secondly, because, for personal and professional reasons, there is an inevitable desire for everything to go well. Keen to promote learning through reflection among their students, Chinese teachers may instead find themselves feeling hurt, impatient, or dissatisfied with the nature and level of grasp evident in what students report, or wanting to jump in and protect the image of their home country and compatriots from what seems like thoughtless criticism. It takes considerable intercultural maturity on the part of the teacher and deep professional understanding to resist the temptation to make all impressions and interpretations positive, especially those that derive from ignorance, and to allow students to work through negative opinions and maybe come to reconsider earlier criticism as they learn more. A teacher who understands this process and can manage their own patriotic urges, can offer much to mediate intercultural growth in the students.

## References

Bennett, M. (1998) 'Intercultural Communication: A Current Perspective', in M.J. Bennett (ed.), *Basic Concepts of Intercultural Communication Selected Readings*, 1–34. Yarmouth: Intercultural Press, Inc.

Brislin, R. (1993) *Understanding Culture's Influence on Behavior*. Orlando: Harcourt, Brace College Publishers.

Byram, M. (1997) *Teaching and Assessing Intercultural Communicative Competence*. Clevedon: Multilingual Matters.

CTTC. (2011) *Getting the Most You Can From Your School's China Trip*. Melbourne: Chinese Teacher Training Centre, The University of Melbourne, Victoria, Australia.

Dewey, J. (1921) *Democracy and Education: An Introduction to the Philosophy of Education*. New York: MacMillan.

Gochenour, T. and Janeway, A. (1993) 'Seven Concepts in Cross-Cultural Interaction: A Training Design', in T. Gochenour (ed.), *Beyond Experience*. 2nd edition. Yarmouth: Intercultural Press, Inc.

Herbert, D. (1999) 'What Do Students Remember From Lectures? The Role of Episodic Memory on Early Learning', Paper presented at the combined *Australian Association for Research in Education—New Zealand Association for Research in Education Conference*, Melbourne, November 29–December 2, 1999.

Martin, J. (1993) 'Episodic Memory: The Neglected Phenomenon in the Psychology of Education', *Educational Psychologist*, 28(2): 169–183.

Orton, J. (1998) 'Intercultural Learning in a Short-Term Program', in K. Knapp, B. Kappel, K. Eubel-Kasper, and L. Salo-Lee (eds.), *Meeting the Intercultural Challenge Proceedings From the SIETAR Congress '96*, 284–298. Berlin: Sternenfels, Verlag Wissenschaft and Praxis.

Orton, J. and Mansell, D. (2011) *Learning From Short-Term Sojourns in China*. Melbourne: Chinese Teacher Training Centre, The University of Melbourne, Victoria, Australia.

Orton, J., Pavlidis, M., and Cui, X. (2013) *The Clear River Sojourn: A Study of the Experience and Learning of a Group of Secondary Students on a Short Sojourn to China*. Melbourne: Chinese Teacher Training Centre, The University of Melbourne, Victoria, Australia.

Pritchard, M. (2017) *Empowering Learning the Importance of Being Experiential*. Woodbridge: John Catt Educational Ltd.

Tulving, E. (2002) 'Episodic Memory: From Mind to Brain', in *Annual Review of Psychology*, xvi. Palo Alto: Annual Reviews.

Tulving, E. (2004) 'Episodic Memory and Autonoesis: Uniquely Human?', in H.S. Terrace and J. Metcalfe (eds.), *The Missing Link in Cognition: Origins of Self-reflective Consciousness*. Oxford and New York: Oxford University Press.

Vygotsky, L. (1994 [1934]) 'The Problem of the Environment', in R. van de Veer and J. Valsiner (eds.), *The Vygotsky Reader*. Leiden: Blackwell.

Wang, J. (2009) *How to Build Meaningful and Sustainable School Partnerships*. New York: Asia Society. Retrieved 10 September 2018 from https://asiasociety.org/china-learning-initiatives/how-build-school-partnerships

Wang, J. (2010) *Improving School Partnership: Some Insight and Evidence*. New York: Asia Society. Retrieved 10 September 2018 from https://asiasociety.org/china-learning-initiatives/improving-school-partnerships

Weekes, W., Pedersen, P., and Brislin, R. (eds.). (1977) *A Manual of Structured Experiences for Cross-Cultural Learning*. Yarmouth: Intercultural Press, Inc.

# AFTERWORD

The chapters in this book consider essential research in the various areas addressed. The findings of studies and accounts of best practice provide knowledge of Chinese language and thus of what is to be learned. The nature of the learning involved is analysed and the challenges it represents for speakers of English and other European languages are identified. Teaching which aims to start where the learners are and assist them to develop a path towards competence in the learning area is presented. At the same time, through these learning activities, students are to be engaged in a broader educational endeavour, one which will open up an understanding of language and its use as a human endeavour. The interaction in the classrooms described is dialogical between teacher and student, while each has a separate role: the students work on the content and the teacher works on the students, observing and guiding them towards a level just a little ahead of current competence. Students also engage in dialogue among themselves.

In planning a series of lessons (e.g. five or six classes over a two-week period), a minute of surrender listening using a news broadcast, conversation, poem, or story being read is included at the start of each so as to provide learners with a chance to reengage with the language and to subject their entire body to the flow of rhythm and intonation. Each lesson also includes a rhythm and tone exercise, lasting no more than a minute. Over a period of two weeks there will be a period of 20 minutes of dedicated work on rhythm, tone, intonation and fluency, and twice that time dedicated to specific work on literacy development—perception exercises, component study, reading lines of Chinese; writing script; discourse. There will also be work carried out in the students' first language on comparing their languages, discussing learning issues and strategies, and pondering the concept that languages are constructed entities, carrying culture, history, and geography, and shaped to serve and represent the dominant groups in societies, yet open to challenge and change.

Within their two weeks of lessons, students learn to expand their control of expression in speaking and writing. They read texts not only sentences, and they work on developing their writing, firstly as script but quite quickly also as discourse. Oral work contributes to competence in self-presentation and interaction in real social situations, with native speaking visitors to their class and with sister school students on the Internet and face-to-face. Knowledge about China and Chinese society is embedded in language work. Scaffolded language exercises are available online for independent student use and guided access to the Internet opens up games, videos and targeted Chinese websites providing songs, cartoons, information about the country, sport and variety programs.

Within any sequence of lessons, wherever learners have the opportunity to observe interactions and texts in native speaker contexts or engage in real time interactions in the classroom, the issue of cultural influences on language use may arise. Whether it be explicit references to everyday cultural practices or subtle indications of how cultural values impact on interactions and meaning making between speakers of Chinese, these opportunities to identify and reflect on the way culture and communication interact are an important part of learning to communicate accurately and appropriately in Chinese. Every opportunity to pause and reflect on how Chinese see their world and how that is expressed through language is a vital element of powerful learning in the Chinese classroom.

While Chinese teachers have a common focus on teaching modern standard Chinese to their classes, those classes are typically and increasingly diverse in the nature of the language and culture background and experience that learners bring to the study of Chinese. As the teacher's role is to encourage learners to work on the content, it becomes increasingly important to understand where each learner is at in terms of their current capabilities and potential to progress further with Chinese. Finding synergies and commonalities within the classroom is an important part of creating an inclusive and collaborative space where learners find ways to work together and support each other in their learning and use of Chinese.

Chinese language learning is a long-term task. Planning for effective and engaging learning opportunities means addressing the real challenges that all learners face in coming to grips with the particular characteristics of Chinese. Planning must begin with a longer term, conceptual framing of these challenges as a path along which learners develop the knowledge and skills to take greater control of their learning as they mature and progress. Successful study of Chinese requires accumulating examples of concepts introduced early and reinforced as they arise incidentally which develop into a coherent whole over time. Setting up a long-term program in which bigger picture concepts are foregrounded, then addressed as they arise in the shorter-term units of work, provides for overall continuity and coherence and a clear roadmap to success for learners. Working in this way, learners can find connections between what they engage with today and their developing understanding of the overall nature of the task. Quality curriculum planning is an essential element for motivating and engaging students, and retaining them in the Chinese classroom. A long-term plan is a blueprint for action, progress, and success that can provide learners with a greater sense of where they are at and how they can create the pathway on which to take their knowledge forward.

# INDEX

Note: Page numbers in italic indicate a figure and page numbers in bold indicate a table on the corresponding page.